Richard Ne[...]

Richard Nelson's plays include *Goodnight Children Everywhere* (RSC), *The General From America* (RSC), *New England* (RSC, Manhattan Theatre Club), *Misha's Party* (co-written with Alexander Gelman for the Royal Shakespeare Company and the Moscow Art Theatre), *Colombus and the Discovery of Japan* (RSC), *Two Shakespearean Actors* (RSC, Lincoln Center Theatre), *Some Americans Abroad* (RSC, Lincoln Center Theatre), *Sensibility and Sense* (American Playhouse Television), *Principia Scriptoriae* (RSC, Manhattan Theatre Club), *Between East and West, Life Sentences, The Return of Pinocchio, Rip van Winkle or The Works, The Vienna Notes* and *An American Comedy*. Radio plays include *Languages Spoken Here* (BBC Radio 3), *Eating Words* (Radio 4 and the World Service), *Roots in Water* (Radio 3), *Advice to Eastern Europe* (Radio 4) and *The American Wife* (Radio 3). He has written a television play, *End of a Sentence* (American Playhouse), and a film, *Ethan Frome*. Among his awards are the prestigious Lila Wallace Readers' Digest Award in 1991, a London *Time Out* award, two Obies, two Giles Cooper Awards, a Guggenheim Fellowship, two Rockefeller playwriting grants and two National Endowment for the Arts playwriting fellowships. He is an Honorary Associate Artist of the RSC.

Making Plays – The Writer–Director Relationship in the Theatre Today, co-written by David Jones and edited by Colin Chambers, was published in 1995 by Faber and Faber.

In Print
@ £20

RICHARD NELSON

Plays One

Some Americans Abroad

Two Shakespearean Actors

New England

Principia Scriptoriae

Left

Introduced by
the author

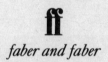

faber and faber

This collection first published in 1999
by Faber and Faber Limited
3 Queen Square London WC1N 3AU

Photoset by Wakewing, High Wycombe
Printed and bound in Great Britain by Mackays of Chatham plc,
Chatham, Kent

A CIP record for this book
is available from the British Library

ISBN 0–571–19708–6

2 4 6 8 10 9 7 5 3 1

Contents

Introduction: Where These Plays Came From

SOME AMERICANS ABROAD

The Royal Shakespeare Company asked me to write a play for them. This was a week or so after the opening of their production of my play, *Principia Scriptoriae*, in the Barbican Pit in October 1986. I was fantastically flattered and thrilled, but soon stumped. What, as an American, would I write about? England? The English? What did I know about English people? It's pretty presumptuous to write about another's culture. I had recently seen a one-act play at the National Theatre written by a very well-known British playwright which was about Americans and set in the tiny village where I live in upstate New York. I found it full of misunderstandings of America and Americans, to say nothing of a setting which completely misrepresented the geography of my village. I swore not to make the same mistake for my RSC play. So – I decided to write only about Americans. But then why should a British theatre company wish to commission an American to write a play only about Americans? And so the basic premise of *Some Americans Abroad* presented itself; I would write about Americans in England.

When I was at college, I went with a school group to England (my first trip abroad) to 'explore' the world of British theatre and see plays, lots and lots and lots of plays – thirty-five, I seem to remember, in but twenty-nine days. *Some Americans Abroad* must have come from this trip. At least so thought the professor who led the group, when years later he turned up at the final performance of the play at the Pit, without a ticket, and attempted to jump the returns queue by shouting to the house manager: 'You must let me in. Don't you understand, this play is about me!'

The house manager let him in. And years later still, he himself played the role of the retired professor, Baldwin, in a staged reading of the play at the college. And he was very good, I thought, very authentic.

TWO SHAKESPEAREAN ACTORS

Some years ago, while wandering through a used bookshop near my home – actually, not really a shop, but a barn filled with books – I came across a very old edition of the diaries of the nineteenth-century British actor William Charles Macready, a name I scarcely knew at the time. I think months went by before I looked through the book at home and happened upon Macready's own description of the Astor Place Theatre riots in New York and his feud with the American actor, Edwin Forrest, which precipitated them.

For a couple of years I had been making periodic abortive stabs at a novel about the nineteenth-century writer Nathaniel Hawthorne. One such stab had focused upon the year 1849, when Hawthorne first met Herman Melville. 1849 was also, I learned, the year of the Astor Place riots. My bookshelves were already crammed with wonderful and useful materials. So I grabbed at this new excuse to lose myself in the mid-nineteenth century, which I did for more months than I can now explain or justify.

Also at this time I wrote what is essentially a two-character radio play for the BBC called *Eating Words*, about an American writer and an English writer meeting for a lunch in London which turns into a long, boozy pub crawl. I think I wrote this play in preparation for writing the last, longest and most difficult scene in *Two Shakespearean Actors*. The scene where Macready and Forrest are alone in the dressing-room, talking about art and acting, while the world erupts just outside. It is a scene which attempts to explore the many contradictions of being an artist in our world. This was also a central concern of the unfinished novel.

During this period of writing and escape into the past, I kept a quotation over my desk:

> 'Writer – beware the political gesture.'
> (A. Chekhov)

NEW ENGLAND

Some have seen *New England* as the companion piece to, or rather 'flip-side' of, *Some Americans Abroad*: where one showed Americans in England, *New England* put the English in America. I don't think this occurred to me while writing it. A friend of mine needed a place to stay for a while. A friend of his offered a room in the house she shared with a man. My friend briefly met this man as he moved in. Two days later, the man died of a heart attack while on a business trip abroad. My friend's friend was also out of town at this time, so my friend took the phone call from the police. He greeted the man's grieving friends, all of whom assumed my friend knew the man extremely well, as he was living in the man's house.

American culture outside of America means so many things. As an American, you don't realize this.

I was invited to a dinner party in London, where I was the only American. Halfway through the dinner, the man next to me started to 'do' his American accent for me.

It was the 4th of July, American Independence Day, and I was in London. I had a party for both American and British friends. One British friend spent half of the party attacking America and its culture, all in his outrageous 'American' accent.

English friends visit us in our home in upstate New York. Every single guest asks the same things: why don't we have fences around our property?, why are the houses made of wood?, etc.

A man from an English newspaper visits in early spring when the leaves aren't yet out on the trees. The Englishman assumes that the trees are all dead. He says he is not surprised, as this is how he imagined America.

The year before writing *New England* I made numerous trips to Russia. With each visit I felt a profound sense of cultural confusion among Russians, the feeling of loss, fear, anxiety, of living on the edge of a giant yawning abyss.

In Moscow I sat inside the hard currency Pizza Hut – at the time a very chic place, because it was one of the few hard currency places to eat. Around me were Western businessmen and Russians dressed in mink coats. Years ago I set a scene of a play (*Some Americans Abroad*) inside the Pizza Hut in Stratford-upon-Avon.

My visits to Russia brought me back to thinking about culture. It also brought me back, for the umpteenth time in my life, to the greatness in the plays of Anton Chekhov. To their universal wisdom. These plays stormed back into my life and work, with a greater force than ever before, and perhaps with a better understanding. They provide me with both professional and personal benchmarks of decency and honesty, as well as a guiding, helping hand through confusion and uncertainty.

So *New England* seems to me to be a darker play, sadder than *Some Americans Abroad*, as it does begin with suicide. And self-destruction, or perhaps the destruction of the self, is ever-present in this play of homeless people.

My village, my home, is only a few miles from the Connecticut border and the scene of this play.

PRINCIPIA SCRIPTORIAE

Principia is the earliest of these plays, and, as I wrote in a separate introduction to the play, I have come to see that it is about fathers and sons, parents and children, and about growing up. It was written around the time of my mother's death and my daughter's birth, hence at a time when parents and children, growing and not growing, were sensitive issues for me.

I have never been to Central America.

I did translate the *Seafarer* in college. It is my translation that Bill Howell keeps in his wallet.

I did not sell T-shirts on a protest march in Washington, as Bill Howell did. I sold my T-shirts during the student strike at my college after the killings at Kent State. And we made a heck of a lot of money too.

I wanted, and want, to be nothing more or less than the best writer I can be, like Bill Howell in Part One.

As for Part Two, at the time of writing *Principia* I had recently adapted a play by Dario Fo, which was first presented in Washington, D.C., then subsequently on Broadway. Though Fo approved my version (after it was successful in Washington), he later criticized it publicly and blamed it for the play's failure in New York. I found his actions disheartening and upsetting. I am sure that my disappointment in this writer coloured my attitude toward the established writers in Part Two of *Principia*.

LEFT

Left, originally titled *Sensibility and Sense*, is very much *Principia*'s companion play and was written immediately after (before *Principia* was even produced). It is preoccupied with many of the same concerns – the child in the adult, the adult in the child, the place of friendship, friendship over time, the personal and the political, the need and fear of being a part of something greater than oneself.

Re-reading it now, for some reason, I see my mother in this play, though she was neither a leftist nor an intellectual, just a clever, complicated lady whose small gestures carried big weight and baggage.

My mother died from the same disease that the Older Marianne is dying from.

Around the time I was beginning to think about this play, I heard Mary McCarthy speak on the lawn of Vassar College.

Around this time, I went to a theatre conference at Smith College.

Around this time, I came across an extraordinary four-page footnote in Diana Trilling's *We Must March My Darlings*, which begins:

> In September 1976 I was informed by the publishers with whom I was originally under contract for this volume that unless I removed my critical reference to Miss [Lillian] Hellman, author of *Scoundrel Time* and one of their best-selling writers, they would not publish my book.

She then goes on to point out the lies in Hellman's memoirs, in a manner that reads like a legal brief.

Around this time, we spent a few wonderful days with friends at their camp on Long Lake in the Adirondacks. The camp has no electricity. And its only access is by boat or seaplane.

These five plays are set in very different places, even different continents, at very different times, even different centuries. But how different are they?

One is set in upstate New York, a second just across the

New York State border in Connecticut, a third in New York City, and a fourth concerns visitors whose home is a Vermont college campus.

The characters in these plays are all actors or writers or artists or teachers. The plays are all about culture and cultures, with American culture being the prime point of reference.

Three were written for the Royal Shakespeare Company, though all five have also been produced by American theatres.

Set side by side, these plays, I hope, complement each other, argue with each other, explain and even contradict each other, and expose each for what it is – the product of one writer.

A play, I believe, is but an attempt – often a very wilful attempt – to organize one's life and thoughts and understandings in ways that life itself doesn't supply us with. These are five of my wilful attempts.

Richard Nelson
Summer 1998

SOME AMERICANS ABROAD

for Colin Chambers and Frank Pike

*This play was commissioned by the
Royal Shakespeare Company*

Characters

Joe Taylor, *thirty-eight, recently appointed Chairman of the English Department*
Katie Taylor, *his daughter, eighteen, attends the College*
Philip Brown, *thirty-seven, a Professor of English*
Frankie Lewis, *forty-one, an Associate Professor of English*
Orson Baldwin, *late sixties, retired Chairman of the English Department*
Harriet Baldwin, *his wife, sixties*
Henry McNeil, *thirty-five, Assistant Professor of English*
Betty McNeil, *his wife, thirty-six*
Donna Silliman, *twenty, a student at the College*
Joanne Smith, *twenty-six, a graduate of the College*
An American, *forties*

All the characters are American.

Some Americans Abroad is set at approximately the present time in various locations in England. Each scene has a title – the location of the scene – which should be projected moments before the scene begins.

Some Americans Abroad was first performed at The Pit, London, on 19 July 1989. The cast was as follows:

Joe Taylor Anton Lesser
Philip Brown Oliver Cotton
Henry McNeil Simon Russell Beale
Betty McNeil Amanda Root
Frankie Lewis Diane Fletcher
Katie Taylor Kate Byers
Harriet Baldwin Patricia Lawrence
Orson Baldwin John Bott
Joanne Smith Candida Gubbins
An American Joe Melia
Donna Silliman Caroline Harding

Directed by Roger Michell
Designed by Alexandra Byrne
Lighting by Rick Fisher
Music by Jeremy Sams
Stage Management Eric Lumsden, Sheonagh Darby, Sarah West Stevens
Musicians Pip Hinton, Christopher Nightingale, Sandy Burnett

Some Americans Abroad was subsequently produced by Lincoln Center Theater (Gregory Mosher, Director, Bernard Gersten, Executive Producer) at The Mitzi E. Newhouse Theater on 11 February 1990. The cast was as follows:

Joe Taylor Colin Stinton
Philip Brown John Bedford Lloyd
Henry McNeil Bob Balaban
Betty McNeil Kate Burton
Frankie Lewis Frances Conroy
Katie Taylor Cara Buono
Harriet Baldwin Jane Hoffman
Orson Baldwin Henderson Forsythe
Joanne Smith Ann Talman
An American John Rothman
Donna Silliman Elisabeth Shue

Directed by Roger Michell
Designed by Alexandra Byrne
Lighting by Rick Fisher
Music by Jeremy Sams
Stage Management Michael F. Ritchie, Sarah Manley
Musicians Michelle Johnson, Joshua Rosenblum, Michael Goetz

Act One

SCENE ONE

Projection: LUIGI'S RESTAURANT IN COVENT GARDEN.

Joe Taylor, Henry and Betty McNeil, Frankie Lewis, Philip Brown and Katie Taylor around a table, towards the end of their meal.

Joe (*to Philip*) First, that does not mean I am in favour of a nuclear war –

Philip You are arguing for a situation that will make such a war more –

Joe Let me finish!

The rest of the table only half-heartedly listens to this conversation as they finish their meals, sip their coffee, finish their wine, etc.

(*to the others*) He twists everything. Anyone else want to jump in, go right ahead. Put me out of my misery. (*He laughs.*)

Philip (*to the others*) I'm waiting for him to get to Gorbachev –

Joe Gorbachev supports me! The whole idea of Gorbachev supports my argument! (*to the others*) We got Gorbachev, didn't we? (*He turns to Philip.*) Philip, what could be clearer? Please. What I have been saying, the point to be made here is – to go out and protest –. To –. What? Chain yourself to some gate of some plant or some boat or whatever –

Philip Frankie, pass me the last of that wine, please.

That's if no one –

Henry No, no. It's yours. (*He turns to his wife.*) Betty?

Betty I'm fine.

Frankie passes the wine. Philip pours into his glass.

Joe If you don't want to –

Philip Go ahead.

Beat.

Joe I want to know what's the purpose in all that? In the protesting. What? (*Beat.*) Disarmament??? (*Beat.*) Come on, what does that mean?

Frankie What does dis –?

Joe When one says one is quote unquote for disarmament, what does one mean? Peace???? (*Beat.*) Who the hell isn't interested in peace?

Philip It's about creating a pressure . . .

Joe A unilateral pressure? What the hell is that? Is anyone really suggesting – seriously suggesting – that we should just junk our bombs? (*Beat.*) Of course they're not. They are suggesting – demanding that we keep negotiating. Well – I agree! (*Beat.*) If that is the purpose of these adventures, then I agree with them. I agree with the purpose.

Philip But now you'll argue that such actions as these protests, they only make the country weaker which only makes real negotiations less –

Joe I'm not saying that. Don't paint me into that corner, OK? (*Beat.*) Jesus Christ, I am a goddamn liberal, Philip. (*Beat.*) Listen to me. You are not listening. (*Beat. To the others*) Am I that hard to understand? (*to Philip*) If the

8

point of protesting is simply to pressure negotiations. Fine.
I understand this. This is not what I'm criticizing. (*He
finishes his wine.*) My point is the intellectual dishonesty
involved in saying one is for disarmament when everyone
is for disarmament. It's like saying you're *for* love!

Philip (*to the others*) There was a time actually not too
many years ago – (*He laughs.*)

Joe I know. And we learned something from that, didn't
we? (*Beat.*) I did. Let's not delude ourselves that we are
actually changing things. Or changing much. It is truth,
honesty that I'm after. *Say* what you're doing! *Say* what
you mean! For Christ's sake is it so hard to be honest?
(*Beat.*) I know things are complicated these days, but you
know what I think – I think things have always been
complicated. (*Beat.*) The man who wrote *Hamlet*
understood that the world was complicated.

   Short pause.

Philip This is true. Good point.

Henry Are we off political science and on to literature now?

Philip If we are, then the perfect example which refutes
you, Joe, is that piece of intellectual mush we sat through
this afternoon. Talk about idiotic debates.

Joe (*to the others*) I knew he was getting to this. (*He
smiles.*) Look, it's a beautiful play. And that's not just my
opinion.

Henry It's anthologized –

Philip Straw men – set up to be knocked down. That's
how Shaw works. The world presented in that play was
tricky, not complicated. Shaw enjoyed trickiness, not real
thinking.

Joe And that is one opinion. (*to the others*) Shaw's

reputation this half-century has gone up and down, up and down, up and down. (*He laughs.*)

Philip The world today makes such a play ridiculous.

Joe Come on, it was funny. You laughed.

Philip I laughed. At a play. I didn't appreciate the effort at political argument. Or rather the trivialization of political argument. (*Beat.*) Look, in the end I think we're saying the same thing. The world is complicated. Too complicated for a George Bernard Shaw to express –

Joe I think that play is very profound.

Henry You teach it in your Modern Brit. class, don't you?

Joe Yes, I do, Henry, thank you. (*Beat. To Philip*) It may be a little schematic –

Philip You mean a little watered down.

Joe But a schematic argument sometimes is the best way to present a complex moral position. Breaking the argument apart piece by piece, it illuminates the position. Or the conundrum. If that's what it is. Often in surprising ways. If you'd like I'll show you what I mean.

Philip Look everyone, I'm sorry for getting him started.

Frankie I doubt if you could have stopped him.

Joe That's not funny.

Henry It's interesting, really.

Betty Very interesting.

Joe Thank you. (*to Philip and Frankie*) You want me to show you or not? (*Beat.*) So – capital punishment. I'll make my point with that. Let me ask Frankie. A woman we all know who has strong moral opinions.

Frankie Since when? (*She laughs.*) He must have got me confused with someone else. How much wine *are* we drinking?

Laughter.

Joe Capital punishment, Frankie. Good or bad? (*Beat.*) Come on, good or bad?

Frankie Bad. Of course. Morally indefensible.

Joe You are sure of that?

Frankie Yes. Yes I am sure, Joe.

Joe But if I were to present an argument –

Frankie For vengeance? If you believe in vengeance then of course –

Joe Not vengeance. (*to the others*) Here now is our complicated world at work. (*Beat.*) While I was in grad. school, I was moonlighting for a small paper. I interviewed a guy in prison. A killer. Sentenced to *life* imprisonment. He was first sentenced to death, but now it was life imprisonment.

Philip After the Supreme Court knocked down –.

Joe Yeh. Whatever. Well, Buddy – that's the guy's name; I went to see Buddy. And he started to tell me that *he* favoured the death penalty. A killer in prison!

Frankie Well – a death wish. Like that man in –. Where was it? Utah? Nevada?

Joe No. No, there's no death wish, Frankie. When his sentence was changed to life, he was very very happy about that. He did not want to die. (*Beat.*) Here's what he said: because he was under a life sentence – actually three, he'd murdered three people and he'd no possibility for parole – the guards in the prison, they knew there was nothing, no recourse left for them if Buddy tried to do something. I mean, he was there for good, for *ever*. There was *no* deterrent. Get it? (*Beat.*) So they treated Buddy like an animal. (*Beat.*) Why wouldn't they, right? (*Beat.*) And this – as you can imagine – dehumanized our Buddy. So – he told me – he thought there should be a death penalty for people who were in prison for life but who *then* kill a prison guard. This would be his one case when the death penalty would apply.

Short pause.

Philip Interesting.

Joe Isn't it?

Frankie I'd never heard –

Joe Buddy's argument is in favour of treating people like human beings. In this case the threat of death *helps* the prisoner.

Henry You should write an article, Joe; you've got something that's publishable.

Joe Thank you. (*to Frankie*) Now you see the problem. As any philosopher knows – you find *one* case that is acceptable, in this case where *killing* is acceptable; then the *moral* argument falls by the wayside. It's all case by case then, instead of a debate about *morality*.

Frankie Which is what we're always trying to achieve with abortion.

Joe Exactly. (*Short pause.*) Don't get me wrong, I think the death penalty is inhuman. I'm just saying, see how tricky things can get? (*Beat.*) Not to wax pretentious, but I do think the mind is really quite extraordinary. (*Beat.*) The pursuit of truth is a bumpy road. But one we all have chosen to follow. Or we wouldn't be teachers.

Henry Beautifully said, Joe.

Philip But what the hell does any of that have to do with a hack playwright like Shaw?

He laughs; the others laugh.

Joe (*laughing*) Nothing. Nothing at all, Phil!

Pause. They sip their coffee.

Henry What a provocative discussion.

Frankie Katie, this must be very boring for you.

Joe Nah, she's used to it. She can take it.

Katie You should see him at home. Dinner's like a senior seminar.

Some light laughter.

Philip Lunch with Joe in the canteen is like a senior seminar.

Frankie Mary says being married to him is like living a senior seminar!

Laughter.

Joe OK. OK. It's not all that funny. (*Beat. To Katie*) I hope, young lady, you do not treat all of your teachers with such disrespect.

Katie I promise I save all of my disrespect for my father.

Laughter.

Betty Very good!

Henry (*shushing her, under his breath*) Betty!

Frankie (*over this exchange*) As any child should!

Laughter.

Philip Or does, you mean!

Laughter. Pause.
  Philip picks up the bill and looks at it.

Henry Is that the check?

Philip Yes.

He hands Henry the bill.

Betty Katie, your father was telling me this afternoon that you've not been to England before.

Katie No I haven't.

Betty How exciting it all must be for you.

Katie I'm having a good time. (*Beat.*) The plays are great.

Henry Aren't they. (*He puts the bill back down.*) When do we go to Stratford?

Joe Next Thursday. (*to Frankie*) Next Thursday?

She nods.

Betty (*to Katie*) You'll love Stratford.

Henry (*to Katie*) You'll come back to England in maybe ten years, Katie, and it'll all still be here. That's what I love about England. (*Beat.*) We first came ten years ago.

Short pause.

Frankie Last year's plays were better, I think.

Betty Do you? Then they must have been really marvellous because so far – (*She stops herself.*)

Frankie I wasn't saying that this year's –

Betty No, no. I know you weren't.

Short pause.

Katie The play today wasn't bad.

Joe Hear that, Phil? That's one for me. (*to Katie*) Good for you.

Katie The woman who played Barbara, she was great, I thought.

Frankie She *was* good.

Henry Excellent.

Short pause.

Katie The Undershaft, wasn't he in *Jewel in the Crown*?

Henry Was he?

Katie I think so.

Philip Hmmmmmm. (*to Henry*) You saw *Jewel in the Crown*, didn't you?

Henry Not all of it.

Philip Treat yourself. When it comes back on –

Betty We will.

Short pause.

Joe Mary sends her best.

Frankie You talked to her?

Joe Katie and I did. (*Beat.*) It's her birthday.

Philip Really? What a shame not to have you –

Joe She understands. (*Beat.*) It was important to her that Katie could come. So she's happy.

Short pause.

Philip Well – happy birthday, Mary!

The others Yes, happy birthday.

Pause.

Joe Maybe we should pay this. (*He takes the bill. Short pause. He turns to Frankie.*) What did you have Frankie?

Frankie The veal.

Joe Right. So should I be banker? (*Beat.*) Let's see that's . . .

Frankie (*taking out money*) Will this cover it?

Joe One second.

Betty (*to Henry*) What did we have?

Henry I had the lasagne. That was six pounds ten pence.

Philip Plus tax and tip.

Frankie I forgot about the tip. (*She reaches into her purse for more money.*)

Betty (*putting money down*) This I'm sure will be plenty. (*Beat.*) Won't it?

Joe And the wine? Do we all put in for the wine?

Philip I certainly do. I must have had –

Henry I only had one glass. How much is one glass?

Joe I'll figure it out. A bottle was –. How many glasses in a bottle?

Betty Five. No more than five. They're big glasses.

Katie Dad –

Joe Put your money away, I'll pay for you.

Katie But I have money.

Joe Save it. In this town, you'll need it, trust me.

Frankie Did the salad come with the entrée?

Katie I had ice-cream.

Joe I have that.

Katie And a coffee.

Philip So did I.

Betty Wasn't that an espresso?

Philip Yes, yes, I'm sorry. Is that more?

Joe One at a time. I have to do one at a time. This is getting too complicated.

SCENE TWO

Projection: RYE, EAST SUSSEX.

A garden behind a small cottage. A few tables, chairs. A path leads off in one direction. Harriet Baldwin, with a tray of tea, cups, etc., and Katie Taylor.

Harriet They must have gone down the path. He must be showing them Lamb House. If you want to catch up –

Katie No, thanks.

Short pause, Katie rubs her shoulders as Harriet begins to set a table for tea.

Harriet You're not chilled, are you? We could sit inside. I suppose it may seem a little nippy.

Katie I'm fine. I have the sweater. And my coat is just –

Harriet (*not listening*) I find it –. Such weather. I don't know. Just bloody invigorating. One learns after all these years what the British see in their gardens. (*She almost drops a teacup.*)

Katie Mrs Baldwin, you're sure I can't –

Harriet Lamb House is where Henry James lived.

Katie I know. Dad read all about it to me on the train.

Harriet It's much bigger than this house. He got the gout there. (*Short pause.*) I suppose it's half the reason Professor Baldwin and I have retired to here, if the truth be told.

Katie So Dad says.

Harriet Jamesian Sussex. (*Beat.*) Just the name is quite seductive. Though we very seriously considered Dickensian London. At first I favoured this. We even checked out a flat near the East End. (*Beat.*) The Barbican Towers. Lovely. (*Beat.*) Beautiful fountain. (*Beat.*) Daniel Defoe Tower it was in. We both feel Defoe a very underrated writer. But they gave him a nice tower though. Your father, of course, Katie, kept suggesting Liverpool because of Hawthorne having been consul there. (*Beat.*) We took the train up. (*Beat.*) I don't think your father's ever really been to Liverpool.

Katie I don't know.

Harriet There's Wordsworth country, of course. We thought of this. (*Beat.*) Stratford obviously was out of the question. One might as well be living in Connecticut. (*Beat. She blows on her hands.*) It's not that much warmer in there. The central heating is being put in. If we had known how much that would cost –. But we did get all this for a very modest price. Something like this in the States –. Something historic like this –. (*Beat.*) You couldn't touch it. We couldn't have touched it. (*Beat.*) We consider ourselves very lucky, Katie. Very lucky. (*She finishes setting the table.*) English, isn't it?

Katie I'm sorry?

Harriet Joe's hooked you for the Department, I understand.

Katie Oh. Yes. I'm an English major now.

Harriet Excellent. A great Department. Professor Baldwin knew how to pick teachers. So even though we're retired . . . (*Beat.*) You will not be sorry. Our English Department is one of the best Departments in the whole College.

Orson Baldwin, Joe Taylor and Philip Brown enter from the path.

Philip (*to Orson*) I stood right up and said – Remember, I was only a sophomore. But I stood there and said to Professor Wilson –. (*to Joe*) Did I ever tell you this?

Joe What story are you telling now?

Philip About quoting Gandhi to Professor Wilson.

Joe Oh, that one.

Philip I said to Professor Wilson – something like: Let the judges be judged by the laws they enforce. I don't remember the exact quote. (*Beat.*) But what I meant was: If this faculty disciplinary committee was going to kick me out of school for stopping an army recruiter, then they were going to be judged by the war that recruiter was working for.

Joe Wasn't he clever, Orson?

Orson Who was going to judge them? I don't get it.

Philip I was talking – morally. I was after their consciences.

Joe Wilson, I'm sure, would have been very upset.

Philip The most liberal Professor on the campus at the time. Half of my philosophy class with him was on pacifism.

Joe I took the class. That's why Gandhi's just a brilliant idea.

Philip Let's say I made my point.

Joe It must have blown his mind.

Philip He hated the war as much as –

Orson I'll find the sherry.

Beat.

Joe Orson, I'm sorry, we're –

Orson Please. Every generation needs its war stories. Sherry, Katie?

Joe I don't think she's ever even had sherry, have you?

Katie I'll pass. But thanks for asking, Professor Baldwin.

Orson leaves in the direction of the house. Short pause.

Harriet I'm also making tea.

Philip You're spoiling us.

Short pause.

Joe Now if I'd tried Gandhi on the town judge . . . (*Beat.*) When *we* stopped our recruiter.

Philip (*to Katie*) This is a different recruiter. (*to Joe*) He'd either have tarred and feathered you –

Joe Dumb as a brick, that man. Hated anyone from the College. You know he gave me a suspended sentence. It's still on my record. In some people's eyes even today I'm a criminal, a radical criminal.

Harriet In whose eyes? I'm sorry, but I don't understand what you're –

Katie They stopped a soldier from recruiting students for the war.

Philip We each did. At different times.

Joe I had already graduated. But I was still in Middlebury because Mary was still a student. (*Beat.*) Phil was also still a student.

Harriet When was this? I haven't heard anything about this.

Joe Years and years ago, Harriet. The dark ages. (*Beat. To Katie and Philip*) And I didn't get any faculty committee, I was arrested. By the police. (*Beat.*) Mary was pregnant with Katie. Fifty dollars for bail. That's what I made in a week at the bookshop.

Harriet I'm sorry – which bookshop?

Joe At the Grange. Before it was a movie theatre.

Harriet I loved that bookshop. (*to Katie*) It had a fireplace.

Joe It was gas. There wasn't a chimney.

Harriet And big chairs. And a cat.

Joe That was our cat. Before we had Katie, Mary and I had a cat.

Philip I remember that cat. What was its name? Che?

Joe I don't remember.

Katie I think Mom said it was Che.

Joe Who can remember? (*to Philip*) You had a dog named Fidel.

Philip It wasn't my dog. I didn't feed it.

Joe You named it.

Short pause.

Philip How did we get on to . . .?

Joe I don't know. (*Beat.*) Orson's Henry James class. And to that from Lamb House.

Philip That's right.

Joe Philip was saying how he had to cut Orson's class so he could go and stop the recruiter.

Philip I didn't ask. I just did it. I was a sophomore.

Harriet You had to have been a good student to get into his James seminar as a sophomore.

Philip This was second semester.

Harriet Still.

Katie And Professor Baldwin, he was understanding . . . about your cutting the class.

Orson enters with the sherry and glasses.

Philip No, he tried to flunk me. He didn't even stop there, he tried to get me kicked out of school. I thought he was a fascist. To this day, I can't help tying Henry James to fascism. (*He laughs.*)

Joe Not completely off the mark.

Harriet (*to Orson*) Dear, I think these young men are calling you a fascist.

Orson shrugs and sets down the drinks.

Joe Orson, you really tried to kick Philip out of school?

Orson I tried to kick them all out. (*Beat.*) As for you, maybe I even talked to the town judge. I thought you should get at least six months. In a prison. (*Short pause.*) You weren't a student any more so of course I was speaking only as a concerned citizen. (*Beat.*) I think I talked to him. I wanted to at least.

Pause.

Joe (*suddenly laughs*) You're joking.

Orson No.

Pause.

Philip (*to Joe*) He tried to get you thrown into –?

Joe But you hired me – both of us – right out of grad. school. You brought us into the Department.

Orson In life, you take one thing at a time. (*He downs his sherry.*) My understanding was that my students were in college to study. Those who wished not to or had better, more relevant things to do, were welcome to go do them.

Pause.

Philip (*changing the subject*) Lamb House is quite beautiful, Katie. If you feel like it you really should go and take a look. (*to Orson*) James spent what? Maybe twenty years there.

Orson Didn't you read the plaque?

Frankie Lewis comes out of the house; as she does she puts on her coat.

Frankie No one's been murdered by terrorists today. Though Donna Silliman has left her passport on a bus.

Orson Silliman? Is that Jewish?

Joe No. (*Beat. Confused, he looks at the others.*) I think her background's Greek. But what does that have to do with anything?

Orson shrugs.

Frankie Henry's taking her to the Embassy.

Orson Henry?

Philip Henry McNeil. He and his wife are with us as well.

Orson Really? The Department is that affluent now? (*He laughs to himself and shakes his head.*)

Short pause.

Philip (*to Frankie*) If you feel like it, Lamb House is just –

Harriet No one ever lost their passport when we ran the trip. (*Beat.*) What sort of girl is this one?

Orson She's not Jewish.

Harriet I heard this, Orson.

Beat.

Joe Well –. She's –. (*Beat.*) She's smart. (*Beat.*) She's fine. Isn't she, Katie? Katie knows her.

Katie I don't *know* her. I've talked to her a few times. She's OK. She's really OK. (*Beat.*) I like her.

Short pause.

Joe (*to Orson*) Katie likes her.

Orson nods and pours himself another sherry. Joe looks to Frankie and to Philip.

Orson, since Henry McNeil's name has come up on its own. Would you have a minute or two for business?

Short pause.

Orson (*nodding towards Katie*) What about . . .?

Joe Katie, maybe you should go take a look at Lamb House now.

Harriet Or come inside with me. I was just about to make the salad.

Katie I'd be happy to help, Mrs Baldwin. (*to the others, as they go*) I understand. Department business.

They go into the house.

Joe It was easier, Orson, when she wasn't going to the College. She wasn't interested in anything we talked about then. Anyway, about Henry.

Orson I know what you –

Joe You probably do, but let me say it anyway.

Orson And I told you –

Joe I know you did, but please, Orson, I'm the Chairman of the Department now, not you. (*Short pause.*) Sorry.

Orson Never be sorry for saying the truth.

Short pause.

Joe The Dean says –. (*to Philip and Frankie*) Correct me if I misstate. (*to Orson*) He says that we either release Henry after this term or offer him tenure track. It's no more one-year contracts for him. (*Beat.*) Of course he's right. It isn't fair to anyone.

Orson No. It isn't. (*Beat.*) But I gather, Mr Chairman, that you don't wish to offer him –

Joe His degree, Orson, it's from Case Western Reserve. That's not exactly Harvard.

Orson No.

Joe That is not our standard.

Orson No.

Philip He's been great to have though. Really filled the gaps. Who else was going to teach Milton?

Frankie He's a dear, lovely man.

Philip And Betty –. Everyone adores her.

Joe They paid their own way here. He wanted that much to come. (*Beat.*) I guess he felt if he came then –

Orson He's here to kiss ass, is that what you want to say?

Joe No. I'm not –. I wouldn't put it that way. (*Beat.*) He's not official. His being here. That's all I meant to say.

   Pause.

Philip (*finally*) Any advice, Orson?

Orson (*turning to them*) If you're talking about next year –

Joe We are.

Orson Then you'd better start interviewing, it's already –

Joe We have.

   Beat.

Orson Then McNeil already knows.

Joe No. (*Beat.*) No, he doesn't.

Philip He's hoping for one more year. He's been applying all over the place. But he's set his sights a little too high, we think.

Orson Of course! We've spoiled him!

Frankie He's had a couple of close calls.

Joe Henry getting something, that would be the answer. That's the hope.

Orson Yes, that would let you off the hook. (*He laughs to himself. Short pause.*) I don't see what choice you have but to tell him. Especially as you've begun to interview.

Joe We've offered someone his job actually.

Orson Then –

Joe (*turning to Philip and Frankie*) Young woman out of Yale. Very bright, isn't she? She'll teach Milton as well. Seems to be he's even a hobby of hers, if you can believe that. (*He laughs. No one else does. To Orson*) She hasn't *signed* the contract. I guess we could lose her. I had thought that maybe we shouldn't tell Henry until we were absolutely sure we had this new person. I didn't want to get the Department in a hole.

Orson No. You don't want to do that. Never do that. (*Beat.*) The problem then is – what to tell Henry now.

Joe I know you've had to deal with things like this before.

Philip He's spent a lot of money, just the airfares for him and Betty –

Orson Have you thought about telling McNeil the truth?

Joe looks to Frankie and Philip.

Joe We've been telling him the truth, Orson. You don't think that we've been lying –?

Orson I mean all the truth. Everything. Tell him he's out. Come next year that is the fact, isn't it?

Joe Yes, but –. (*He looks to Philip and Frankie.*) Yes. That is the fact. Even if this woman from Yale doesn't –. I have a file of at least ten others.

Orson I'm thinking of the Department now. (*He turns and points his finger at Joe.*) As you should be, Joe. (*Beat.*) The longer you wait the more resentful he's going to be. This sort of situation, it can cause a lot of shit. Suddenly you have a teacher who isn't bothering to teach any more. This has happened, Joe.

Joe I know the case you're talking about.

Philip If that's the thinking, why not just tell Henry the last day of classes when he can't do any harm? (*Beat.*) I'm not suggesting this.

Orson It wouldn't work. He'd have forced the issue weeks before with the Dean. (*Beat.*) You tell him now, you also tell him he's got a recommendation from you whenever he needs it. Whether he's resentful or not *there's* his reason for behaving himself.

    Pause.

Joe Then the right thing seems to be to tell him. (*Beat.*) The truth.

Orson If I were you.

    Short pause.

Philip I agree with Orson. We should tell him.

Frankie We have to, Joe. (*Beat. To Philip*) I love Henry, don't you?

    Short pause.

Joe Then – OK. (*to Frankie and Philip*) I'll do it. While we're here, I'll do it. (*Beat.*) This week I'll – (*Beat.*) Tomorrow I will do it. (*Beat.*) Thanks, Orson. Thanks for your wisdom.

    Orson nods and pours himself more sherry.

Orson (*as he pours*) Too bad Henry's not black. He'd get a job like that. (*He snaps his fingers.*)

Philip Orson, that's – (*He stops himself.*)

Orson How are the children, Frankie?

Frankie Great. (*Beat.*) And Howard's great too. Sends his best.

Joe Howard was given the Stirling Biology Chair, you know.

Orson I read this in the *Alumni Review*. Congratulations.

Harriet and Katie come out.

Harriet Can we come out now? You looked from the window like you were winding down.

Orson I'm sorry, we didn't mean to –

Harriet Dinner will be ready in ten minutes.

They sit. Pause.

Orson Anyone want more sherry?

They shake their heads.

Harriet So how many students do you have with you this year?

Joe It's twenty-two, isn't it? Counting Katie.

Katie Why wouldn't you count me, I'm a student.

Joe And we've seen what? Fifteen plays so far, in the first two and a half weeks. Another, I think –

Philip Twelve or thirteen to go.

Frankie We've seen some wonderful things. We'll be in Stratford later this week.

Orson The students will love that. When I ran this course Stratford was always the highpoint. (*Short pause. He laughs to himself.*) I remember a *Much Ado* we saw –

Joe I think I was with you that year.

Frankie We saw a *Misanthrope* that was very funny, Orson.

Orson I don't like French plays. I don't know why.

Philip There was the Shaw. Katie just loved the Shaw.

Katie (*smiling*) I didn't say I loved it that much!

Joe Don't back down now!

He laughs. All except the Baldwins laugh.

Orson Shaw is very underestimated today. Very. You know they've discovered some letters between James and Shaw. Very interesting.

Harriet You've been to the National, I suppose.

Frankie A few times already. It's like nothing else, is it?

Short pause.

Philip At one of the buffets we had a main course and wine and it cost what?

Frankie Five pounds at the most.

Joe Not even that much.

Philip It was under three. I mean, it was cheap.

SCENE THREE

Projection: FOYLE'S BOOKSHOP, STREET LEVEL.

A large table full of books with only their spines showing (the sale table). Joe Taylor, Philip Brown and Henry McNeil browse through the books on the table. Pause. Philip picks out a book.

Philip (*to Joe*) Have you read this?

Joe Oh God.

Philip I know what you mean.

He puts the book back. Pause.

Henry (*with a book*) This I found pretty interesting.

Joe Did you?

Pause. They browse.

Philip (*with another book*) I think he really missed the boat on Whitman.

Joe He's good on Irving though.

Philip I didn't realize anyone even read him on Irving any more. (*Beat.*) I didn't realize anyone read Irving any more. (*He looks to Henry.*)

Henry I don't.

Joe picks up a book.

Philip What's that?

Joe (*putting it back*) Second printing. (*He picks up another.*) Ever met him?

Philip Booth? No.

Joe You should, it's an experience.

Henry I question some of the things he has had to say about Conrad.

Philip You do?

Beat.

Henry You know I did my thesis on Conrad.

Philip Then you should know. (*Short pause. He looks at the picture of Booth on the book.*) We shared a table at the MLA one day. If you'd had to watch him eat, you'd never read a word he wrote again. (*Philip has taken the book and now puts it back.*) At least not on art.

Joe (*without looking up*) In Chicago? (*Beat.*) Was the

MLA that year in Chicago?

Philip (*browsing*) Atlanta.

Beat.

Henry I was at the one in Chicago.

Pause.

Joe Philip was there too, weren't you? You brought that native American Indian woman to dinner with us. To this day, Mary thinks he's interested in native American literature.

Philip I've done some research! (*He laughs.*) She was beautiful. Made Chicago almost bearable. Though I do remember being tired all the time. (*He laughs.*)

Joe (*to Henry*) And Mary keeps saying he needs to be fixed up. That's how little she understands men.

They browse.

Jesus Christ. (*He picks up a book.*) This is the sort of thing that should be burned. (*He opens it.*) I know for a fact that he spent just two years on Hawthorne at the Princeton Library. In and out of Hawthorne scholarship in two years! And he writes a book. (*Beat.*) Junk. Nothing's digested. This is the sort of thing that drives me crazy. (*Beat. He puts book back, continues to browse. Without looking up*) I reviewed it for the *Hawthorne Quarterly*. You'd think I'd raped his daughter, the letter he wrote me. (*He laughs.*)

Philip I don't see anything I want here. I'm going upstairs to drama.

Joe I'll stay down here with Henry.

Henry I was thinking of going –

Joe Stay with me. Come on.

Henry looks to Philip.

I'd like the company.

Beat.

Philip We'll meet here in an hour and then go to Dillons.

Joe Fine.

Philip (*to Henry*) OK?

Henry Sure. Yeh. I didn't know we were –

Philip Where's Betty?

Henry She's probably in fiction.

Philip Good for her. That's where I'd be if I only had the time. (*As he leaves:*) She can come to Dillons as well of course.

He goes. Short pause.

Joe I thought that went without saying. About Betty coming with us.

Henry It does. Of course it does.

Joe Show me what you're getting?

Henry (*picking up the pile of paperbacks at his feet*) I'll probably put a few back.

Joe Huh. (*Beat.*) Nice. The Penguins though you probably can get half off. There are a million places that –. Just down the street, at the Penguin Shop, in the basement. They're used, but . . .

Henry I wouldn't care about that. I happen to even prefer used paperbacks. It's sort of a thing of mine . . .

Joe I'd look there first.

Henry Thanks. I'll put these back.

Joe Henry? (*Beat.*) Also, on the corner –

Henry The used shop. I've been –

Joe With the green front.

Henry Right. I know, when you go in –

Joe Also in the cellar. There's a whole room of Penguins.

Henry There are? (*Beat.*) Terrific.

Long pause. Joe slowly checks out Henry's pile of books. Henry pretends to browse.

Joe Just wanted to save you some money.

Henry I appreciate it. I do. (*Beat.*) So I guess now I can buy a few more books. (*He laughs.*) It's a disease, it really is, isn't it? That's what Betty calls it. She says that if I were given the choice between a last meal or a last book, I'd –

Joe (*not listening; looking through one of his books*) I hadn't realized . . .

Henry What? (*Beat.*) Looks interesting, doesn't it? I figure if I'm teaching Milton I might as well –. You know.

Joe That's quite admirable.

Pause.

Henry I love teaching Milton actually.

Joe That's – lucky.

Joe laughs, then Henry joins in, a little nervously. Short pause.

(*going back to browsing*) No luck with the job hunt, I suppose.

Henry You'd be the first to hear, Joe. After Betty. Of course.

Joe Right, I didn't think –. (*He stops himself.*) She's incredibly well liked, you know. One hears that all the time.

Henry nods.

Henry Joe. I know it'd make life a lot easier for you, if I got –

Joe That is so like you, Henry! (*Beat.*) Here you are, with a problem, and what do you do? You worry about me? (*He pats him on the back.*) You are something.

Henry It's a tight market out there.

Joe Tell me about it. The number of applications I get . . . You wouldn't want to know. (*Beat.*) But I've got to think, you –. Henry, you!

Pause. Joe pretends to browse again.

Henry Joe, if I ask you something, you'll be honest with me won't you?

Joe You have to ask that??

Henry I mean it. The truth, OK? (*Beat.*) Not just for me, but for Betty and the kids. I just need to know.

Joe Henry, what are you talking about?

Henry I know maybe I should have waited for you to bring it up. But it's why you wanted to talk to me, isn't it? Why you didn't want me to go with –?

Joe Henry, you're not making any sense.

Pause.

Henry Joe, is there any chance of my keeping my job past

35

June? (*Beat.*) Look, I've accepted that tenure track is out of the question. I've put that out of my mind.

Joe That – was a good thing to do. (*Beat.*) I would not count on getting tenure track.

Henry No. (*He laughs to himself.*) I don't any more. But still with one more year under my belt. One more year and, Joe, I'd be pretty damn attractive to a lot of colleges.

Joe You're attractive to a lot of colleges already, Henry. You just need to get a little lucky.

Henry I do have two interviews lined up.

Joe (*big smile*) Now that's good to hear! Great for you, Henry. I told everyone it would only be a matter of time.

Henry They're both with high schools, Joe.

Short pause.

Joe Oh Shit.

Henry Is there *any* chance at all of my staying on for one more year? I'm not asking for a definite yes, just is there a chance? (*Beat.*) You know I'd teach anything.

Joe That's never been an issue.

Henry If I had a whole year more. You see what I'm saying. There's hardly anything out there now. Whereas next year, I know for sure of three positions, because of retirements . . .

Joe is looking back at the table of books.

I'm sorry, if this isn't the right time. You want to look at –

Joe (*looking up*) No. No.

Short pause.

36

Henry Have you already hired someone to replace me? (*Beat.*) You have, haven't you?

Joe Who told you that? Henry, with you still thinking that you could be hired back?

Henry Then you haven't?

Joe We've interviewed. Of course.

Henry I've heard this. This does not surprise me. That's OK.

Joe I wouldn't want to give you a lot of hope.

Henry I'm not asking for a lot. (*Short pause.*) Joe. Look at me and tell me.

Joe (*looking at him*) No one's been hired yet. No.

Henry OK. Good. (*He breathes deeply.*) Excellent. Thank you. Just to have this talk has made this trip worthwhile. I'll go find Betty and tell her we're going to Dillons.

Joe And put those Penguins back and save yourself some money.

Henry I will. I'll do that. Thanks. Thanks a lot, Joe. (*He turns to go and sees Betty who has just entered.*) There you are.

Betty The system they have in this store, it drives me crazy. First you have to find the book. Then you stand in one line to get a bill, you take the bill to the cash line, you pay the cash person, then you go back –

Henry Buy it at Dillons. We're going there next.

Betty Are we?

Joe Actually I'm set to go any time. We just have to find Philip.

Henry I'll find him. I have to put these books back anyway.

Joe He's up in drama.

Henry That's what he said. (*He turns to go, then back to Betty.*) You don't mind? About Dillons?

Betty No.

Henry Good. Thanks. (*He hurries off.*)

Joe goes back to looking through the books. Pause.

Betty You didn't tell him, did you, Joe?

Joe looks up.

Joe About?

Betty You've hired his replacement. (*Beat.*) Frankie told me last night after all of you got back from the Baldwins'.

Joe She did, did she.

Betty I asked her and she told me. I knew you'd have been talking about Henry's situation. And Frankie had the guts to tell me the truth.

Joe Betty, how do you know what I've told Henry and what I haven't told –

Betty He won't even go to his interviews, Joe! He's dreaming. And what are we supposed to do? I don't even know where we'll live. Do you know how much this trip cost? Do you know why he insisted we come? (*Beat.*) He was hoping if we hung around with –

Joe I know!!! (*Short pause.*) It's going to break his heart to teach high school.

Betty True enough.

Joe (*turning to her*) You want to break his heart?!!!

Betty That doesn't make sense, Joe.

Pause.

Joe I only want to be kind. I think there is a place for kindness in this world! A place for caring! For decency! (*Short pause. He rubs his eyes, then leans on the table, sighs.*) Look. I talked to him, OK? Two minutes ago.

Betty You told him? You actually told him you'd hired –?

Joe You saw how he looked. You can thank me for being so gentle with him.

Betty And he understood you? (*Beat.*) And he understood you?!

Joe I was as clear as I could be, Betty. I can't do any more than that.

Betty I suppose not.

Short pause.

Joe You know Henry. He dreams. He hears what he wants to hear sometimes.

Betty OK.

Joe But if you're saying what I should have done was shove the fact in his face, well –

Betty No, Joe, no.

Joe I did the best I could. And it was one of the hardest things I've ever had to do to a friend. And Henry is my friend, Betty.

Beat. She nods.

So it is done. It's done. Now enough is enough. (*He starts to browse again.*) I even saved him some money on some books.

Betty Thank you.

Joe (*picking up a book*) Catch!

He throws her the book. She catches it.

I understand you like fiction. I hear that's good. I don't have much time for fiction myself . . . (*Beat.*) Let me buy that for you. I think it's only 5op.

SCENE FOUR

Projection: LYTTELTON BUFFET.

Joe Taylor and Joanne Smith sit at a table; pastry and tea in front of them; Joanne has a small shoebox beside her.

Joanne No, I didn't mean that! I love Stratford. I really do. And the Royal Shakespeare Company, it's –. It's world famous, isn't it? What more could you want? (*Beat.*) It's just –

Joe Joanne, I know what you're going to say.

Joanne I don't think you can –

Joe You're going to say, the problem with Stratford is –. Well, to be brutally blunt, it's all the Americans. Right?

Joanne How did you –?

Joe Look, I feel the same way. Every time I go there it drives me crazy.

Joanne You too? Professor Taylor, I can't tell you how –

Joe I don't know what it is about the place. Attracts them like flies.

Joanne London's not nearly so bad.

Joe They at least hesitate in London.

Joanne By and large they do.

Joe But in Stratford! Last year I think six different people came up to me. I hadn't said anything. I had even avoided eye contact. But if they sniff you out as an American –

Joanne Which in Stratford does not take a bloodhound.

Joe I tried once wearing a nice tweed cap. I loved this cap. Some guy from Louisiana nearly knocks me down, he was so excited to tell me he'd bought the same sort of cap in Edinburgh.*

Joanne I know they come right at you.

Joe Why do I care where they're from, this is what I don't understand. So they happen to be American and so am I. So big deal.

Joanne Right.

Joe We have nothing in common. I don't know –. They make the whole thing feel cheap.

Joanne By 'the whole thing' you mean being here.

Joe Absolutely.

Joanne I get that same feeling.

Joe For you it must be –. Because you're actually living here. You're a resident and everything. (*Beat.*) Then to be taken for a tourist.

Joanne It drives me crazy. So I hardly go to Stratford any more. And never. Never in the summer.

Joe *That* must be a nightmare. The summer.

Joanne Imagine your worst nightmare and then double it.

Pause. They sip their tea.

*Joe pronounces the gh as a strong g.

Joe (*taking a bite of a pastry*) Delicious. Would you like to try –?

She shakes her head.

Joanne I used to feel a little funny about it. They are after all from my country. But –. (*Beat.*) Then you hear them shout.

Joe (*eating*) If they just acted like they were guests.

Joanne My husband doesn't mind. He finds them sort of –

Joe But he's not American. So he's not the one being embarrassed.

Joanne That's true. Well put. (*Beat.*) I'll explain it that way to him. (*Short pause.*) Sometimes when I'm in a shop I try not to say anything. I just point. Maybe they'll think I'm English or something. Maybe that I don't even speak English. That I'm foreign. So I point.

Joe The accents some people have.

Joanne They don't hear themselves. (*Beat.*) Sometimes it's funny, but sometimes – (*Short pause.*) Anyway.

Joe Right. Anyway.

She starts to open the box.

Joanne It's good to talk to someone who –. Well –. You know.

Joe I know. (*He offers her the last bit of pastry.*) Are you sure?

Joanne No, thanks. (*She starts to take out piles of tickets with rubber bands around them.*)

Joe (*eating the last bite*) Incredible, the calibre of food sold in a theatre.

Joanne Here's the last lot.

Joe (*eating*) Everyone – by the way – has been raving about the seats we've had.

Joanne Good, I'm pleased to hear that. You never really know what you'll get.

Joe I don't think we've had one bad seat.

Joanne Knock wood. So – here's for this afternoon, the Lyttelton. It's wonderful by the way. You'll have a great time.

Joe Terrific.

Joanne (*handing over bunches of tickets*) The Simon Gray is tonight. (*Beat.*) It's short. (*Beat.*) Tomorrow's Stratford. Friday's Stratford again. Then the day off. That's correct, isn't it?

Joe (*going over his list that he has taken out*) That's correct.

Joanne Good. (*Beat.*) Then there's Saturday night back at the Barbican. I finally got *Les Mis*. on Monday.

Joe Thank you. Mary and I saw it in New York. The kids'll love it.

Joanne Tuesday, the Royal Court.

Joe What's there?

Joanne I forget. It's in previews.

Joe Oh really. That could be fun.

Joanne Something very Royal Courtish to be sure.

Joe I know what you mean. (*He laughs to himself.*)

Joanne Something at Wyndham's on Wednesday afternoon, then a free evening and you're gone on

43

Thursday. So there you have the rest of it. (*She pushes the tickets toward him.*) James, I'm afraid, is working late these days in the City. He sends his regrets about Wednesday night.

Joe (*looking at the tickets*) I'm sorry to hear –

Joanne But if you wouldn't mind my coming alone . . .

Joe (*looking up*) Alone? Of course not! Why would we mind? (*Beat.*) James must be doing very well.

Joanne He is. He is. (*Beat.*) We're going to buy a boat.

Beat.

Joe We haven't decided on the restaurant. But I'll –

Joanne There's no rush. I'm home most nights. (*Beat.*) And there's a machine.

Joe I'll call. When we've decided.

Joanne Good.

Philip Brown has entered with a tray.

Philip Joe, would you excuse me for a second? (*to Joanne*) Sorry to interrupt.

Joe Philip, you haven't met Joanne Smith.

Philip I don't believe I –

Joe Joanne, Philip Brown.

Joanne How do you do?

Philip How do you do? (*to Joe*) I don't mean to –

Joe Joanne's the one who bought us the theatre tickets.

Philip Oh right! Joe's former student. Wonderful seats. Every show's been great.

Joe (*to Joanne*) See what I mean? (*to Philip*) Come and sit with us.

Philip Frankie's in line –

Joe She can join us too. Sit down. Come on, there's room.

Philip puts his tray down.

And now – tell us what's the news on the Rialto? (*He laughs. No one else does.*)

Philip Donna Silliman's still missing.

Joe (*looking at his watch*) She's going to miss another play. What do some of these kids think they're here for?!

Joanne What's this –?

Philip One of our students, she wasn't in her room last night, and –. Well, you heard.

Joe I just do not understand this kind of thing!

Joanne But I guess it's got to happen all the time.

Philip Every year. Something happens every year.

Joe This one's already lost her passport once.

Joanne There's always one.

Philip We got from one of the students that she's been seeing some boy. From Amherst, if you can believe it. He's with another school group. We're trying to find out what hotel they're staying in.

Joe You've called Amherst?

Philip Frankie did. She charged it to your room. It didn't seem fair to have it on her expenses.

Joe That's fair.

Philip It seems that yesterday and today – Frankie should tell you herself – but these are their free days and the students have been encouraged to travel around a little bit. So Donna probably went with the guy somewhere.

Joe So she'll be back tomorrow. When we're in Stratford. (*Beat.*) Great.

Philip She probably hasn't thought to look at the schedule.

Joanne I am sure it will all work out.

Joe (*to Philip*) Speaking of Frankie, where was she last night?

Philip Last night? We were all at the theatre. What was the name of that play? After a while they begin to blur, don't they?

Joanne I can check the –. (*She takes out her schedule.*)

Joe I mean later. After Katie told me about Donna, I knocked on Frankie's door.

Philip And she didn't answer?

Joe shakes his head.

That's funny. (*He shrugs.*) I don't know. Maybe she's a sound sleeper, Joe. (*Beat.*) Why are you asking me?

Joanne It was *Les Liaisons Dangereuses*.

Philip What was?

Joanne The play you saw last night.

Philip That's right. With the girl with the naked back. I remember that one.

Frankie Lewis enters with a tray.

Frankie Is there room for –

Joe Of course there is. Philip, move over.

Frankie I could sit –

Joe No. No. (*to Joanne*) Frankie Lewis, Joanne Smith.

Philip Joanne's the woman who –

Frankie Yes, we met the other day. Katie introduced us.

Joanne Yes, that's right.

Frankie Each day the seats get even better. (*She nods to Philip.*) Philip.

Philip Frankie.

Frankie Phil's told you, I gather.

Philip Told what?

Joe That we have a runaway.

Philip That. Yes, he knows.

Frankie I wouldn't say 'runaway'. That's a little melodramatic, wouldn't you say? She'll be back.

Joe When we're in Stratford.

Frankie They're not children, Joe. (*to Joanne*) You were a student of Joe's.

Joe My first year teaching.

Joanne I even babysat for Katie. (*to Joe*) I didn't tell you, we had tea one afternoon last week. She's really –. She's grown up.

Frankie (*to Joe*) That's where we ran into each other. At the Tate.

Joanne Right. And Katie introduced us.

Frankie (*picking up the Hamleys bag that she brought with her*) This is in your way.

47

Joanne No, it's –

Frankie I'll set it over here. (*She does.*) Something for the boys from Hamleys.

Joe Frankie has two beautiful boys.

Joanne Congratulations.

Short pause. Suddenly Philip laughs to himself.

Philip It's funny – but when I first came in and saw Joe talking with a strange attractive young woman –

Joe Joanne Smith.

Philip I know. But I didn't know then. I didn't know you knew her, Joe. (*He shakes his head and laughs.*) So my first thought, seeing these two, was – now that is so unlike Joe Taylor. (*He laughs.*) But then it turns out you do know her. She even used to babysit . . . (*He laughs. The others are confused about what he is saying.*) Never mind.

Pause.

Frankie (*to Joe*) Donna Silliman will come back to the hotel, find we're gone, we'll leave a message and she can take a train and join us or wait for us. (*Beat.*) What else can we do?

Philip Oh Joe, you wanted to ask Frankie about last night?

Frankie (*turning to Philip*) What about last night?

Joe I knocked –

Philip He knocked on your door. What time was that?

Joe About – four.

Philip About four, he knocked. *I* told him you must be a very sound sleeper.

48

Frankie Well I am, Joe. (*Beat.*) I am a very sound sleeper. Everyone knows that.

Philip Hopefully, not everyone.

He laughs. Then the others laugh. Finally Frankie joins in.

Frankie I don't know about anyone else, but I'm still getting over my jet lag. (*Beat.*) But at least I don't go dozing off in the middle of a show.

Joe Once! The second night we're here!

Frankie (*to Joanne*) He refused to take a nap.

Philip He kept saying he'd taken this trip so many times, he didn't need a –

Joe OK! OK! (*Beat.*) Christ, will you ever let me forget it?

Short pause.

Frankie I'm sorry I didn't hear you knock.

Joe nods. Beat.

Joe Joanne's been to the play we're seeing this afternoon. She loved it.

Joanne It's very funny. I love those old Aldwych farces. They're so English.

Joe They really are.

Joanne I don't think they'd work at all in America today, do you?

Joe I can't see how. It takes a special . . .

Joanne I know what you mean. (*Beat.*) James's family is right out of one of those plays actually. (*She laughs to herself.*) The first time I met them –. They don't live posh or anything like that, but there is a cook. She used to be

James's nanny. (*Beat.*) One of the family, she is. And everyone is always saying that. Helen from Glasgow. (*Beat.*) They could not have been kinder to me. James's father, Freddy – he insists I call him Freddy – and once he gets into a chair you begin to wonder if he'll ever move out of it. (*Beat.*) Or so his mother says. James's sister made us all watch the telly. James tried to argue but I said I'd love to. I'd only been here a month and I'd hardly got used to English telly so I thought here was my chance to ask questions. (*Beat.*) So this man comes on; he tries to make some jokes which are not funny, I think to myself. Then he says something like: 'The girl went up to the boy and put her hand into his –.' He paused and a middle-aged woman completes the sentence with: '– her hand into his *golf bag*!' And everyone laughs. (*Beat.*) Even James laughed I noticed. This is peculiar I think to myself. (*Beat.*) 'Into his golf bag.' She continues now '– and pulls out a club which she used to wiggle his –.' She pauses and a middle-aged man now completes the sentence with: 'Wiggle his tee out of the ground.' (*Short pause. She sips her tea.*)

Joe Huh.

Joanne This goes on and on. And when it ends the man who started it all drops his trousers to reveal that his underpants look like the British flag. (*Short pause.*) What's amazing about England is that in time you begin to find this sort of thing funny as well. (*Beat.*) Or so I'm told. James says it's the weather. (*Beat.*) In any event, I don't think a good old Aldwych farce would work in America.

Joe No.

Philip No.

Pause.

Frankie Have you lived in London long, Joanne?

Joanne About sixteen and a half months.

Short pause.

Philip It must have been a lot of work getting us the tickets.

Joanne It was fun. I love it. (*Beat.*) I love going to the theatre. Even going to the box office. It's something to do. (*Beat.*) Professor Taylor, I'd love to do it again next year.

Joe (*hardly before she's finished*) Consider yourself hired! (*to the others*) Right?

Frankie Absolutely.

Philip You're the Chairman!

Joanne Thanks. Thank you. (*Beat. She begins to stand up.*) I should be going. You all probably have a million things to do.

Joe Us? No. We have nothing to do. What time's the show?

Frankie Two thirty.

Joe Two thirty. We've got another hour.

Joanne sits back down. Pause.

(*finally*) Frankie, I'm sure I don't need to say this, but I do think we should try to keep it to ourselves.

Frankie Keep what to ourselves??

Joe That Katie was the one who told us about Donna Silliman not being in her room. (*Beat.*) Last night. Before I knocked on your door. And you were asleep. (*Beat.*) I don't want the kids to start thinking she's a . . .

Philip Spy?

Joe Yeh. I guess. Yeh.

Joanne That must be hard for Katie.

Joe She handles it well.

Joanne Oh, I'm sure she –

Joe There's Henry and Betty.

Henry and Betty McNeil enter with trays.

Over here! There's room over here! (*to the others*) Let's squish together a little more.

They do.

Betty You're too crowded. We'll sit outside.

Joe It's raining.

Betty It stopped.

Joe It's wet then.

Henry If you think there's room.

Joe Of course there's room.

Everyone starts to squeeze together; Joanne stands.

Joanne Actually, look at the time. I should be off.

Henry I hope that we're not –

Joe There's plenty of –

Joanne Really. I just noticed the time. Thanks.

She goes. They sit.

Philip She's the one who bought the tickets.

Henry Oh. (*He stands and shouts.*) Beautiful seats!!!

Joe Don't shout.

Henry What?

Joe Never mind.

Long pause.

(*to Philip*) What if she gets pregnant?

Philip quickly turns to Frankie then back to Joe.

Philip What?

Joe Donna Silliman. On this trip. What if she got pregnant? She could you know.

Philip Perhaps even as we speak.

Frankie Philip!

Philip But really is that our problem? (*Beat.*) You're not leading up to a discussion of abortion rights, are you?

Joe No. (*He laughs.*) No. (*Beat.*) I could if you want.

Frankie That's OK.

Pause. Betty and Henry eat.

Joe Look, while I have you all together like this.

Frankie Like what?

Philip He means – so uncomfortable.

Betty If we're in the way –

Joe I just want you all to know that *I* know I'm the Chairman of the Department. So you can relax. (*Beat.*) For better or worse that is the case. And as the Chairman I personally will accept full responsibility for what happens to any of the students. OK? Do you hear me – I accept full responsibility. So the rest of you can relax.

Philip Good for you.

Frankie Thanks.

Short pause.

Henry Baldwin, when he was Chairman, would never have had the guts to say that.

Betty sighs and turns away.

What? What did I say?

Awkward pause as they try to eat and drink their tea crammed together like this.

Joe (*who has been hiding his face in the box full of tickets*) Who's going to keep the tickets? If they're left with me they're sure to end up lost. (*He laughs. No one else does.*)

SCENE FIVE

Projection: WATERLOO BRIDGE.

Joe Taylor and Henry McNeil, as they walk back across the bridge from the National Theatre. Late afternoon.

Joe Let's stop here. Wait for them to catch up. (*Beat.*) It's just drizzling.

Henry I didn't even notice.

Short pause. Joe looks back. Henry looks back.

They're taking pictures.

Beat.

Joe It was a wonderful performance, didn't you think? (*He laughs to himself.*) The English have such a delicious sense of humour.

Henry Very well put. (*Beat.*) When he hid under the table –

Joe You heard me laughing?

Henry I think I was laughing even louder.

Joe That I very much doubt. (*He laughs. Short pause.*)
The butler was excellent. He never changed his
expression.

Henry A very good actor.

Short pause.

Joe We could keep . . . (*He nods ahead.*) If you want.

Henry I don't mind waiting.

Short pause.

Joe Quite the view.

Henry nods. Beat.

Henry Though I think it's even more impressive from the
National's side.

Short pause.

Joe (*suddenly turning to Henry*) While I have you like –

Henry (*who has turned at the same time, and speaks at
the same time*) Joe, I just want to –

They both stop. They laugh.

Go ahead.

Joe No, no. Please.

Beat.

Henry I only wanted to say that –. I want to apologize
for the way Betty's been acting.

Joe Why? How has she been –?

Henry I don't know what's gotten into her. I've told her I think she's being quite a drag on the whole –

Joe Henry, she's –

Henry Why, I don't know. Maybe it's the pressure about the job. I try to tell her things do work out. (*He laughs.*) But – (*He smiles and shrugs.*) Maybe she's just a little homesick.

Joe Maybe.

   Beat.

Henry When this whole trip is over I'm sure she'll realize what a good time she had.

Joe Of course she will. (*Short pause.*) Quite the view. (*Beat.*) Sometimes I think it all looks like a postcard. That I'm inside a postcard. You ever feel that way? (*He turns and faces Henry, putting his hand on his shoulders.*)

Henry A lot.

   Joe smiles and nods and begins to turn back.

So what were you –? You were going to say something. (*Beat.*) You started –

Joe Henry . . . (*Beat.*) Look, I have no right to ask you for a favour.

Henry What are you talking about? You can say this with all the favours you have done me?

Joe I've done nothing. (*Beat.*) You paid your own way here. What you do with your time –

Henry Ask me the favour, Joe. Ask me!

Joe Promise me, if you don't want to –

Henry Ask, for Christ's sake.

Short pause.

Joe (*turning and looking over the Thames*) Philip is staying behind tomorrow. To wait for Donna Silliman. (*Beat.*) The Amherst class is due to check back into their hotel by two tomorrow. We think it's a fair guess that Donna will be at ours around the same time.

Henry So Phil's going to be waiting for her at the hotel. I think that is a very good idea. I support this, Joe.

Joe Good. (*Beat.*) I'm pleased you agree. I am. I need your support.

Henry You can always count on that.

Joe I know. I do. (*Short pause.*) But that wasn't the favour, Henry. (*Beat.*) Phil, I think, should have some company while he's waiting.

Henry And that's what you want me to do.

Joe I have no right to ask this.

Henry You have every right. Donna's been one of my students. I have a responsibility here as well.

Joe That's very very generous, Henry.

Henry Bull. It's what anyone would do. So – it's settled. I'll stay behind. Have you talked to Phil about this?

Joe He suggested it.

Henry I'm flattered.

Joe He wanted company. (*Beat.*) He wanted your company.

Henry Who likes to be alone? Should we keep our hotel rooms for the day?

Joe No. I don't want this costing you anything. You can

wait in the lobby. And the second she shows up, you and Phil bring Donna to Stratford.

Henry By train?

Joe I suppose so. I leave that up to you. Maybe there's a bus. I don't know. (*Beat.*) Henry, you do this and I think the Department will owe you at least a dinner.

Henry I don't expect anything.

Joe And we'll make sure Betty's –

Henry She won't give you any trouble.

Joe I meant, we'll look after her. (*Short pause.*) Beautiful night. The rain makes it very impressionistic. (*Beat.*) I wonder how much a sign like that cost.

Henry Just the electricity. The number of flashing bulbs.

Joe The National Theatre really must have money.

Henry (*looking back*) They're coming now.

Joe (*ignoring him, recites*)
This City now doth, like a garment, wear
The beauty of the morning; silent, bare,
   Ships, towers, domes, theatres, and temples lie
   Open unto the fields, and to the sky . . .

  Beat.

Henry Wrong bridge.

Joe Yes. I know.

Henry I didn't mean to –

Joe (*ignoring him*) The last time I was on this trip, I tried to get Baldwin to get a group, students, some of the teachers, whoever wanted to, nothing formal, and we'd all get up very early and go to Westminster Bridge, and just as the sun began to rise, we'd read –

Henry That poem.

Joe (*turning to Henry*) Just how Wordsworth wrote it. But Baldwin said who the hell would get up at dawn.

Henry He's wrong. I would. (*Beat.*) Maybe when we get back to London –

Joe You think others would come?

Betty McNeil and Frankie Lewis enter, both under umbrellas.

Betty (*to Henry*) Others would come where? And how much does it cost?

Frankie (*to Joe*) Aren't you soaked? Here, get under the umbrella.

He does.

Henry It's a surprise. Right, Joe? For when we all get back.

Philip enters with his camera.

Philip Wait a minute. Let me get one of the four of you.

They stop and turn to him.

Frankie When we get back from where?

Joe From Stratford.

Frankie Right, now we go to Stratford.

As she finished her line, flash from camera.

Joe Another one.

Awkward pause as they wait for Philip to take the photo.

Act Two

SCENE SIX

Projection: IN FRONT OF THE ROYAL SHAKESPEARE
THEATRE, STRATFORD-UPON-AVON.

*Joe Taylor and an American man, during the interval of
the matinee. Joe has a rolled-up poster under his arm and
eats ice-cream from a cup; the American smokes a
cigarette and looks through a programme.*

American They don't have any pictures of the actors in
their costumes. (*Beat.*) Did you notice?

Joe shakes his head.

A shame. The costumes are terrific.

Joe Please. (*Beat.*) Please, don't shout.

American He's good. (*He points to a picture.*) Don't you
think he's good?

Joe eats and nods.

What a costume he's got. (*Beat.*) You got a poster. I was
thinking of getting one. Which one did you get?

Joe hesitates, then shows him.

Maybe I'll get that one too.

Joe There are plenty of other –

American Look here. (*He shows him an advertisement in
the programme.*) They seem to have all kinds of shit. (*He
reads.*) 'RSC Merchandise'. (*Beat.*) Posters. T-shirts.
Records. Here's an RSC shopping bag. RSC address book.
The Game of Shakespeare. What do you think that's about?

Joe shrugs, looks away.

Maybe my niece would like that, she loves Monopoly. She kills me at it. (*He laughs.*) She's ruthless. I wonder what kind of skills this game teaches. (*Beat.*) So what part of the States do you come from?

Joe I'm British. I'm a naturalized British citizen. (*Beat.*) I tutor at Oxford.

American No kidding. I'm in insurance. (*Beat.*) So for someone like you all this must be pretty old hat.

Joe nods without looking at him.

Would you believe this was my first time? It is. Every year for years I've been promising myself . . . (*Beat.*) Finally –. Here I am. (*He laughs to himself.*) The thrill of a lifetime. (*He turns to Joe.*) Doesn't eating that stuff make you even colder?

Joe Not if you're English

American nods, shrugs, looks at the programme, then up.

American Theatre's my hobby, you know. We've got a very successful little theatre back home. The high school lets us use the auditorium. I've seen some so-called professionals that weren't any better, really. (*He laughs to himself.*) Last summer we did Thornton Wilder's *Our Town.* You want to know whose arm they twisted to play the Stage Manager? (*He laughs.*) I wasn't half bad either! (*Beat.*) Nothing like these guys, of course. (*He nods towards the theatre.*) These guys are real pros. I'm not even in their league, let me tell you. I don't even deserve to wipe the sweat off these guys' faces. You know what I mean? (*He laughs to himself.*)

Frankie hurries in.

Frankie (*as she enters*) It's just the intermission? How long *is* the play?

Joe They're saying all the words. Every now and then they have to do that. So have they called?

Frankie They're here.

Joe Here? When? They were supposed to call first.

Frankie They rented a car.

Joe A car?! I told them to take a train or a bus. I'm not sure we have it in the Department budget to rent a –

Frankie Joe, Donna Silliman wants to talk to you.

Joe Sure. And I want to talk to her. As soon as this is over, I'll –

Frankie Now.

Short pause.

Joe Now?? (*He looks towards the theatre.*) But there's still –

Frankie I think you should go.

Joe In my whole life I've only seen one professional production of –

Frankie I think it is important.

He hesitates.

Joe Why? What happened?

Frankie She's in my room. Come and talk to her.

Joe And Phil and Henry?

Frankie They went off sight-seeing. Since they missed the start of the play.

Joe hesitates, then goes back to the American.

Joe My programme, could I have it back, please? I have to leave.

American Sneaking out?

Joe No, I am not 'sneaking out'.

American They do go on and on –

Joe I am not sneaking out!

American (*handing the programme to him*) I'm not sure I would have paid a pound for that.

Joe And now there is no need, is there? (*He turns and goes off with Frankie.*)

Announcement Ladies and gentlemen, will you please take your seats. The performance is about to begin.

The American puts out his cigarette and goes off towards the theatre.

SCENE SEVEN

Projection: TRINITY CHURCH GARDEN, STRATFORD-UPON-AVON.

A garden bench. Henry McNeil and Philip Brown sit; Philip holds a piece of paper. A large book is next to Henry.

Philip (*referring to the paper*) I tell you they cheated us. And I'm not saying that because we only had the car for a few hours. I knew we had to pay for the full day.

Henry I can't believe they would –

Philip Why not? (*Beat.*) Because William Shakespeare

63

lived here? Wise up, Henry. (*Beat.*) What insurance did you agree to?

Henry I don't know. Whatever –

Philip You don't know. So first, without even asking, they stick us for the maximum insurance.

Henry How do you know that's the maximum?

Philip Because why wouldn't they?

Beat.

Henry If it was up to me to ask for less insurance then it's our fault.

Philip He saw we were in a hurry. So he took advantage. Did you add this up? (*Beat.*) I just did. Add it up. (*He hands the paper to Henry.*) Are you adding it up?

Henry Yeh. (*Short pause.*) OK. (*He hands the paper back.*)

Philip Now what excuses are you going to make for them?

Henry So they overcharged us by five pounds, big deal.

Philip Five pounds *is* a big deal to a lot of people, Henry.

Henry They made a mistake. I doubt if they'd bother to cheat someone for five pounds.

Philip Five pounds is five pounds! Five pounds adds up! First thing in the morning I'm going down there and get that five pounds back.

Henry Do what you want. If it'll make you happy.

Philip It's not my five pounds. It's the Department's five pounds. (*Beat.*) And you're coming with me.

Henry I'm not going to act like that for five pounds.

Philip You mean like you've been cheated? You have been cheated, Henry.

Henry Spend half a day to get back five pounds? Who's being foolish now?

Philip It's the principle, Henry!

Henry You'll embarrass yourself!!

Philip Have some guts, will you?!!!

Henry turns away. Pause.

OK. Sorry. (*He pats Henry on the leg.*) Sorry. I didn't mean . . . Hey, I guess we're just different people, that's all.

Henry turns back to him, nods and then smiles.

(*folding up the bill*) Forty-nine pounds for three hours. Fuck. (*He puts the bill in his pocket. Short pause.*)

Henry You should have been the one to choose the insurance.

Philip You did fine. You did.

Short pause. Henry picks up the large book – it is The Collected Works of William Shakespeare – *and begins to thumb through it.*

Henry (*without looking up*) Joe got the message, I hope.

Philip He must have.

Henry (*looking at his watch*) We said five thirty. It's almost six.

Philip (*shrugging*) Maybe the idea didn't interest him.

Henry It was his idea. In London he was the one who suggested we do this. (*Beat.*) This kind of thing. (*Beat.*)

65

Philip Well, I think we should have started with just the three of us.

Betty McNeil enters from the direction of the church. She carries a small bag.

Betty No Joe or Frankie?

They shake their heads.

Philip (*standing*) Sit down. I dried the bench with my handkerchief.

Betty No, Phil, don't –

Philip Please, I've been sitting and driving all afternoon.

Henry (*suddenly standing*) So have I. (*He offers his seat.*) Please –

Betty I don't want to sit.

They are all standing now.

Henry (*nodding towards her bag*) What'd you get?

Betty opens the bag and takes out some postcards.

Betty They were thirty pence each. But I figure since it's going to a church.

Philip Thirty pence?! (*He shakes his head in disgust. Short pause.*) It's the same in the States though. Ever been to the gift shop at say the Statue of Liberty? They rip you off there too.

Pause.

Henry (*having looked at the cards, now hands them back*) They're nice. You should have bought more.

Short pause.

Betty I thought this idea to read the poem was Joe's.

Philip We were just commenting on that. (*Short pause.*)
So how was the play this afternoon? It broke my heart to
miss it, you know.

Betty I think two Shakespeares in one day is asking for
trouble. But the kids seemed to follow this one. But we'll
see what they're like after tonight. (*Beat.*) It was three and
a half hours long.

Philip But I'll bet it seemed like an hour, right?

*Philip turns to Henry and laughs. Henry laughs
lightly.*

Betty Why is that funny?

Frankie Lewis hurries in.

Frankie Joe said to go on without him.

Philip What's the matter?

Henry What's going on?

Frankie Donna Silliman is . . . She's pretty hysterical
actually. I have to go back.

Philip Wait a minute. (*to Henry*) She was fine in the car,
wasn't she?

Henry Fine.

Philip What's she saying?

Frankie Henry, Joe would like you to drop by the hotel
before the play. Just for a second.

Henry Sure. I can go now if –

Philip Hey, if you're going then –

Frankie Stay. He just needs a minute. There's plenty of time. (*Beat.*) He's trying not to make this into a big thing.

Henry Make what into a big thing –?

Betty What happened?

Philip (*trying to take Frankie's hand*) Frankie, are you OK? You look –

Frankie (*pulling her hand away*) I'm great. I'm feeling just great, Philip. (*Beat.*) How are you feeling? (*Beat. She turns to go.*) Please just read the poem . . .

She hesitates, then hurries off. Pause. They look at each other.

Philip And I thought we were finished with Donna Silliman for the day, but I guess not. (*Short pause.*) I wonder what Joe wants to see us about.

Betty Henry. He wants to see Henry.

Short pause.

Henry We better start if I'm going to see Joe before the show. (*Beat.*) Who wants to begin? (*Beat.*) How about Betty? (*No response.*) Betty?

He holds out the book to her, after a moment she takes it. And begins to read.

Betty 'To the memory of My Beloved, The Author, Mr William Shakespeare: and what he hath left us.'

> To draw no envy (Shakespeare) on thy name
>> Am I thus ample to thy Booke, and Fame;
> While I confesse thy writings to be such,
>> As neither Man, nor Muse, can praise too much.
> 'Tis true, and all mens suffrage. But these wayes
>> Were not the paths I meant unto thy praise:
> For seeliest Ignorance on these may light,

Which, when it sounds at best, but eccho's right . . .

She hands the book to Henry.

Henry (*reading*)
Or blinde Affection, which doth ne're advance
    The truth, but gropes, and urgeth all by chance;
Or crafty Malice, might pretend this praise,
    And thinke to ruine, where it seem'd to raise.
These are, as some infamous Baud, or Whore,
    Should praise a Matron. What could hurt her more?
But thou art proofe against them, and indeed
    Above th'ill fortune of them, or the need . . .

He hands the book to Philip.

Philip (*reading*)
I therefore will begin. Soule of the Age!
    The applause! delight! the wonder of our Stage!
My Shakespeare, rise; I will not lodge thee by
    Chaucer, or Spenser, or bid Beaumont lye
A little further, to make thee a roome:
    Thou art a Moniment, without a tombe . . .

SCENE EIGHT

Projection: BAR OF THE ARDEN HOTEL, STRATFORD-UPON-AVON.

Night. The bar is closed. Joe Taylor sits at a table with Katie Taylor and Donna Silliman. They are laughing.

Joe (*to Donna*) Sounds like his theatre class was studying Harrods a lot more closely than they were the Royal Shakespeare Company. (*He laughs.*)

Donna I think they were. (*Beat.*) Looking at the kids, some of the kids and the clothes they were wearing, I think a basic knowledge of Harrods may have been a prerequisite for the class.

Joe Yeh. (*He laughs.*) What a waste of money. I don't know, maybe I'm old-fashioned but here is this opportunity –. It's like a living education. That's what England could be. I think that's what our course tries to realize. (*Beat.*) I don't know if we succeed. (*No response.*) We try. (*Beat.*) I think we come quite close to succeeding. (*Beat.*)

Donna Sure. You mind if I –?

She takes out a packet of cigarettes from her purse. Joe shakes his head.

Katie? (*She offers her one.*)

Katie Thanks.

She takes one. Joe looks at her.

For Christ's sake, it's a cigarette!

Donna Every week they had three days off to do what they wanted. No classes or anything.

Katie For travel?

Donna For farting around. That's how I met Chip. (*Beat.*) He was bored. He'd *bought* a ticket to one of the plays we were seeing. (*Beat.*) Do you believe that?

Katie shakes her head.

Joe Why is that so –?

Donna On his own he bought a ticket!

Joe I don't find that –

Donna He could have done anything. But he went to see this play. (*Beat.*) You'd really like him, Professor Taylor. He's a very good student. Reads a lot. Likes to go to bookstores. (*Beat.*) He wants to teach. (*Beat.*) We were walking out of the theatre and he sort of tapped me on the shoulder and asked for a light. (*She smokes.*) I asked where he was from. He asked where I was from. You're in a foreign country, it's nice to see someone from home. (*Beat.*) It makes you feel relaxed.

Katie I feel the same way. I've met two, three Americans on this trip.

Donna They're not –. I don't know, critical.

Katie They see the same things you see.

Donna That's it. Exactly. (*Beat.*) Though there's always . . . (*She laughs.*) One afternoon last week I went with Chip and his class on a quote unquote walking tour of Kensington. The teacher got everyone to count Rolls-Royces. Unbelievable.

Katie You're kidding!

Joe I'm sure there was –

Donna I'll bet I know more about the English theatre than his teachers do.

Joe Donna, you –

Donna OK, I missed a few plays. OK, I missed a few classes. (*Beat.*) OK, I missed a lot of plays and a lot of classes, but I'll tell you what, I'm going to see everything we see for the rest of the time we're here.

Joe We go home in six days, Donna.

Donna In those six days, then. (*Short pause. She smokes.*) Chip's now gone to Paris. (*Beat.*) His girlfriend made him go. It was either me or Paris. So I was really upset. That's why that stuff in the car – (*Beat.*) I didn't need that.

Joe No.

Katie No one does.

Donna I was vulnerable.

Joe We understand.

Donna He scared me. Professor Brown scared the hell out of me.

Beat.

Joe Talk about it as much as you want.

Long pause. Donna rubs her eyes and almost cries.

Donna (*suddenly turning*) You're not going to get Chip into trouble? It wasn't his fault. I forgot about Stratford. (*Beat.*) Chip's not his real name, you know.

Joe As we said at dinner, if you're willing to forget about it, Donna, we're willing to. (*Beat.*) At dinner you seemed to be willing to.

Donna I am. (*Beat.*) But what Professor Brown did –. Nothing like that ever happened to me –

Joe A misunderstanding.

Donna How do you misunderstand –?

Joe (*turning to Katie*) I thought this was over. We had dinner. We talked about this.

Donna And my parents? You'll talk to my parents?!

Joe Why do you assume that? (*Beat.*) We have six more days. They can be lovely days, Donna. But that will be mostly up to you. (*Short pause.*) I'm not trying to treat this lightly. I don't want you saying that's what I did. If there's more you want to say? (*Beat.*) We can stay up all night if you like. I don't want you to be unhappy with the way I have handled what's happened. (*Beat.*) What you say has happened.

Donna You do think I'm lying –

Joe I don't want you to get home and start complaining! I don't want you saying –. Look, Katie's been here. She's heard everything.

Katie Is that why you wanted me here?

Pause.

Joe We know his name isn't Chip. We know his name. (*Short pause. He looks at his watch.*) The play's over. Maybe you and Katie would like to –

Katie The rest of the class was going to a pub. I know which one.

Katie hesitates, then gets up. Philip Brown and Henry McNeil enter.

Henry Joe, you missed the whole play. I thought *Antony and* –

Joe We got talking. (*to Donna*) We finished, right? (*Beat.*) Right?

Donna (*standing*) I think we should go.

Joe Donna, before you do. (*Beat.*) I think if for no other reason than for my sake, you should say what you recall happened in the car. To Professor Brown. (*Beat.*) To his face. (*to Philip*) I don't want you saying I put words in her mouth.

Philip What's this about?

Joe Phil, please. (*Beat.*) Donna.

Donna (*after a long sigh*) I told Professor Taylor what you tried to do to me in the car on our way up here.

73

Short pause.

Philip Which was??

Donna That you tried to touch me. In fact, he did touch my breast. Actually he grabbed it. I had to push him away.

Philip Joe, this is –

Joe Wait. (*Beat.*) Donna. Is there anything else you wish to tell me? Anything at all?

She shakes her head.

You're satisfied that you've had an honest hearing? (*Beat.*) Then you can go.

Katie and Donna start to go.

Katie?

Katie What, Dad?

Joe You have money?

Katie Yes.

Joe Buy her what she wants.

Katie and Donna leave. Pause.

Sorry that the bar's closed.

Philip (*stunned*) You don't believe that girl.

Henry She's lying, isn't she?

Philip Of course. (*He laughs to himself.*) Why would I –? How could I –? (*Beat.*) Henry was in the car the whole time.

Henry Except for about three minutes when I went into a gas station for directions. I already told Joe this.

74

Philip You already . . .? You knew about this? When did Donna –?

Joe As soon as you got here. I talked to Henry before the show.

Philip (*to Henry*) So throughout the play –

Henry Joe made me promise not to say anything. He wanted to get to the truth first. (*Beat.*) And I think that was the right decision, Joe.

Philip But you told Betty?

Henry I've always made it clear, you tell me something, you are telling her something. I do not keep secrets from her.

Philip (*to Joe*) He tells Betty. (*Beat.*) And it wasn't three minutes in that gas station! It was more like thirty, forty seconds, Henry. (*Short pause.*) Anyway, I didn't do anything. Why would I do something like that? What am I crazy, Joe?

   Long pause.

Joe I don't think she's going to make a fuss. She was as scared about being yelled at for staying out and missing the bus here . . . (*Beat.*) Katie and I took her out for dinner this evening. That's why I missed the play. I figured something had to be done.

Philip To bribe her you mean?

Joe She's quite relaxed about it all now, I think. You saw her. (*Beat.*) A few hours ago . . . Sit down, Phil.

   Philip hesitates, then sits.

Henry Betty's waiting in the lobby. She wants to take a walk. After sitting all day in the theatre – (*Beat.*) It's hardly even drizzling any more.

Joe Good.

Henry hesitates, then leaves.

God, what an evening!

Philip What I do not understand is: are you saying you believe this girl.

Joe No. (*Beat.*) Of course not.

Philip Thank you. Thank you.

Joe Frankie called the Dean –

Philip The Dean? Frankie? She also knew?

Joe She's the one who got me. As a woman I think Donna –

Philip Bullshit!!

Joe As a woman I think Donna found it easier to talk to her. Initially. Then I came into the picture. As the Chairman of the Department.

Philip What did the Dean say?

Joe Donna's been having a lot of trouble of late. She's close to failing. This course – if we decided to flunk her . . . (*Beat.*) I promised her we wouldn't by the way.

Philip Another bribe?

Joe I just didn't think it was right. A whole academic career should not come down to a course like –. I mean, you can't force someone to go to the theatre. (*He laughs. Beat.*) The Dean respects you, Phil. (*Beat.*) Not once did he suggest anything but respect for you. He said that if you denied trying to molest –

Philip (*standing up*) Of course I deny it! What am I now, a rapist?!!

76

Short pause; he hesitates then sits down.

Joe Then when you have this sort of thing, where it's one person's word against another's. And there's no proof. And there isn't, Phil. She couldn't show Frankie one scratch or anything. Then it's the Dean's policy to not get involved if he can help it. (*Beat.*) I respect him for that. He said basically that I should ignore the matter as best I could. (*Beat.*) He even said we shouldn't have called. This sort of thing, it's best to keep it –. You know. You see I'm learning my job. (*He smiles.*) Things get so damn complicated. And then there's the fact that we're friends. I wouldn't want people to have accused me of –

Philip You're not the one being accused!! (*Short pause.*) Henry's wrong about the three minutes.

Joe He just wanted to be safe. He didn't want to underestimate.

Philip Fuck. (*Beat.*) One messed-up girl accuses me of pawing her and you, Henry, Frankie, the Dean, Betty –. Who else did you call? Baldwin?

Joe Yes.

Philip You called Baldwin? (*Beat.*) You called Baldwin? I don't believe it.

Joe He said he remembers warning you once about –

Philip About what?!

Joe Something about a girl, he couldn't remember.

Philip When I was a student!

Joe Ah. He didn't say that.

Philip I was fucked up over this girl. Another student! I wasn't fucking molesting anyone!!!

Joe I just had to be sure. (*Beat.*) I didn't know what to do. Baldwin suggested I call the Dean. That's where that came from. So blame him, Phil. He said I should protect myself. (*Beat.*) I talked it over with Frankie. She agreed to make the call. I think hearing about it from a woman . . . We didn't want to scare the Dean. (*Beat.*) We thought this was a great idea. I was happy to have her the one who called. (*Beat.*) The Dean could have said – get her on the next plane. Get you on the next plane. He could have said a million things. We didn't know. But now – it's over. There will be no report, nothing. This I have learned. (*Beat.*) Katie, by the way, was here the whole time tonight. Donna can't change her story. Or add to it now. Katie heard everything. This was my idea.

Philip (*quietly*) But you thought that I could –

Joe Let's go to a restaurant. I think we can still get a drink in a restaurant. Let me buy you a drink. (*Beat. Not looking at him*) How was the play? You know I felt awful letting my ticket just waste like that. I wish I could have found somebody. There must have been somebody. If I had know I'd have given it to our maid. She'd have been thrilled. A free ticket to *Antony and Cleopatra*. (*Beat.*) I feel bad. You're hurt. I don't want you to be hurt.

Philip You know, Henry probably said three minutes hoping it'd get me into trouble. He's going to need a job soon after all.

Joe Phil, Henry wouldn't –

Philip I'm joking.

Joe Don't even joke like that. People don't act that way. (*Short pause.*) So – should we go?

Philip I did touch her shoulder. I remember this. She was staring out of the car. I asked her if she needed to go to the bathroom. She said nothing. So I touched her shoulder.

Joe There's nothing wrong with that. You were trying to get her attention, right? (*Short pause.*) Frankie said she'd leave a note at the desk about where she'd be eating. So if we felt like joining her . . . (*Beat.*) Do you feel like joining her? She was a great help with Donna. You should know this. She never let up for a minute. Even more than me she never believed Donna Silliman for a second. She was right there – demanding to know which breast. Everything. She even yelled at her. Right from the beginning, she – (*Beat.*) She cared, Phil. (*Beat.*) But that shouldn't come as a surprise, because she –

Philip Sleeps with me? Is that what you're going to say? That it took a woman I sleep with to defend me from attempted rape?!! (*Beat.*) Thanks. Thanks a lot. That makes me feel a whole lot better.

Pause.

Joe No. (*Beat.*) I wasn't going to say . . .

Short pause.

Philip (*looking up at Joe*) You knew about us, didn't you? You assume everyone knows that sort of thing. We haven't exactly been subtle about it. I think even Howard knows.

Joe Of course I knew. (*He laughs.*) Sure.

He didn't know and now Philip knows this.

But what I was *going* to say was . . . Well, she's a friend. (*Beat.*) That's what I wanted to say. The other –. That has nothing to do with this, I'm sure. (*Pause.*) How was the play? I can't tell you how much I wanted to see if. Of all the plays to miss. You know I'm working on an article on *Antony and Cleopatra*. How often do you get the chance . . .

Philip (*without looking at him*) There's a matinee tomorrow. I could take over the class.

Joe No, no. It's my turn. (*Beat.*) Let me think about it. (*Beat.*) Anyway, this morning I was working on it. Amazing what you can still discover. Things hidden everywhere! (*Beat.*) You read and read and read and still you find things. (*Beat.*) In the fourth act there's a scene. Eros is putting armour on Antony and Cleopatra's there? (*He turns to Philip who nods.*) Well this is – iconographically speaking – *The Arming of Mars*, Phil. It's the painting brought to life! Eros is Cupid, see. Antony is Mars, of course. And Cleopatra, she's even referred to as Venus in the play, isn't she? (*Beat.*) She is. So what I've discovered is: Shakespeare has gone and written a scene and based it on a painting! (*He shakes his head.*) Structurally then, here is a representation not of life, but of another representation!!

Short pause.

Philip That's –. Publishable.

Short pause.

Joe Maybe I should clean up this mess.

He begins to pick up the glasses off the table; dumps the ashes from the ashtray into a glass; crumples up little bits of garbage, etc.

SCENE NINE

Projection: PIZZA HUT, UNION STREET, STRATFORD-UPON-AVON.

Later that night. Frankie Lewis at a table; Joe Taylor is

*taking off his coat and sitting down. Frankie has a pizza
and a pitcher of beer in front of her.*

Frankie I think it's supposed to close in –

Joe He's just taking a short walk. But if you want to go,
we –

Frankie No, I was just –. When I ordered they said they
close in – (*She looks at her watch.*)

Joe I don't want anything anyway.

He starts to stand up.

Frankie (*looking around*) But I guess they'll tell us.

Joe True enough.

He sits back down. Frankie eats.

Take your time. (*Short pause.*) He said he'd only be a
minute or so. (*Beat.*) He wanted a few minutes by himself.

Frankie How's he doing? How did he take it?

Joe What was there to take? Everything was settled.
Wasn't it?

Frankie Still just to be accused of something like . . . (*She
shrugs. Eats.*) That's got to make you . . . I don't know.
(*Beat.*) A little bitch tries to save her butt and almost ruins
your career? I mean, in different hands, Joe, something
like this –. His heart must have stopped for a few beats.
Mine would have. (*Beat.*) The world can start to look
pretty scary if you let it.

Joe Yeh. (*Beat.*) But he must have known that you and I
would never . . .

Frankie Once he caught his breath, but before that . . .
What a nightmare for him. (*She pours some beer.*) You're
sure you don't want –.

81

Joe shakes his head.

Joe Save it for Phil. (*Short pause.*) I think taking her out to dinner helped out a lot. Good idea.

Frankie Thanks.

Joe Once she relaxed.

Frankie Once you said we weren't going to flunk her.

He shrugs.

The Department I think should pay for –. And not just hers, but your dinner as well, Joe.

He shrugs.

I'm serious. Did Katie go with you too?

Joe She was a big help.

Frankie I told you she would be. So then the Department should pay for her dinner as well. It was business, Joe, remember that. (*Beat.*) Keep the receipt. (*Short pause.*) How much was dinner?

Joe We ate at a pub.

Short pause.

Frankie Henry says they got cheated on the car rental.

Joe Shit.

Frankie They were in a hurry, so –. He and Phil are going to argue with them tomorrow.

Joe Good luck.

Frankie They should have kept it until tomorrow. We could have all gone for a drive. Wouldn't have cost any more, except for the mileage.

Joe They weren't thinking.

Frankie Henry didn't want to park it on the street.

Joe Oh.

Frankie Makes sense.

He nods. Short pause.

Joe How was the play tonight?

Frankie That's right, of all the plays for you to have missed –.

Joe I'm thinking of seeing the matinee. Phil offered to –

Frankie Do it, you won't regret it.

Joe What with the article I'm writing –

Frankie You told me. That's why I said of all the plays . . .

Joe Oh right.

Pause.

Frankie Joe. I want to say that I think you handled this whole – problem – perfectly. I thought you should hear someone say that.

Joe Thank you. I appreciate it. (*Beat.*) We try. (*He laughs.*) Thanks, Frankie.

Frankie The worst-case scenario would have been to try and keep it from the School. Better have the Dean think you're too cautious than –. No one likes surprises. You can't be too careful.

Joe No.

Frankie You've really got to protect yourself, don't you? Even when it's a silly obvious lie like this; it still could have snowballed. That little bitch . . . (*Beat.*) I couldn't have had dinner with her, Joe. I lied when I said since you weren't, then I should be at the play. I couldn't have even sat and looked at her. (*Beat.*) To accuse Phil. A man I –

Joe (*interrupting*) Respect.

Frankie I think we both do. Why not one of us next?

Joe You can't be too careful, you're right.

Frankie It's frightening.

Joe Absolutely. (*Short pause. Without looking at her*) We're sure he didn't do what she said he did?

Frankie Joe?? How can you –?

Joe We're positive?

Frankie He's our friend! He's your best friend!

Joe Who knows anything about their friends?

Frankie That's a sad admission. (*She looks at him.*) What don't you think you know?

Finally he turns away and shrugs.

Joe I will have a little of that. (*He pours some beer into a glass.*) What's important is that we have been fair to all sides.

Frankie I can agree with that.

Joe I'm sure Phil understood what I had to do.

Frankie If he doesn't, he will. Come on, you're already a ten times better Chairman than Baldwin ever was.

Joe I agree. (*He laughs to himself.*) He was an asshole. (*Beat.*) He is an asshole.

He laughs. She laughs.

Frankie It's going to be a pleasure serving under you, sir.

She smiles and salutes. He smiles, shrugs, then nods.
Pause.

By the way, Joe, the other day when you asked why I hadn't answered the door when you had knocked? Late at night? (*Beat.*) Remember that?

Joe I remember.

Frankie I realized later – (*Beat.*) I'm not that sound a sleeper to sleep through a guy knocking for –. I'll bet you knocked for a while.

Joe I did.

Frankie Anyway, I realized that I hadn't been in my room at that time. What time was it?

Joe About four.

Frankie I'd had trouble sleeping. Jet lag. I guess. And so I'd gone out walking. Imagine a woman going out walking say in New York. (*She laughs.*)

Joe She wouldn't.

Frankie No. (*Beat.*) So if it ever comes up, why it would I don't know – I was out walking. (*Beat.*) Howard knows I'm not a sound sleeper.

Joe looks down.

I called Howard today. There's two feet of snow.

Joe There's always two feet of snow.

Frankie So – nothing's changed. I told him we were having a wonderful time.

Joe Except for all the girls claiming Phil's trying to rape them.

She hesitates, then laughs. He does not laugh.

Frankie (*laughing*) At least we can laugh about it now. (*Short pause.*) I also told Howard how you and I had been palling around a lot together. Spending a lot of time –. He liked to hear that.

Frankie looks at Joe, who looks back. Philip Brown enters.

Philip You're still here.

Joe They're about to close.

Frankie Sit down. We have a few minutes yet. Here, finish my beer. I'm sure you can use it.

Philip sits.

Joe How was the walk?

Philip nods.

Frankie Must have been a traumatic night.

Philip I'm fine.

Frankie Joe was saying how well you took –

Philip I just wish to God someone would have just asked me. That's all.

Joe Come on, I did ask –

Philip To be the last person on the goddamn earth to know! You know what that feels like?!

Frankie Joe did what he thought was best.

Philip For Joe!

Joe That's not fair.

Frankie He's just learning his job.

Joe Don't apologize for me. A minute ago –

Philip He still has a lot to learn about how to treat people.

Frankie He's sorry, Phil.

Joe I'm not! (*Beat.*) How the hell did I know you didn't try to fuck her?!! (*Short pause.*) I know now of course. (*Beat. He whispers.*) I wished to avoid accusing you. I was trying to do what was right.

Frankie He was, Phil. That's what Joe was trying to do.

Short pause. Philip takes the crust left from Frankie's pizza and eats.

Joe Frankie called Howard today.

Philip looks at Frankie.

There's two feet of snow.

Frankie He sends his best to everyone.

Beat.

Philip Nice guy, Howard.

Joe Phil, Frankie was saying that the other night – when I knocked on her door, she *wasn't* asleep. She was out – walking.

Philip Frankie, he knows about –

Joe I don't know anything!

Frankie looks to Philip, then to Joe. Pause.

Frankie I don't know about you two but I'm exhausted. How long was that play? (*Beat.*) To be honest, I think it was about a week ago that I suddenly started to feel that if I had to see one more play – (*Beat.*) One more three-and-a-half-hour play. (*Beat.*) The fannies the English must have. Tough as leather. (*Short pause.*) But that passed. Once I saw the light at the end of the tunnel. Once I had that feeling of being over the hump. (*She laughs.*) Come on, they're closing.

Philip We can finish our beers. (*Beat.*) The play we're seeing on Tuesday is supposed to be very interesting. I was reading about it.

Frankie Which one is that?

Philip I forget the title. But it's a new play. Very political they say.

Joe That'll be fascinating. That's very English.

Frankie True.

   Beat.

Joe In the tradition of Shaw.

Philip Please God, don't let it be that!

   He laughs; Frankie laughs; then Joe laughs lightly.

Joe (*after a big yawn*) I don't know about you but I'm ready to go home.

SCENE TEN

Projection: WESTMINSTER BRIDGE.

Early morning. It is raining, cold and windy. Henry McNeil, Frankie Lewis, Betty McNeil, Philip Brown and Katie Taylor have come with Joe Taylor to Westminster Bridge. They all hold a single piece of paper. Joe reads from a book of poetry by Wordsworth.

Joe (*reading*)
   This City now doth like a garment wear
   The beauty of the morning; silent, bare,
      Ships, towers, domes, theatres, and temples lie

Open unto the fields, and to the sky;
All bright and glittering in the smokeless air.
Never did sun more beautifully steep
   In his first splendour valley, rock or hill;
Ne'er saw I, never felt, a calm so deep!
   The river glideth at his own sweet will;
Dear God! The very houses seem asleep;
   And all that mighty heart is lying still.

*He slowly closes the book. In the near distance, Big
Ben begins to strike six. No one looks at anyone else;
six people alone in their own thoughts. One wipes the
rain off his face, one puts up an umbrella but then takes
it down – it is too windy; a portrait of loneliness. When
the clock finishes, Joe opens his single piece of paper,
and everyone – following Joe's lead – begins to sing
quietly, so as not to embarrass themselves (and of
course in their American accents).*

Everyone (*singing*)
  God save our gracious Queen
  Long live our noble Queen,
    God save the Queen!
  Send her victorious,
  Happy and glorious,
  Long to reign over us,
    God save the Queen!

*Joe starts the second stanza, others follow, though with
a little more difficulty.*

O Lord our God, arise
Scatter her enemies,
  And make them fall.
Confound their politics,
Frustrate their knavish tricks,
On Thee our hearts we fix,
  God save us all!

Pause.

Joe Third stanza. (*He looks down at the paper.*)

SCENE ELEVEN

Projection: LUIGI'S RESTAURANT, COVENT GARDEN.

The same restaurant as in the first scene, though a larger table. Towards the end of their meal: Joe Taylor, Henry and Betty McNeil, Frankie Lewis, Philip Brown, Katie Taylor, Orson and Harriet Baldwin, and Joanne Smith.

Frankie It will be nice to get home.

Joe Back to the real world. Back to work! (*He laughs to himself.*)

Philip Don't remind me. Now we have all those journals to read. (*Beat.*) Orson, not only do we have to see the plays, but then we have to read what our students thought about them.

Orson I know the system.

Henry Phil, I enjoy reading what my students –

Philip I'm kidding, Henry.

He looks at Henry who looks away.

Frankie It has been a great time.

Joe I think we've all enjoyed ourselves.

Pause. They eat.

Harriet Has everyone tried to pack? I remember – when was that, dear?

Orson I don't know what the hell you're talking about.

Harriet Yes you do. (*Beat.*) I don't remember the year, but our things didn't fit. We had to buy a whole new suitcase at the very last minute. (*She laughs.*)

Orson The suitcase broke. We bought a new one because it had broken.

Harriet That was another year.

Orson (*shaking his head*) Oh forget it. What does it matter? So we bought a suitcase. Who cares? (*He drinks from his wineglass. Short pause.*)

Harriet (*to the others*) It's those Martinis.

Orson It is not those Martinis!

Short pause.

Frankie (*to Henry and Betty*) You never did get down to their home in East Sussex, did you? (*Beat.*) It's very beautiful. Historic, I should say.

Joanne (*to Orson*) You must be very pleased.

Betty (*to Frankie*) We were never invited.

Beat.

Harriet You weren't –. Oh, I'm terribly –. You weren't waiting for a formal –?

Beat.

Betty No. We weren't waiting for anything formal. (*Beat.*) I suppose there was just so much we wanted to do. And the time just vanished.

Short pause.

Henry Well *we've* packed everything. Except what we'll use tonight. (*Beat.*) Everything fits. We tried to restrain ourselves – (*He laughs.*)

Betty The trip cost us enough as it was.

Pause.

Joe I suspect tomorrow morning will be a real madhouse. How did *you* handle it, Orson? Some of the students say they'll take the tube to the airport.

Frankie But the luggage some of them now have.

Joe That's what I'm saying. And half of them I'm sure are down to their last 50p.

Orson That's their problem.

Beat.

Philip Orson's right. Let them find their own way. It's good training.

Short pause.

Frankie What time are we supposed to meet?

Joe In the lobby at eight. No later than eight.

Philip We better say seven thirty.

Pause.

Frankie (*to Joanne*) We're really sorry we didn't get the chance to meet your husband, Joanne. It's funny, in the beginning it seemed like there was going to be so much time –

Philip Where did the time go?

Joe looks at Philip, then at Frankie. Philip turns away.

Joanne He's hoping maybe next year.

No one seems to understand.

My husband. He's –

Orson What does your husband do?

Joanne He works in the financial City. (*Beat.*) Near St Paul's.

Orson Good for him.

Frankie I love St Paul's.

Joe (*to Joanne*) Of course, whenever you're back in the States –

Joanne We're talking about a trip –

Frankie We'd love to see you. Both of you.

Joe Katie would even let her old babysitter have her room, I suppose.

Katie I'm never there. I'm in a dorm.

Joe And why I don't know. (*to Joanne*) Do you know how much housing is now? Everything's gone crazy. (*Beat.*) But Mary said Katie should have the whole experience of college. I means, how's she going to have bull sessions with her friends until three in the morning if her parents are right next door? (*He laughs.*) That sort of thing. Right, Katie?

Orson (*eating*) Or how's she going to have boys in her bed when her parents are in the next room?

Short awkward pause.

Katie (*to Orson*) That didn't stop me in high school.

Beat, then laughter.

Harriet Good for you. Give it back to him.

Joe By the way, I was reading through Katie's journal this morning –

Katie Dad –!

Joe You let me. I wasn't doing anything you didn't know about. She's got some real interesting things to say about the RSC's *As You Like It*. Very interesting.

Philip Really . . .?

Joe You'll have to read it.

Henry I'd like to.

Joe (*to Katie*) *The Tempest* I think you missed the point of though.

Frankie That's easy enough to do.

Harriet Especially at her age.

The others nod. Pause. They eat.

Joe What did anyone think of the play last night?

Philip There's a loaded question.

Joe No. Really. I haven't heard anyone say a word.

Orson What was the play last night?

Joe What was the title? I don't remember. That says something. (*He laughs.*) Some new play, Orson. I wouldn't rush out.

Philip I liked it.

Beat.

Joe Good. (*He shrugs, then laughs.*)

Philip Look, your problem is that you don't think politics belongs in the theatre.

Joe First, I've never said that. In fact, I have often argued the opposite. Who defends Shaw?

Frankie Please, keep Shaw out of this.

94

Joe And second, I happen to believe there is a difference between politics and sentimental whining. (*Beat.*) I would kill to see real political thinking on the stage. Where real problems are really addressed, Phil. Where I can be engaged! I am not a dumb person. We should not be treated like we were. This is all I'm saying.

Philip And last night –

Joe If someone is going to start preaching to me then he – or she – better have something very very interesting to say. That's all. But to be a captive audience, forced to listen either to what I already know or what I know to be a very simplistic, you know, explanation, then – well, I want to run screaming into the night. Period.

Philip Bullshit. I repeat, your problem is that you don't think politics, today's politics, even belong in a play.

Orson Why is that a problem?!!

Pause.

Katie (*standing*) Excuse me. Before you get started again, I promised some of the women I'd join up with them. It's our last night as well.

Joe Yes. You told me you'd have to leave early.

Henry It was our pleasure to have you, even if for a short time.

Harriet She's our godchild, you know.

Betty I didn't know.

Katie has opened her purse.

Joe No, no, no! Please, Katie. I'm not that poor. I'm not rich, God knows, but I'm not so poor as that.

Katie Thanks, Dad. (*She turns to leave.*) Don't stay up too late.

Harriet (*laughing*) Listen to her.

Joe Katie, wait a minute. You still have your camera?

Katie Yes.

Joe Come on, of all of us. Come on. (*He starts moving people together.*)

Katie I don't know if there's enough –

Joe Try. What's to lose? A little closer. (*Beat.*) Of our last night.

Katie OK.

Everyone is posed.

Ready? One. Two. Three.

Joe Everyone smile. Are we smiling?

Clicks. Everyone moves.

Another one.

Orson No, no. One's enough.

Philip Please, Joe. We're still eating.

Joe It's probably too dark anyway.

He waves Katie off. She leaves.

Frankie Thanks, Katie!

Henry Thanks!

Short pause.

Joe So in this play, we're meant to feel sympathy for miners. Good. Fine. Who doesn't like miners?

Orson In my day –

Philip Anyone with a political view you tried to arrest, Orson.

Orson Only when it got in the way of –

Harriet Please.

Joe And it gave me goosebumps. This play. Why?

Philip Because it touched –

Joe Because it pushed obvious buttons! Things in this world are complicated. Not simplistic. You don't help yourself or anyone else by not recognizing that. By not using the mind you've got. (*Beat.*) Isn't that what we teach? Isn't that why we have our students read what we do – so that they can learn to think? (*Beat.*) A mind is not a reflex, it is a living thing.

Henry The President of the College said that at last year's graduation.

Joe I know. And I liked it.

   Short pause.

Philip And I liked the play. So that's that.

Frankie I liked it too.

Joe Who doesn't like a good cry?

Frankie I learned something about miners.

Joe You learned what you already believed, Frankie. Period. (*Beat.*) Trust me, this sort of theatre is old fashioned. We went through that twenty years ago. (*Beat.*) You certainly don't find it in the States any more. (*Beat.*) And in another five, ten years you won't find it here either. (*Beat.*) I don't want to see it. Americans don't want to see it. (*Pause.*) Sorry, I'm dominating the –

Philip We argue like this all the time.

Frankie (*to Orson and Harriet*) They do. This I can swear to.

Orson Nice to see ideas still being discussed in the Department. (*Beat.*) I was afraid after I'd left . . .

Beat.

Joe (*nodding towards Philip*) He's fun to argue with. He really is. He never seems to learn, Philip. And I can't help but play devil's advocate. Five kids with armbands walking around telling the College to disinvest in South Africa, and you'd think from listening to Phil that it's the sixties all over again. (*He laughs.*)

Philip Disinvestment has a point.

Joe Of course it has a point. I don't argue with that. It's your Polyanna-ish hope that is so irritating! It's like he never learns! (*Beat.*) Of course South Africa's bad! Of course!!!

Long pause. They eat.

Betty Professor Baldwin, how is your book coming? Frankie was telling me a little about it.

Joanne What is the book about?

Harriet Orson is editing the collected letters of Harold Frederic for Cornell University Press.

Orson I'm writing the introduction as well.

Frankie That I didn't know.

Short pause.

Joanne I'll be ignorant, who's Harold Frederic?

Henry (*before anyone else can answer*) Nineteenth-century American novelist. Very interesting. Very important.

Joanne Never heard of him.

Philip Edmund Wilson liked him.

Pause.

Harriet We've gotten the proofs.

Frankie You're that close?

Orson Mmmmmmmmmmmmm. (*Short pause.*) Harriet's been helping, haven't you? (*Beat.*) We read them out loud to each other, as we proof. Every night from six to nine. We do about fourteen pages an evening that way. (*Beat.*) Harriet has a lovely voice. (*Pause.*) Henry James helped raise money for Frederic's family when he died.

Harriet He died drunk. (*Beat.*) He had a drinking problem.

Short pause.

Orson He was a good friend of James. He lived quite a long time in England.

Harriet He is said to have called Henry James an effeminate old donkey who lives with a herd of other donkeys around him and insists on being treated as if he were the Pope. (*Beat. To Orson*) I think I got that right.

Orson I doubt if Frederic either said it or felt that way. It is part of the Frederic myth though. (*Beat.*) He had two wives, though only one officially. Two sets of children. One in America, one here. He liked women. They liked him.

Harriet Though both families he stuck in the country while he himself went off to carouse in the city. (*She shakes her head.*)

Joanne Sounds very –

Orson He wrote *The Damnation of Theron Ware*. Do you know it?

99

Joanne shakes her head.

A very sexy book. (*Beat*.) I reread it all the time.

Pause.

Joanne While I have all of you here, I was wondering if there was anything different or whatever that I could do for next year. If you don't mind I'd like to pick your brains.

Philip I don't know.

Henry We had great seats.

Joanne I'm sorry I couldn't get any speakers.

Frankie I think it worked out just fine like it did.

Joe Sometimes a speaker, well, if they don't know the class . . .

Joanne I wanted to get an actor.

Betty That would have been interesting.

Joanne There's a friend of a friend who knows someone who is with the Royal Shakespeare Company.

Philip Really? The students would have loved that.

Joanne But he wanted fifty pounds.

Philip For one class? Forget it.

Joanne That's what I said. I had thought that they'd do this sort of thing for free.

Frankie I would too.

Philip You'd think they'd want to meet their audience.

Joe Or just for the publicity.

Joanne But if you are interested for next year . . .

Joe We'd have to put it in the budget.

Philip Absolutely.

Joanne Then I guess it was a good thing I didn't tell the guy it was OK.

Philip For next year? He needs to know now?

Joanne For this time. He said he needed an answer right then and there.

Joe That would have been a disaster, really. I think we're what? Quite a lot in the red already. What with the car rental.

Frankie Oh and I said the Department should pay for Joe's dinner in Stratford.

Henry With Donna Silliman?

Orson Who's Donna Silliman?

Betty That girl who said Phil –

Orson Oh yes. The Department should pay for that sort of thing. (*Beat.*) Got caught with your pants down, did you, Philip? (*He laughs.*)

Philip She made it up, Orson.

Orson (*laughing*) I'm sure she did! I'm sure! (*Short pause.*) Henry, I hear you have to move on. All I can say is you shall be missed, dear boy.

Henry I don't think that is totally settled as yet. For next year, I mean. (*He looks around. No one looks at him.*)

Orson Too bad you're not black.

Joe I don't know about anyone else, but I'm beginning to feel the wine.

Orson Yes, we should get another bottle!

Frankie No, no! (*Beat.*) I think I wouldn't mind getting back. I haven't even started to pack.

Joe I thought you were going to pack this afternoon. What did you do all day if you didn't pack? (*He suddenly turns to Philip.*)

Philip We should get the check.

Joe (*staring at him*) We already have.

Henry Let me see. (*He takes the bill.*)

Philip I think we should treat Joanne.

Frankie Yes, for all her tireless work.

Joanne No, really.

Joe Out of the Department?

Philip We should split hers.

Joanne No, no please, it's I who –

Philip We insist.

Joe If she wants to pay, Phil.

   Short pause.

Joanne I'm serious. Let me pay for myself.

   Philip hesitates, then nods.

Orson (*to Betty*) Within twenty-four hours of Henry James having two strokes, he was calling for a thesaurus; the doctor had called his condition paralytic and he thought there was a more accurate word. (*He laughs.*) He loved words. I suppose you have to.

Harriet Orson.

   He is quite drunk now.

I'll pay ours. What did you have, the beef spaghetti?

He shrugs.

At least one of these four bottles is yours. We'll pay for one whole bottle.

Betty Actually, I think he drank –

Philip I'll buy your drinks, Joe. You bought me drinks at the Barbican.

Joe But only because you bought me drinks at the National. No, no, you don't owe me.

Philip Still, that's OK.

Joe No. (*Beat.*) Katie didn't have anything to drink, did she? Did anyone notice?

Betty She must have. Her glass has been used.

Henry Put in something. Don't put in much.

Joe Let's say seven pounds twenty. What's the VAT on that?

Philip Just estimate, Joe.

Betty (*to Henry*) Here's some money.

Joe Let me look at that. (*He takes the bill.*) I say we leave no more than 10 per cent. I mean we're leaving tomorrow, right? We're not coming back for a year.

TWO SHAKESPEAREAN ACTORS

for Anton Lesser and Roger Michell

This play was commissioned by the
Royal Shakespeare Company

Characters

ACTORS AT THE BROADWAY THEATRE
(*in parentheses, the parts they play*)
Edwin Forrest (Macbeth; Metamora), *early forties*
Miss Jane Bass (1st Witch), *twenties*
Miss Helen Burton (2nd Witch; Goodenough), *twenties*
Miss Anne Holland (3rd Witch; Nahmeokee), *twenties*
Tilton (Porter; Church), *sixties*
Thomas Fisher (Young Siward; Kaweshine), *late twenties*
Fanny Wallack (Lady Macbeth), *forties*
Robert Jones (Banquo, Malcolm; Anrawandah),
early thirties
Mr Blakely (Duncan; Errington), *fifties*
Scott (normally plays Macduff, but is injured), *thirties*
John Ryder (fills in as Macduff), *English and the
travelling companion of Macready, thirties*

ACTORS AT THE ASTOR PLACE OPERA HOUSE
(*in parentheses, the parts they play*)
William Charles Macready (Macbeth), *English, late fifties*
Charles Clark (Macduff), *forties*
Mrs Pope (Lady Macbeth), *thirties*
George Bradshaw (Banquo), *forties*
Frederick Wemyss (Siward, Old Man), *sixties*
James Bridges (Young Siward, 3rd Witch, Ross),
early twenties
John Sefton (1st Witch, Donalbain), *forties*
Mr Chippindale (2nd Witch), *forties*
Peter Arnold (Malcolm), *twenties*

OTHERS
Catherine Forrest, *wife of Edwin, English, thirties*
Miss Wemyss, *an aspiring actress,*
daughter of Frederick Wemyss, late teens
Dion Boucicault, *playwright and actor,*
English/Irish, thirties
Agnes Robertson, *actress and Boucicault's wife, late*
twenties
Washington Irving, *writer and amateur actor, sixties*
Other actors, and servants

This play concerns imagined events surrounding the
following true incident: on Thursday 10 May 1849,
while the English actor William Charles Macready was
performing Macbeth *at the Astor Place Opera House*
in New York City, a riot erupted which resulted in the
death of thirty-four people and the injury of over a
hundred more.

Two Shakespearean Actors opened at the Swan Theatre, Stratford-upon-Avon, on 29 August 1990. The cast was as follows:

Mrs Catherine Forrest Mary Chater
Mrs Pope Penny Jones
Miss Jane Bass Polly Kemp
Mrs Agnes Boucicault Yolanda Vazquez
Miss Helen Burton Catherine White
Thomas Fisher George Anton
Washington Irving John Bott
John Sefton Michael Bott
Frederick Wemyss Alfred Burke
Charles Clark Michael Gardiner
Dion Boucicault Ciaran Hinds
John Ryder Paul Jesson
Edwin Forrest Anton Lesser
Scott Trevor Martin
Tilton George Raistrick
James Bridges Vincent Regan
Robert Jones Ken Shorter
George Bradshaw John Warnaby
William Charles Macready John Carlisle
Mr Blakely Arnold Yarrow
Miss Ann Holland Georgiana Dacombe
Peter Arnold Andrew Havill
Mr Chippindale Bill McGuirk
Miss Wemyss Rowena King

Directed by Roger Michell
Assistant Director Clarissa Brown
Designed by Alexandra Byrne
Lighting Design by Rick Fisher
Music by Jeremy Sams
Stage Management Jondon Gourkan, David Mann, Liz Lawrence

Two Shakespearean Actors was subsequently produced by Lincoln Center Theatre (Gregory Mosher, Director, Bernard Gersten, Executive Producer) at The Cort Theatre on 17 December 1991. The cast was as follows:

William Charles Macready Brian Bedford
Edwin Forrest Victor Garber
Catherine Forrest Frances Conroy
John Ryder Željko Ivanek
Dion Boucicault Eric Stoltz
Agnes Robertson Laura Innes
Washington Irving Tom Aldredge
Jane Bass Jennifer Van Dyck
Helen Burton Judy Kuhn
Anne Holland Hope Davis
Tilton Tom Lacy
Thomas Fisher Graham Winton
Robert Jones John Wojda
Mr Blakeley Richard Clarke
Scott Jeffrey Allan Chandler
Mrs Pope Le Clanché Du Rand
Charles Clark Alan Brasington
George Bradshaw Micahel Butler
James Bridges Tim MacDonald
John Sefton James Murtaugh
Mr Chippindale Mitchell Edmonds
Peter Arnold Ben Bodé

Frederick Wemyss Bill Moor
Miss Wemyss Katie Finneran
Other actors and servants played by David Andrew
MacDonald, Katie MacNichol, Susan Pellegrino, Thomas
Schall

Directed by Jack O'Brien
Set Design by David Jenkins
Costume Design by Jane Greenwood
Lighting Design by Jules Fisher
Sound Design by Jeff Ladman
Original Score by Bob James
Fight Director Steve Rankin
Production Stage Manager Alan Hall
Stage Manager Deborah Clelland

Act One

SCENE ONE

Projection: THURSDAY 3 MAY 1849. 11 P.M.

A tavern, New York. Two large tables.

At one table: six men and two women: William Charles Macready, John Ryder, Charles Clark, George Bradshaw, James Bridges, Frederick Wemyss, and Mrs Pope and Miss Wemyss. With the exceptions of Miss Wemyss and John Ryder, all are members of Macready's acting company, that is now rehearsing a production of Macbeth *at the Astor Place Opera House.*

At the other table: Tilton, an older actor, who is a member of the acting company Edwin Forrest is now performing with at the Broadway Theatre.

The Macready group has been here for some time; beer, wine, etc. on the table. Tilton has only just arrived.

Clark (*to Tilton as he sits down*) How did it happen?

Bradshaw Before you answer that, who was he playing?

Tilton Cassio.

Beat.

Bradshaw Scott as Cassio? I thought he was Forrest's Iago?

Mrs Pope Not this season. (*Beat.*) Earlier in the season.

Tilton Who told you that?

Mrs Pope In Baltimore wasn't he Iago?

Tilton Scott told you that.

Mrs Pope Didn't he sit here, at this very table and say he was born to play Iago? (*Beat.*) I heard him say this. Did anyone else hear him say this? (*Beat.*) He said this is what he learned from playing the part in Baltimore. Or maybe it was Philadelphia.

Tilton He's never played Iago in his life. (*Beat.*) Once he played it. Something like five people had to get sick at the same time. It took that sort of luck. And then he knew about every third line. That's not playing Iago. (*Beat.*) He's never actually played the part.

Mrs Pope You played Iago, didn't you, Tilton?

Tilton For years and years. (*Short pause.*) Anyway, he slipped. Playing Cassio he slipped. And . . . (*Beat.*) I wasn't on stage. This is what everyone was telling me.

Clark How much of the finger did he cut off?

Tilton All of it! (*Beat.*) I don't know. There was blood everywhere, though. I saw his shirt. After he left, it was there lying across a chair. (*Beat.*) Blood all over it. (*Beat.*) Someone said the dagger cut it all off and it was still on stage. (*Beat.*) But I didn't see it. So . . . (*He shrugs.*)

   Short pause.

Bradshaw What else was Scott playing, Tilton?

Tilton Let me think. In *Jack Cade* – what? What does he play? (*Beat.*) I'm not in *Jack Cade*. I don't remember. (*Beat.*) He's very good in it, they say. (*Beat.*) But we don't do *Jack Cade* for – two weeks? I don't remember. I think that. And then there's his Macduff. He does play Macduff. I don't know what Ned'll do about losing a Macduff. There's a part I also used to play.

Mrs Pope I can see how that would have been a very good role for you.

Tilton My wife always said that same thing. She loved my Macduff. (*Beat.*) I always thought that odd – for a wife to like such a part – what with all that happens to his family in the play.

Mrs Pope I doubt if she was thinking about it that way.

Tilton She was a smart woman, Mrs Pope.

Mrs Pope I remember her well.

Beat.

Ryder (*suddenly standing and calling*) If you need a Macduff! If this –. If he –.

Others look at him.

I know the part. I've played . . . I'm not doing anything at this –. Now. (*He turns to Macready.*) Unless you think –.

Beat.

Clark (*introducing*) Mr John Ryder.

Tilton nods.

And Mr Macready, I'm sure you –.

Tilton I have seen you on stage many many times, sir.

Macready smiles, then turns to Ryder.

Macready (*nodding towards Tilton*) What's his –?

Ryder shrugs.

Mrs Pope Tilton.

*Macready shakes his head, not knowing who he is.
Short pause.*

Tilton I shall pass this information along to Mr Forrest.

Ryder Thank you. I would appreciate it. (*He sits. Beat.*

Suddenly he stands again.) Would you care to join us? If that's all –.

Tilton I am supposed to save –. (*He gestures 'this table'.*)

Ryder nods and sits. Pause.

Bradshaw I wonder how long he'll be out.

Beat. Mrs Pope looks at him.

Scott.

Wemyss I wonder if he was drinking. Scott drinks.

Mrs Pope Not any more. Not like when he did drink.

Wemyss He was drinking like that last week.

Macready (*interrupting, not having listened to what anyone has been saying*) I only want to say – to all of you – that I am having a wonderful time. So thank you.

Others nod at him.

Mrs Pope (*to Wemyss*) When did you see him last week?

Macready (*interrupting again*) I think our rehearsals . . . I want you to know I could not be more pleased. And I am not speaking as an Englishman to –. (*Beat.*) No, I happen to love American –. Everything here is so –. It's rich. It's –. I was telling John just the other day, wasn't it? I was saying that *I* think American accents, they are so much closer to what Shakespeare himself spoke. You are so much closer. I think this has almost been proven. I mean, you – as American actors –. I appreciate the way you have taken me in. The warmth. I feel this. I –. (*Beat.*) Thank you. (*Beat. He stares at Clark.*) Much closer to what Shakespeare himself spoke. You! Without even –. Just instinctively. All one's sophistication it really can get in the way, can't it?! (*He laughs.*) We poor English actors – right, John? Well, it's so much hard work and practice and study, and then one comes here and sees you –. How you –. The energy it comes so easy for you. (*Short pause. He looks at each actor at his table, one by one.*) Anyway, I salute you. I have wanted to say this all week. Every night I tell John, I meant to say this. Here I have found in New York, an American group of –. Which is almost like a group of English actors. I can't say more. (*Short pause.*) Let me get some more to drink. (*He reaches for money.*) I won't stay long, I promise you. Don't worry. (*He laughs to himself.*) I want to buy –. I want to pay. (*He takes out some money and turns to Ryder.*) John, would you . . .?

> *He hands money to Ryder, who hesitates. Macready drinks. Ryder goes off to the bar. Pause.*

Wemyss (*to Mrs Pope*) Last week. Maybe Tuesday. He was in here drinking like he used to.

Mrs Pope I'm sorry to hear that.

Bradshaw And after he slipped and cut himself –.

Tilton Cut it off. The whole finger's off.

Bradshaw He then what? What happened to the –.

Tilton They finished the scene. Everyone. Scott too. Like nothing had happened. Blood was spurting and he stays.

Mrs Pope Incredible.

Macready Good for him! Good for him!

Mrs Pope (*to herself, shaking her head*) For two dollars a performance.

Clark Something like that happens, you don't think, you act instinctively.

Mrs Pope Stupidly.

Macready (*banging the table, ignoring everyone*) Good

for him! (*He laughs.*) John's like that too. My good friend
John. (*He gestures towards where Ryder left, then
laughs.*) He was in *Spartacus*. With me. This was with me
in Leeds. (*He coughs, getting everyone's attention.*) Listen
to this. He needs to come on with his arm on fire. And we
have worked this out. Carefully. (*Beat.*) His arm on fire.
(*Beat.*) A metal band is put around his arm. And he carries a blanket – so if anything does happen . . . Which it
shouldn't, but you want to be safe. This is an actor that I
employ. I must be safe. The blanket he is to take and pat
out the flame if –. Whatever. If he needs to, has to.
Anyway, he lights the flame just before his entrance. And
he comes on now. (*Beat.*) Fire blazing. Great effect. But
someone this time has missed a cue. So we wait a
moment. This happens even in the English theatre, let me
tell you. Someone misses an entrance. (*Beat.*) So the fire
blazes for a little longer than it is supposed to. But John,
he –. He does nothing. Then he leaves. And so on. But
then later we hear that his whole arm is quite badly
burned. (*Beat.*) He had let it burn! And why? Because he
said –. (*Beat.*) The line he is to speak – he has a line which
normally comes only a few seconds after he enters, but –
and now this line, because of the mistake, it's coming a bit
later, he says it – the line – I forget the line, but he says it.
And it gets a nice little laugh. It always gets a nice little
laugh. (*Beat.*) And he says, that's why he didn't want to
pat out the fire. Because he needed the blaze, he thought,
to get that nice laugh. (*Beat.*) So he let his arm burn! (*He
laughs. Short pause. He adds:*) Just to get the laugh!

Mrs Pope We understood.

No one else is laughing.

Macready (*laughing*) I love John. From that day, I have
loved him. That's the sort of –. I don't know. (*Beat.*)
Nothing deceptive about him. Very rare for an actor.

(*Beat.*) A good friend. (*He smiles.*) A good man to have around. (*He drinks.*)

Long pause.

Tilton (*finally*) Scott's wife was nearly hysterical. (*Beat.*) She's pregnant.

Bradshaw (*to Mrs Pope*) You know his wife.

She nods.

Macready (*suddenly hitting the table again*) In England, acting is a noble profession, gentlemen! (*Beat.*) And ladies.

Ryder enters with more to drink. No one says anything as he sets the drinks down. Awkward pause.

I won't ask you to show your scar, John. (*He laughs.*)

Mrs Pope (*quickly changing the subject*) Anyone else seen Hackett?

Wemyss Why would we –?

Mrs Pope He's offering seasons. He offered me a season.

Wemyss I wouldn't take a season.

Mrs Pope He's doubled what he's paying. At least for me. (*Beat.*) I may take a season.

Bradshaw He never asks me. We socialize. My wife sees his wife. Two three times a month, I think. But he never . . .

Tilton He came around last week after *Richelieu.*

Mrs Pope I heard this.

Tilton He made offers. (*Beat.*) To Jack. To Mary. To Florence.

Bradshaw Why does he need both Mary *and* Florence?

Wemyss Which Jack? Wheatley?

Tilton Hooper. Jack Hooper.

Mrs Pope Jack Wheatley's ill. Didn't you know?

Wemyss No. No, I didn't.

Beat.

Bradshaw I thought you'd worked a lot with Wheatley.

Wemyss No.

Bradshaw Weren't you together in –.

Wemyss Wheatley wasn't in it then. When I was. (*Beat.*) I took over his role. I saw him play the role. We've met. We've been out together. Many times. In groups. Nice man. (*Beat.*) He's not that old.

Clark He is a nice man.

Bridges He has children everywhere.

Mrs Pope I've heard this.

Wemyss Where is he?

Tilton At home. Went back to his wife.

Short pause.

Wemyss (*to his daughter*) We're about the same age. Wheatley and me.

Macready (*grabbing Clark's shoulder*) Mr Clark, it was a very good rehearsal today. Very good.

Beat.

Clark Thank you.

Short pause.

Mrs Pope Mr Macready, as you've brought up the

rehearsals . . . (*She looks at the others for a second.*) Do you happen to know if I'll be needed tomorrow in the afternoon?

Macready I don't know. (*Short pause.*) You have something else to do.

Mrs Pope If I'm needed I will be there. (*Short pause.*) If I'm not my sister has planned a tea –. She would like me to –. She needs some help. (*Beat. She turns to the others.*) But I wouldn't want to –. If it's a bother. I can work all morning. Right through lunch if you wish. If that would help.

Macready I'll do what I can, Mrs Pope.

Mrs Pope I don't want it to be a problem, so if –. (*She turns to the others.*) If it's going to cause anyone any . . . (*Beat.*) Is it? (*Beat.*) I guess it isn't, Mr Macready. No one said –.

Macready I will do what I can, Mrs Pope.

> *Long pause. Only now does it become clear just how drunk Macready is. He holds his head, breathes heavily, then finally and suddenly stands up.*

And now I will go. (*Beat.*) Before I drink too much. I do not want to drink too much. John, will you see me to a cab?

> *Ryder stands and takes his arm. Macready turns to the others and points.*

A good day! A very good day it has been! Do not be disheartened!

Wemyss (*standing*) Actually we can help. We're leaving as well. Let's go, Catherine.

Miss Wemyss (*to the others*) Thank you for letting me join you. I have enjoyed myself very much.

Wemyss takes Macready's arm from Ryder and helps him out. Catherine follows. Ryder watches them go.

Clark Why should we be disheartened? He said he thought rehearsals were going well. I think rehearsals are going well.

Mrs Pope Please sit and stay, Mr Ryder. Unless you have to . . .

Beat.

Ryder No. (*He looks around the table.*) I don't have to . . . Thank you. I'd like to very much. (*He sits back down. Pause.*) Any idea who Mr Forrest will get to play Macduff?

Tilton (*before anyone can answer*) Ever seen Macready act?

Mrs Pope We're rehearsing with –.

Tilton I mean from the audience. I have seen him many many times. (*Beat.*) Each time – it gets even worse.

Mrs Pope (*to Ryder*) Sorry, he's –.

Ryder (*holding up his hand*) No, no, please, don't –. Not for my sake. Just –.

Clark He's been fine to work with. (*Beat.*) I've worked with worse.

Mrs Pope He actually spent some time with me on a scene he isn't even in.

Bridges I saw his Richard in Philadelphia on his last tour. (*Beat.*) I don't much like that sort of acting. It's not why I go to the theatre.

Clark People like it.

Tilton English people like it.

Bradshaw Not just English people. He's performed all around the –.

Tilton Then people who want to be English people. They like it.

Bradshaw Maybe.

Bridges Rich people like it.

Tilton I agree with that too.

Mrs Pope The Astor Place Opera House people will like it. So he'll do fine. We'll do fine.

Bridges As long as there's an audience.

Tilton I wouldn't want such an audience.

Mrs Pope I say take what you can get.

Short pause.

Bridges On my own, I never go to the Astor Place.

Mrs Pope It's expensive.

Bradshaw The dressing-rooms are rather nice though.

Mrs Pope They are, aren't they?

Short pause.

Ryder I've –. (*Beat.*) I have played Macduff.

Bradshaw English actors I'll wager are very different from American actors.

Mrs Pope I hear when they go out – like this, as a group – they only speak in verse to each other.

Ryder (*quickly*) No, that's not true. We don't.

The others laugh.

We really don't. (*He realizes the joke and laughs with the others.*)

Tilton I've worked with English actors. The first thing

you learn is never leave out your money.

Mrs Pope When someone's passing through – when anyone is – and you know you can't find him again, you do not leave our your money. It has nothing to do with being –.

Bridges Are you enjoying America, Mr Ryder?

Clark You've been before?

Ryder No, I haven't. (*Beat.*) That's why Mr Macready, well, besides wanting the company, he thought I should see for myself. He said, John, you are not going to believe this. I want to be there to see your face.

> *Beat. Thomas Fisher, Jane Bass, Helen Burton, and Ann Holland – all actors working with Edwin Forrest at the Broadway Theatre – enter, on their way to Tilton's table, which he has been saving for them.*

Fisher (*while entering*) This one? Is this our table? How many –? (*He starts to count chairs.*)

Miss Bass (*to Mrs Pope at a distance*) Hello. How are you?

> *Mrs Pope smiles and nods.*

Fisher We'll need another chair.

Tilton Who's –?

Fisher Ned and Robert are at the bar getting the drinks.

Clark You can use these chairs.

Fisher (*going to the table for the chairs*) Nice to see you.

Clark And you. (*Beat.*) You know –.

Fisher Of course I do. Why don't you –. If you want.

Mrs Pope We're leaving. I'm leaving. We've been here how long?

Fisher (*taking the chair back to the other tables*) Another time then.

Bradshaw Absolutely.

The Macready table now watches the other table.

Tilton (*to Miss Bass*) How's Scott? Anyone seen Scott?

Miss Bass Ned spoke to him. (*Beat.*) The doctor wants him to sleep.

Miss Burton He wanted to come out with us. (*She smiles and shakes her head.*)

Miss Holland He's going to be fine.

Tilton Someone was saying they'd seen him drinking.

Miss Bass Tonight?

Tilton They said this tonight, yes.

Fisher He didn't seem himself, did he? Even in the dressing-room. (*Beat.*) And he never dries.

Miss Holland He dried tonight?

Fisher I think so. (*Beat.*) I'm not sure, but I think so. Sometimes with Scott it's hard to tell.

Miss Holland (*to Miss Burton*) Save a place for Robert.

Miss Burton looks at her and moves over a chair.
Edwin Forrest and Robert Jones, also an actor with Forrest's Broadway Theatre company, enter carrying the drinks.

Forrest (*while entering*) I'm spilling. (*to Jones, who is behind him*) Watch your step, don't slip. (*Beat.*) Someone should get a cloth and –. I don't want anyone to slip.

Miss Bass (*getting up*) I'll ask at the bar.

Clark We have a cloth. (*to Bridges*) Give me that. Give me the cloth.

    Bridges does.

(*holding up the cloth*) We have one.

Forrest Thank you.

Miss Bass I'll take it.

    She takes the cloth. Forrest looks at Jones.

Jones Clark. Charlie Clark.

Forrest Thank you, Mr Clark. (*He starts to turn, stops, looks back at Clark.*) Have we worked together?

Clark No. No, sir. (*Beat.*) Not yet. (*He laughs.*) Hopefully some day.

    Forrest nods.

Jones Charlie is –. In fact, you all are, aren't you? Working with Mr Macready on his *Macbeth*.

Mrs Pope We are. That's right.

Forrest And it's going well?

    They nod.

Good. (*He winks at them and goes to the other table.*)

Jones (*to the Macready table*) If you'd like to join –.

Ryder I'd love to. Thanks. (*He gets up. Introducing himself*) Ryder. John Ryder.

Jones How do you do? English?

Ryder That's right.

Clark (*to others*) Why don't we . . . He's asked us. I'm going to. (*He gets up.*)

126

Mrs Pope (*getting up*) I can just stay a minute more.

Bradshaw Me too. One minute.

They move towards the other table, carrying their drinks. Forrest is at the table beginning to serve.

Forrest Who doesn't have a glass? Who wants wine? Who wants beer? (*Beat.*) Why don't I just pass it around.

Ryder I heard you had a problem during the performance tonight.

Short pause.

Forrest We did, yes. (*Beat.*) Poor Mr Scott, he –.

Tilton I told them, Ned.

Forrest (*turning to Tilton, then back to Ryder*) Then you know. (*to the others*) Please, help yourselves. (*Beat. To Ryder*) Have we worked together?

Ryder I've never performed in America. Not that I have anything against it. (*Beat.*) I'm a friend of Mr Macready's. I help him.

Forrest I've been to England.

Ryder Of course I know that. I've seen you –.

Forrest Perhaps I saw you do something there.

Ryder Perhaps.

Forrest I'm sure I have. (*He stares at Ryder then turns to Fisher.*) Mr Fisher, I've a few notes about tonight that I'd like to give before I forget them. That's if you have a moment.

Fisher Of course, Ned.

Forrest Bring your chair.

Fisher brings his chair and sits next to Forrest. Others have sat as well, except for Ryder.

Ryder (*a little too loud*) What role was the poor man who hurt himself playing?

Short pause. Others choose to consciously ignore Ryder's question.

Forrest (*barely audible, to Fisher*) First let me say, what I thought you were doing in our first scene was quite laudable . . .

Tilton (*to the others*) You just missed Macready himself.

Bridges He was with us. He bought us . . .

Conversations begin. Small groups of two or three, with only Ryder excluded.

Clark I've got work in Cincinnati whenever I want it.

Miss Burton They all say that. Then you get to Cincinnati.

Clark Not this time. I believe these people. (*Beat.*) These people are different.

Miss Burton Go to Cincinnati then.

Many overlapping conversations now so no one is understandable. This goes on for a few moments and then: blackout.

SCENE TWO

Projection: 1 A.M.

Parlour, Edwin Forrest's house. A few chairs, a bookcase, etc.
Forrest and Miss Bass sit in chairs, fairly near to each other and occasionally glance at each other. They also have glasses in their hands. Bradshaw stands at the bookcase

browsing through the books. Ryder stands looking through a scrapbook. Long pause. Ryder closes the scrapbook, sets it on a table, notices a silver snuffbox and picks it up.

Ryder This is beautiful.

Forrest (*turning to Ryder*) Read what it says. (*Beat.*) Read it out loud so Mr Bradshaw can hear.

Bradshaw stops browsing.

Ryder (*reading from the snuffbox*) 'Presented to Edwin Forrest, Esq., by the members of the Sheffield Theatrical Company, as a mark of their esteem for him as an actor and a man.'

Beat.

Forrest Something to cherish.

Ryder Certainly . . .

Forrest Coming as it does from actors.

Short pause.

Bradshaw This was when you were in England . . .

Forrest The last time. Let me see it. I haven't noticed it for a long time.

Ryder hands him the box. Miss Bass gets up and goes to Forrest to look at the box. Short pause.

(*to Miss Bass*) They had a nice little ceremony. The man who made the speech was a very lousy actor.

He smiles, the others laugh lightly.

Brooke, I think his name was. Do you know him, Mr Ryder?

Ryder I don't know. I –. I don't think so.

Forrest I thought being English . . .

Ryder Maybe I do. I don't know. (*Beat.*) Brooke? I don't know.

Forrest hands Ryder back the box.

It is a beautiful box. (*He goes and puts it back on the table.*)

Forrest (*holding up a decanter*) Would anyone –?

Ryder I'm fine, thank you.

Forrest turns to Bradshaw, who shakes his head and goes back to browsing. He turns to Miss Bass, who now sits on the arm of his chair.

Miss Bass (*holding up her glass*) I haven't touched what I have.

Forrest puts the decanter down without pouring a drink.

Forrest (*without looking at Ryder*) Have you already gone through both scrapbooks, Mr Ryder?

Ryder I –. Both? No. I didn't know there were two. I've only seen this –.

Forrest Miss Bass knows where the other one is kept.

Miss Bass I'll get it. (*She goes to a table, opens a drawer, takes out a book.*)

Forrest I call that section the Shakespeare Corner, Mr Bradshaw.

Bradshaw I can see why. (*He laughs.*)

Forrest Warburton's edition is certainly worth a look.

Bradshaw Which is . . .?

Forrest To your left. (*Beat.*) Up one. Two over. There. That's right.

Bradshaw takes out a book.

I have nearly all the editions of Shakespeare's work. Even –. (*He stops himself and smiles.*) But we'll get to that. (*He turns to Miss Bass, who has the scrapbook.*) I'll take that, please. (*He turns back to Bradshaw.*) The actor's work – I don't have to tell you – is much more than what is on the stage. These are but some necessary tools for one's investigations. (*He takes the scrapbook and opens it.*) Come here, Mr Ryder. I plan to exhaust all of your enthusiasm as well as your patience.

Ryder I'm the one who asked to see –.

Forrest (*pointing out things in the scrapbook*) Here I am as Richard III. (*He smiles.*) This was in Dublin, you'll be interested to know.

Forrest stares at the picture. Pause. Ryder looks to Miss Bass and then to Bradshaw who has come to look over Forrest's shoulder. Finally, he turns the page.

Romeo.

Forrest stares at the picture, then sniffles, takes out a handkerchief and wipes a tearing eye. Ryder watches this, aware that he has no idea what is going on and uncomfortable because of this.

I also played Mercutio. First I played Mercutio. I was only a boy then.

He smiles at Miss Bass, who smiles and takes his hand.

Mr Wallack was the Romeo. He was much too old. Much. He should have known better. (*Beat.*) Someone should have told him. Been honest with him. (*He sighs and stands.*) I promised to show you something, didn't I,

Mr Bradshaw. Excuse me. (*He goes off.*)

Bradshaw (*to Ryder*) What's he . . .?

Ryder shrugs.

I think I will have a little of that.

He pours himself a drink. The atmosphere in the room has suddenly relaxed.

Ryder (*to Miss Bass*) Have you worked with Mr Forrest before? (*Beat.*) I mean before this season.

She looks at Bradshaw, then back at Ryder.

Miss Bass Yes. Yes I have.

Ryder Then maybe you can help me. Do you think he was being serious when he said he wanted me for Macduff?

Miss Bass Yes, I'm sure he was being serious, Mr Ryder. (*Beat.*) He needs a –.

Ryder Sometimes you don't know. People say all sorts of things. (*Beat.*) Especially late at night.

Miss Bass Rehearsals are tomorrow. I'm sure he expects you there.

Bradshaw You know the part.

Ryder In England I've played it a hundred –.

He stops himself as Mrs Catherine Forrest enters: she is in her dressing-gown. Awkward pause.

Mrs Forrest I thought I heard voices. (*Beat.*) Is my husband here or do you just come on your own now, Miss Bass?

Bradshaw He went to get something.

Mrs Forrest begins to go off in that direction.

Miss Bass How are you, Mrs Forrest?

She ignores this and goes off. Beat.

Ryder I hadn't realized he had a wife.

From off: the sound of an argument, Forrest and his wife shouting at each other; though exactly what they are shouting about cannot be heard. Ryder, Bradshaw, and Miss Bass try to ignore what they hear is happening. Ryder pours himself a drink.

Bradshaw (*to Ryder*) Have you seen the –? (*He nods towards the bookcase.*)

Ryder I haven't had the chance yet. But I'd love to. (*He goes to the bookcase.*)

Bradshaw An extraordinary collection.

They pretend to browse, as the argument continues off. Finally Forrest enters alone, carrying a large book.

Forrest (*while entering*) Pope's edition is also worth looking through. But before that . . . (*Beat. He holds up the book.*) Here is what I wanted to show you. (*He sits.*) The most precious thing I own.

Ryder and Bradshaw come closer.

I dare say, I believe it to be the only First Folio in the New World.

Ryder First Folio –? (*He instinctively reaches for it.*)

Forrest Gentle. Gentle, Mr Ryder. (*Beat.*) She breathes. This book. She lives. (*He opens it and reads.*) 'Mr William Shakespeare's Comedies, Histories & Tragedies. Published according to the True original copies. London. Printed by Issac Jaggard and Ed. Blout, 1623.'

Pause. Forrest has heard something.

Now she's crying.

Mrs Forrest can be heard crying in the next room.

(*to Ryder*) Feel the cover.

He does.

As smooth as a child's face. As smooth as a face. (*He rubs his hand across Miss Bass's face.*) What one needs to study to be a Shakespearean actor. (*He gently pats the book.*) The truth lies in our hands. (*Beat.*) The ignorance of the world knows no bounds, Mr Ryder. I have twice been criticized for reading 'dead vast' instead of saying 'dead waste'. Some quartos have it even as 'wast' – whatever that is supposed to mean – and also as 'waist' – w–a–i–s–t. (*He laughs.*) But in here, Mr Ryder, our true authority, it is 'vast'. (*Beat.*) 'Vast' for the vacancy and void of night. For the deserted emptiness. Not 'waste'. Not for what has been thrown away. 'Vast'! For the hole, the h–o–l–e! The loss of what is, what was, a loss that shall always remain a loss! (*Beat.*) You study. You learn. (*Beat.*) Like a face. That smooth. Rub your face against the book and feel it. Against your flesh.

Ryder takes the book and rubs it against his face, then hands it to Bradshaw, who does the same. Pause.

(*without looking at Ryder*) Some of Macduff's lines we cut, Mr Ryder. I shall give you such cuts tomorrow. (*Pause.*) Poor Scott, cut his finger off from here. (*He holds up his finger.*) Blood was everywhere. Somehow it even got on the sheets. (*Beat.*) Big stain on Desdemona's sheets. I noticed that as I –. I was holding the pillow. (*He looks up at them.*) Sometimes you lose yourself so much in a role. (*Beat.*) Sometimes you –. (*Beat.*) Sometimes you are so lost.

Mrs Forrest's crying is louder for a moment.

Ryder Maybe we better . . . (*Beat.*) If I'm going to be ready for rehearsal. (*He tries to smile.*)

Forrest I was good as Othello tonight. They got their money's worth.

Short pause. Ryder doesn't know whether to leave or not. Blackout.

SCENE THREE

Projection: 2 A.M.

Parlour of Macready's rooms at the New York Hotel. Miss Wemyss sits alone. Ryder has just entered.

Ryder I'm sorry, I –. Is Mr Macready . . .?

Miss Wemyss He'll be right out. He's just in there.

Ryder nods. Pause. He paces, not knowing whether to stay or go; she watches him, smiling when she catches his eye.

Ryder He left me a note. (*Beat.*) Downstairs. When I came in they gave me the note. (*Beat.*) It said he wanted to see me as soon as I . . . (*Beat.*) I just got in. It's probably too late.

Miss Wemyss I don't know.

Short pause.

Ryder (*putting on his hat*) Tell him I –.

Macready enters in his dressing-gown.

Macready Come in, John, please come in.

Ryder It's very late.

Macready Thank you for coming. Sit down. I'll fix us a drink.

135

Ryder I've had plenty tonight.

Macready A nightcap never hurts. (*Pause. He pours their drinks.*) You've met Miss Wemyss?

Ryder Tonight. At the tavern. With her father –.

Macready Of course you have! Of course! Where is my head? (*He laughs to himself. To Miss Wemyss*) And what about you, my dear, what may I get you?

Miss Wemyss I don't wish anything, Mr Macready. I am content as I am.

He suddenly bursts out laughing.

Macready I don't know what it is about her, John, but everything she says makes me laugh.

Miss Wemyss smiles at Ryder.

Ryder I think we should talk in the morning.

Wemyss enters carrying a teapot.

Wemyss (*while entering*) This is all I could –. From the kitchen. They insisted they put it in a teapot though. I don't understand this thinking. (*Beat.*) I had to stand down there and watch them pour a whole bottle into a teapot. (*He shakes his head.*)

Macready (*holding up the decanter*) Now pour it into here, Mr Wemyss. (*He turns to Ryder.*) We were beginning to get a little low.

Wemyss pours the liquor out of the pot and into the bottle. He is a bit drunk.

Your daughter just said something very funny. Very funny.

Wemyss turns to his daughter and smiles and continues to pour.

(*to Ryder*) What did she say?

Ryder I don't know. Why is Mr Wemyss –? What's he doing here?

Macready (*to Miss Wemyss*) What is it you said?

Miss Wemyss I don't remember any more.

Macready bursts out laughing, then turns to Ryder patting Wemyss on the shoulder.

Macready Frederick here wanted a little advice, didn't you?

Wemyss You've been very helpful, William.

Macready His daughter –. This is his daughter. She wishes to become an actress. Isn't this true, my dear?

She smiles.

Wemyss She has the looks for it, I think. Look at her.

She smiles again at Ryder.

Macready And –. (*Beat.*) You –. What? You wondered, correct? If there might be some place in London –. To learn. He thinks she should learn in London. That says something does it not? (*Beat.*) Someone to learn from.

Wemyss Someone to even befriend . . . (*He turns to his daughter.*) You don't know what can happen when a young woman is that far away from her family. (*He turns to Macready.*) She has a lovely family. Five daughters. They take care of each other.

Macready (*to Ryder*) I am going to look into matters for her. I shall see what there might be for –. I don't know. (*Beat.*) Perhaps an apprenticeship? (*Beat.*) Perhaps at Drury Lane? How would that strike you, my dear? (*He smiles.*)

Wemyss Drury Lane would be excellent.

Macready I cannot promise of course.

Wemyss No one is asking for a promise, William. No one. Are we?

Miss Wemyss I'm not.

Macready looks at her, smiles and finally sighs a drunk sigh. Pause.

Ryder What did you want to see me about?

Macready Drink, John. We have a whole new teapot full of drink.

He gestures for Ryder to take his drink. Ryder doesn't move.

Oh yes. That. (*He turns to Miss Wemyss.*) What would you do, Miss Wemyss? Would you ignore the threats?

Ryder What threats? What are you talking about?

Macready laughs and nods at Ryder.

Macready (*to Miss Wemyss*) Now everyone is getting worried. Don't panic, Mr Ryder, please. (*He laughs. Pause. He stops laughing and turns to Ryder.*) Mr Wemyss has been telling me that we are under threat. Or do I exaggerate?

Wemyss No. (*Beat.*) Mr Macready's life is, I believe, in some danger.

Ryder For what? Who –?

Wemyss There have been letters. I have one here. (*He takes out a letter and hands it to Ryder.*) I didn't want to mention it at the tavern, with –.

Ryder starts to hand the letter to Macready.

Macready I've seen it, John. You read it. See what you think.

Wemyss Though most in the company have been –. *Are* aware at least that something . . . You feel it in the air, I suppose. And we've all heard I guess that there are persons who are upset –.

Ryder For what reason?!

Macready Because I dare to perform the noble Thane on the same night in the same city as does the sainted American, Mr Edwin Forrest! (*He turns to Wemyss.*) Is that not the true reason?

Wemyss I don't know. (*Beat.*) Maybe. I know it's what you think.

Macready Of course it's the reason for these attacks! A perceived competition with their idol, their native idol! (*Beat.*) Ridiculous. (*Beat.*) Sheer effrontery – on my part. This is how they see it. Pure gall. And of course it would be upsetting. On the same night! For all to compare! Of course they are worried! (*He laughs.*) And an Englishman, no less! Look at the spelling. The illiterate bastards. Probably Irish.

Ryder I don't understand what they're demanding.

Macready Short of a complete surrender and my going home immediately, you mean. (*He laughs to himself.*) All in good time. All in good time.

   Beat.

Wemyss The letters are meant to frighten –.

Ryder (*to Macready*) And you take the threats seriously?

Macready I don't. (*He laughs.*) I don't. But others may. (*Beat.*) So I am suggesting that we contact Mr Forrest, present him with this irksome situation we, as guests, now confront in his homeland, and no doubt he shall do the honourable thing and see fit to perform some other of his multitude of roles that evening. (*Beat.*) Let's say *Metamora*. (*Beat.*) I understand he is especially convincing as an Indian. Americans can be, you know. An English- man would be hopeless as a savage. A pity I will not be able to see this performance myself. (*Beat.*) John, I think I am asking you to do this.

Ryder I doubt if Mr Forrest will change his repertoire at this late –.

Macready He has to! (*Short pause.*) He has many plays – they are cast – they can be mounted. I have scheduled only *Macbeth*. I have only a company for *Macbeth*. It would be impossible for me to do anything else. (*Beat.*) Besides, I understand after the accident tonight he doesn't even have a Macduff. So if he needs to explain to the public –.

Ryder He has a new Macduff. (*Pause.*) He asked me. (*Beat.*) You have Clark. You wanted Clark. I didn't have anything to do. I know I'm here to help you, but I can do both. I know the role for Christ's sake! (*Beat.*) I told Forrest I would have to speak with you first. And if you objected . . . (*Beat.*) He was desperate. But . . . Do you object?

Macready (*without looking at him*) We are a fraternity, John – the acting fraternity. We know no borders. Have no flags. (*Beat.*) So how can I object to helping out Mr Forrest. Wouldn't he do the same for me? I'll get someone else to speak with him. Someone with less to lose.

Ryder That's not fair.

Wemyss I'd be happy to.

Ryder Forrest's performance is sold out. It would be nearly impossible at this point to change the schedule.

Macready (*suddenly turning on him*) Men and women are being threatened with violence, John, and you talk about an inconvenience?!! (*Beat.*) I do not say this for myself. Do you understand? (*Beat.*) But these actors work under my protection. I have their safety as my responsibility. (*He sips his drink.*) We have not yet sold out. (*Beat.*) Two *Macbeths* in one evening may be too much for New York to bear. (*Beat.*) I cannot change. I have told you why. If he does not, these scoundrels, these ignorant hooligans have the guts, I'm afraid, to attempt what they have threatened. Does Mr Forrest realize what he will be instigating? Consciously or not. Will he alone accept the responsibility for our well-being? (*Short pause.*) I'm sure we'll be fine. (*He shrugs.*) I'm pleased you found work. I truly am.

Ryder He asked me. I didn't seek it. I must have said no ten times. (*He laughs.*)

Macready So – what else could you do? (*He reaches for the letter, takes it from Ryder, and begins to look at it again.*) I knew nothing of any problems. Any such – tensions. Where did they come from? I should have been warned. To hate one simply because one is accomplished. (*Beat.*) Had I known . . . (*He shakes his head.*)

Ryder You knew – I knew that there's some resentment when any English actor –.

Macready I am not any English actor! (*Beat.*) And I knew of no such resentment, John!! (*He sits and sighs.*) Such incidents make one long for home even more.

   Miss Wemyss starts to stand.

Please everyone, there is no need to hurry off.

She sits. Short pause.

Ryder It's very late.

Macready Yes it is. Yes. (*Pause.*) I wrote Mrs
Macready. (*to Ryder*) This was where I was when you
came in. (*to Miss Wemyss*) You didn't mind, did you?
Being left on your own? (*Short pause.*) I spoke of this
loneliness. Being away from home. (*Beat.*) She must be
getting tired of such letters. (*He laughs to himself.*) But
it is like being suspended upon the edge of a cliff. This
is how much of your country feels to me, Mr Wemyss.
As a cliff.

Wemyss nods.

I try to go to sleep and a hundred devils attack me.
(*Beat.*) And tie me up. (*Beat.*) Little devils. (*He yawns.*)
If I did not know how important what I bring is. (*Beat.*)
The need. When one is hearing Shakespeare spoken correctly for the first time. (*He smiles.*) It is an honour. And
it is a burden. One I shall gladly pass on to younger
men. (*Beat.*) When they emerge. (*Beat.*) I'm tired. Don't
go yet.

Pause.

Wemyss I have been to Drury Lane myself once. This was
years ago when I was a much younger man. (*Beat.*) I
think my daughter could be very comfortable there. I have
told all my children – there is nothing like England.
Nothing in the world.

Miss Wemyss Mr Macready has not offered to . . .

Beat.

Macready (*looking at her and smiling*) I shall. I do.
(*Beat.*) But will I remember I've offered in the morning?
(*He laughs.*) Let me think about it.

*Pause. Macready sits, staring at nothing. Miss Wemyss
smiles. Wemyss stands behind Macready's chair and
sips his drink. Ryder doesn't know whether to leave or
not. Blackout.*

SCENE FOUR

Projection: THE NEXT DAY, THE AFTERNOON.

*A bare stage, which represents the stages of the Astor
Place Opera House and the Broadway Theatre, during
rehearsals of the two* Macbeths.

*a) Broadway Theatre
Drums. Then thunder. The Three Witches (Misses Bass,
Burton and Holland) are on. (Act I.iii)*

1st Witch ... nine times nine,
Shall he dwindle, peak, and pine.
Though his bark cannot be lost.
Yet it shall be tempest-tost.

2nd Witch Show me, show me.

3rd Witch Here I have a pilot's thumb,
Wracked as homeward he did come.

Drum within.

All A drum! A drum!
Macbeth doth come.

Macbeth (Forrest) and Banquo (Jones) enter.

Macbeth So foul and fair a day I have not seen.

Banquo How far is't called to Forres? What are these,
That look not like the inhabitants o' th' earth,
And yet are on't?

Macbeth Speak, if you can. What are you?

1st Witch All hail, Macbeth! Hail to thee, Thane of Glamis!

2nd Witch All hail, Macbeth! Hail to thee, Thane of Cawdor!

3rd Witch All hail, Macbeth, that shalt be King hereafter!

Banquo Good sir, why do you start, and seem to fear
  Things that do sound so fair? To me you speak not,
  Speak then to me, who neither beg nor fear
  Your favours nor your hate.

1st Witch Hail!

2nd Witch Hail!

3rd Witch Hail!

1st Witch Lesser than Macbeth, and greater.

2nd Witch Not so happy, yet much happier.

3rd Witch Thou shalt get kings, though thou be none.
  So all hail, Macbeth and Banquo!

Macbeth Stay, you imperfect speakers, say from whence
  You owe this strange intelligence, or why
  Upon this blasted heath you stop our way
  With such prophetic greeting. Speak, I charge you.

  Witches run off, Macbeth and Banquo give chase.

b) Astor Place Opera House
The Three Witches (all male: Bridges and two older men,
John Sefton and Chippindale), Macbeth (Macready) and
Banquo (Bradshaw).

1st Witch Hail!

2nd Witch Hail!

3rd Witch Hail!

1st Witch Lesser than Macbeth, and greater.

2nd Witch Not so happy, yet much happier.

3rd Witch Thou shalt get kings, though thou be none.
So all hail, Macbeth and Banquo!

Macbeth By Sinell's death I know I am Thane of Glamis,
But how of Cawdor? The Thane of Cawdor lives,
A prosperous gentleman; and to be King
Stands not within the prospect of belief.
No more than to be Cawdor.

Witches run off, Macbeth and Banquo give chase.

c) Broadway Theatre (Act I.vi)
Out of the shadows enters Macbeth (Forrest). (Act I.vii)

Macbeth If it were done when 'tis done, then 'twere well
It were done quickly. If th' assassination
Could trammel up the consequence, and catch
With his surcease success, that but this blow
Might be the be-all and the end-all; here,
But here upon this bank and shoal of time,
We'ld jump the life to come. But in these cases
We still have judgement here, that we but teach
Bloody instructions, which, being taught, return
To plague th' inventor. This even-handed justice
Commends . . .

d) Astor Place Opera House
Macbeth (Macready) alone. (Act I.vii)

Macbeth Will plead like angels, trumpet-tongued against
The deep damnation of his taking-off;
And pity, like a naked new-born babe
Striding the blast, or heaven's cherubim horsed

Upon the sightless couriers of the air,
Shall blow the horrid deed in every eye
That tears shall drown the wind. I have no spur
To prick the sides of my intent, but only
Vaulting ambition, which o'erleaps itself
And falls on th' other –

Pause. Finally Macbeth (Macready) turns towards the wings and gives a small nod, and Lady Macbeth (Mrs Pope) enters.

> How now? What news?

Macready *(to Mrs Pope)* Closer. Closer. There. Now look at me. (*Beat.*) I look at them and you look at me. Thank you.

Beat.

Macbeth   How now? What news?

e) Broadway Theatre (Act II.i)
Macbeth (Forrest) enters with a torch.

Macbeth Is this a dagger which I see before me,
   The handle toward my hand? Come, let me clutch thee!
   I have thee not, and yet I see thee still.
   Art thou not, fatal vision, sensible
   To feeling as to sight? or art thou but
   A dagger of the mind, a false creation,
   Proceeding from the heat-oppressed brain?
   I see thee yet, in form as palpable
   As this which now I draw.
   Thou marshall'st me the way . . .

f) Both theatres are represented.
Both Macbeths (Macready and Forrest) now continue the speech together, though not necessarily in sync.

Both Macbeths   . . . that I was going,
  Mine eyes are made the fools o' th' other senses,
  Or else worth all the rest. I see thee still,
  And on thy blade and dudgeon gouts of blood,
  Which was not so before. There's no such thing.
  It is a bloody business which informs
  This to mine eyes.

  Lights begin to fade on Forrest.

                  Now o'er the one half-world
  Nature seems dead, and wicked dreams abuse
  The curtained sleep.

  *Macready is alone now. The stage represents only the
  Astor Place Opera House.*

Macbeth   Thou sure and firm-set earth,
  Hear not my steps which way they walk, for fear
  The very stones prate on my whereabout
  And take the present horror from the time,
  Which suits with it. Whiles I threat, he lives;
  Words to the heat of deeds too cold breath gives.

g) Broadway Theatre
*Very loud pounding or knocking is suddenly heard. Porter
(Tilton) hurries on. (Act II.iii)*

Porter Here's a knocking indeed! If a man were porter of
hell gate, he should have old turning the key.

  Another knock.

Knock, knock, knock. Who's there, in th' other devil's
name?

  Beat.

Tilton Wait, I think I jumped. It's what? Is it 'knock,
knock'? Or 'knock, knock, knock'? Which is the first, the

147

two or the three knocks? (*Beat.*) Please, which is the first?!

Prompter (*off*) It's the three 'knocks' first.

Tilton Really? (*Beat.*) Thank you. (*Beat.*) Sorry. (*He goes back to his position, then suddenly breaks it.*) Now let me get this straight. It's the three 'knocks', then the two 'knocks', right? And then it's the three again, am I correct? And then it's the two again?

Prompter That is correct.

Tilton So it's three 'knocks' and the devil's name line. Then two 'knocks' and the Belzebub.

Prompter (*off*) The three 'knocks' are with the Belzebub and the two are with the devil's name.

Tilton What?

Prompter (*off*) And it's the devil's name line that comes first. (*Beat.*) After the *three* 'knocks'.

Tilton stares in disbelief.

Then the third one – also after three 'knocks' – is the English tailor bit. Then comes 'too cold for hell'. (*Beat.*) After three more 'knocks'. (*Beat.*) I'm sorry, after *two* more 'knocks'. (*Beat.*) Yes, that's right, it is two more 'knocks' for the last one. Is that clear?

Short pause. Tilton tries to shake off confusion.

Tilton (*rubbing his eyes*) Let me start again. (*As he exits:*) I'm sorry to hold everyone up.

He leaves. Pounding. He hurries on.

Porter Here's a knocking indeed! (*He stops himself.*)

Tilton I don't have the faintest idea what I'm saying now. All I'm thinking about is how many goddamn 'knocks' I have!

Short pause. Forrest enters with others in the company.

Sorry, Ned.

Forrest Take your time.

Tilton I'm fine. I knew it. Ask anyone and they'll tell you
I knew it perfect. (*Beat.*) I was just a little uncertain of the
'knocks'. (*Awkward pause.*) Would you mind if I . . . Just
for now, if I said say as many 'knocks' as I want. As come
out. That's what's . . .

Forrest Say what you want. I mean it. (*to others*) Ready?
Let's continue.

He leaves with the others.

Tilton (*as he exits, to the Prompter, off*) Hear that? I can
say as many 'knocks' as I damn well want! (*He exits.*)

h) Astor Place Opera House
Mrs Pope (Lady Macbeth) stands to one side as Macready
(Macbeth) plays both Macbeth and Lady Macbeth in Act
II.ii.

Macready (*knocking with his foot, as Macbeth*)
                             Whence is that knocking?
  How is't with me when every noise appals me?
  What hands are here? Ha! they pluck out mine eyes.
  Will all great Neptune's ocean wash this blood
  Clean from my hand? No, this my hand will rather
  The multitudinous seas incarnadine,
  Making the green one red.

He hurries to a side and enters now as Lady Macbeth

(*as Lady Macbeth*) My hands are of your colour.

And blah-blah-blah. Whatever the lines. More knocking.
(*He knocks with his foot.*) Something about retiring to the
bedroom. I take you by the hand. Like this. Come here.

Mrs Pope goes to him, he takes her hand.

Macbeth To know my deed, 'twere best not know myself.

He knocks with his foot.

Wake Duncan with thy knocking! I would thou couldst.

Macready Head on my shoulder. And look down. Down.

Beat. As they exit.

And I look out as we leave.

They exit.

i) Broadway Theatre
Porter (Tilton) is alone on stage. Pause.

Tilton I've dried. I've never dried.

Forrest (*entering*) What's the line? Give him the line.

Tilton I don't remember anything. What's my character? What's the name of the play? (*He laughs.*) I'm kidding. (*He laughs.*) I'm sorry everyone. My apologies to all of you. It's one of those days. (*He laughs.*)

Forrest Just say your last line and we'll keep going. (*He turns to go.*)

Tilton What's my last line?

Prompter (*off*) 'I pray you remember the porter.'

Pause. Porter is alone on stage.

Tilton Ready?

He sighs, then, unaware of the mistake he is making:

Porter I pray the porter remember.

Macduff (Ryder) enters.

Macduff Was it so late, friend, ere you went to bed,
That you do lie so late?

Tilton I don't know those lines. We cut those lines. I
wasn't supposed to know them.

Forrest (*entering*) You enter with me, Mr Ryder. Each
from different sides. (*He calls off.*) What's the line?

Prompter (*off*) 'Our knocking has awaken.'

Forrest Our knocking has awaken. (*Beat.*) From different
sides.

Ryder The rest is cut.

Forrest I thought someone was giving Mr Ryder the
cuts?!

> *They go. Tilton is alone.*

Tilton From my last line? (*Beat.*) What was my last line
again?

Prompter (*off*) It's 'I pray you remember the porter.' It's
not 'I pray the porter remember.'

Tilton 'I pray the . . .'

Prompter Which is what you said the last time.

Tilton I said –? (*Beat.*) I couldn't have said . . . (*Beat.*) I
did? I heard –.

Forrest (*off*) Please, Tilton, begin!

> *Short pause.*

Tilton (*He does not know what to say.*) I . . . Uh.

j) Astor Place Opera House.
Thunder and lightning. Macbeth (Macready) and the
Three Witches (Sefton, Bridges, Chippindale). (Act IV.i)

The Witches sit on the ground.

Macbeth I conjure you, but that which you profess,
Howe'er you come to know it, answer me.

1st Witch Speak.

2nd Witch   Demand.

3rd Witch   We'll answer.

1st Witch Say if th' hadst rather hear it from our mouths,
Or from our masters.

Macbeth   Call 'em –.

*He stops himself. He goes to one of the Witches and
pulls his dress down a little so less of his leg can be
seen, then continues.*

                              Call 'em. Let me see 'em.

Thunder and an explosion.

*k) Broadway Theatre
Macbeth (Forrest), the Three Witches (the Misses Bass,
Burton and Holland) and 1st Apparition. (Act IV.i)*

1st Apparition Macbeth, Macbeth, Macbeth, beware
Macduff!
Beward the Thane of Fife! Dismiss me. – Enough.

1st Apparition leaves.

Macbeth Whate'er thou art, for thy good caution,
thanks:
Thou hast harped my –.

*He stops himself. He goes to 1st Witch and pulls her
dress up a little so more of her attractive leg can be
seen, then continues.*

Thou has harp'd my fear aright.

1st Witch   Here's another,
More potent than the first.

Thunder and an explosion.

l) Broadway Theatre
Macduff (Ryder) and Malcolm (Jones) (Act IV.iii)

Macduff *(with great passion)* Fit to govern?
  No, not to live! O nation miserable,
  With an untitled tyrant bloody-sceptred,
  When shalt thou see thy wholesome days again,
  Since that the truest issue of thy throne
  By his own interdiction stands accursed.
  And does blaspheme his breed? Oh my breast,
  Thy hope ends here!

Beat. They begin to walk off.

Jones Calm down, calm down. You've got the part.

They exit.

m) Astor Place Opera House
Macbeth (Macready) enters. (Act V.vii)

Macbeth They have tied me to a stake. I cannot fly,
  But bear-like I must fight the course. What's he
  That was not born of woman? Such a one
  Am I to fear, or none.

Enter Young Siward (Bridges).

Young Siward What is thy name?

Macbeth   Thou'lt be afraid to
hear it. My name's Macbeth.

Young Siward The devil himself could not pronounce a title
  More hateful to mine ear.

They fight. This should be a much stiffer battle than
that which Forrest will fight. Young Siward is slain.
Macbeth drags him off.

n) Broadway Theatre
Macbeth (Forrest) and Young Siward (Fisher) enter fight-
ing. This should be quite a thrilling sword fight. Then
Young Siward is slain.

Macbeth   Thou was born of woman.
But swords I smile at, weapons laugh to scorn,
Brandished by man that's of a woman born.

He drags off the body.

o) Astor Place Opera House
Continuation of previous scene (Act V.vii). Macduff
(Clark) enters, then Macbeth (Macready).

Macbeth Why should I play the Roman fool and die
On mine own sword? Whiles I see lives, the gashes
Do better upon them.

Macduff   Turn, hellhound, turn!

Macbeth Of all men else I have avoided thee.
But get thee back! My soul is much charged
With blood of thine already.

Macduff   I have no words;
My voice is in my sword, thou bloodier villain
Than terms can give thee out!

They fight.

Macbeth I bear a charmed life, which must not yield
To one of woman born.

Macduff   Despair thy charm,
And let the angel whom thou still hast served,

Tell thee, Macduff was from his mother's womb
Untimely ripped.

Macbeth Accursed be that tongue that tells me so,
For it hath cowed my better part of man!

Macduff 'Here may you see the tyrant.'

Macbeth   Before my body
I throw my warlike shield. Lay on, Macduff;
And damned be him that first cries, 'Hold, enough!'

They exit, fighting.
   *Malcolm (Arnold), Siward (Wemyss), and others
enter. (Act V. ix)*
   Macduff enters with the bloody head of Macbeth.

Macduff Hail, King of Scotland!

All   Hail, King of Scotland!

Malcolm We shall not spend a large expense of time
Before we reckon with your several loves
And make us even with you. What's more to do
Which could be planted newly with the time –
As calling home our exiled friends abroad
That fled the snares of watchful tyranny,
Producing forth the cruel ministers
Of this dead butcher and his fiend-like queen.
So thanks to all at once and to each one,
Whom we invite to see us crowned at Scone.

*Flourish. They exit. Then immediately some of the
actors cross the stage, taking off costumes, etc., all a bit
tired. As they exit:*

*p) Broadway Theatre
Macbeth (Forrest) and Macduff (Ryder) enter fighting.*

Macready Watch it. There. That's right. There.

Then as Macbeth.

Macbeth   Before my body
I throw my warlike shield. Lay on, Macduff;
And damned be him that first cries, 'Hold, enough!'

*They fight on stage. Finally at one point Macbeth is
stabbed and falls. Macduff – or rather Ryder – with
some hesitation raises his sword and appears to cut off
Macbeth's head. A head falls on the ground. Macduff
picks it up. Others enter.*

Macduff (*with the head*) Hail, King of Scotland!

All   Hail, King of Scotland!

Tableaux. Blackout.

SCENE FIVE

Projection: 5 P.M.

Forrest's dressing-room, the Broadway Theatre.
   *Table, a couple of chairs, door. Forrest sits, taking off
his make-up; throughout the scene he changes from his
Macbeth costume to his normal clothes. Ryder, still in
costume, stands.*

Forrest I don't know how this is any of my business.

Ryder I think – The basis for the threats – or so Mr
Macready believes – seems to be the fact that you are
both performing the same play on the same –.

Forrest So are you, Mr Ryder. (*Beat.*) So are you.

   Beat.

Ryder On the same night. It's a competition that
these people – whomever they are – are trying to . . . I

156

don't know. Build up?

Forrest According to Mr Macready.

Ryder According to Mr –.

Forrest This is what he has concluded.

Ryder That's right. (*Beat.*) *I'm* only passing it along. I'm the messenger. That's all I am.

Forrest I understand.

Short pause.

Ryder Anyway, a competition. English versus –.

Forrest You're English.

Ryder I'm not saying that it's logical. (*Beat.*) English versus American. There is still, I suppose, a certain lingering –. Passion? It's uncorking this –, these tempers that has Mr Macready truly worried and why he believes there might be truth to the –.

Forrest Do the threats mention me?

Beat.

Ryder No. Not in the letter I saw.

Forrest So the basis for the threats actually remains in some doubt.

Ryder They do criticize him for being foreign.

Forrest I have been criticized in England for being foreign! (*Short pause.*) So they do not mention me. They do not mention that Mr Forrest happens, by coincidence, to be performing the same –.

Ryder Mr Macready believes –.

Forrest He has an opinion! (*Beat.*) And if I were

157

Macready and I held such an opinion, the obvious action to take would be to change my schedule and perform something else.

Ryder *He* can't.

Forrest Too bad. (*Short pause.*) Then cancel.

Knock at the door. Door opens, Tilton peeks in.

Tilton Sorry about this afternoon, I . . .

Forrest (*continuing to Ryder*) But this is Mr Macready's business and it has nothing to do with me. (*Beat. To Tilton*) Sorry about what? What happened? Did something happen?

Tilton I don't know where my mind was. It suddenly went . . .

Forrest I don't know what you're talking about, Tilton. Please. (*He continues to undress. Beat.*)

Tilton Thanks, Ned. Thank you. (*He turns to go and bumps into Fisher.*) Sorry. (*He leaves.*)

Fisher You wanted to see me, Ned?

Forrest Come in, Thomas, come in.

Ryder Would you like me to –.

Forrest Sit down, please. Both of you. (*Beat.*) I was just about to compliment Mr Ryder on his performance. After our little misfortune last night, we seem to have landed on our feet. (*Beat.*) Thanks to Mr Ryder.

Fisher Nice work.

Forrest (*turning to Ryder*) You know I *have* seen you act before. In fact, I do believe I have seen you play this part before. Now where was it? (*Beat.*) Could it have been in Edinburgh?

Ryder I have played in –.

Forrest I recall sneaking in one wet night to catch Mr Macready –.

Ryder Yes, I did play Macduff to Mr Macready's –.

Forrest But it was you whom I remember, Mr Ryder. (*Beat.*) I thought you were magnificent. The best Macduff I have ever seen.

Ryder (*smiling at Fisher*) Thank you.

Forrest You see, most Macduffs don't realize that it is revenge that is driving the man. Passionate revenge. They don't show this. (*Beat.*) The part is not about Good triumphing. Who the hell knows if the man's good or not? It is hate that drives him. (*Beat.*) Ugly, sweaty hate. (*Beat.*) I hardly even remember the performance of the Macbeth.

Ryder Mr Macready –.

Forrest For that one night, the play should have been called *Macduff*.

   Beat.

Ryder (*smiling*) Mr Forrest, I think you're putting me on. To call the play –.

Forrest It would have been justified. By your performance. (*Beat.*) By your energetic and dominating performance. (*Short pause. To himself*) *Macduff*! (*Beat.*) Macbeth need hardly even appear. (*Beat.*) What about a drink? The three of us? (*He takes a bottle and a few glasses.*)

Ryder I don't really think –.

Forrest I insist. Please. (*Pause. He pours and hands out glasses.*) To you. And to our wonderful production which unfortunately we must call – *Macbeth*. (*He drinks.*)

*Fisher laughs at the way Forrest is making his point
with Ryder.*

(*turning quickly to Fisher*) Mr Fisher, you know we are
scheduled to play here for the next five weeks.

Fisher Of course I do, yes. Why do you –?

Forrest I ran into Mr Hackett the other day. Actually I
believe it was just this morning. He said something about
having engaged actors already for a tour. Do you know
anything about this?

Fisher I've met Hackett maybe two or three times in my
whole life.

Forrest I thought you worked for him once. I thought
this is what you told me when I hired you for here.

Fisher I worked for him. I did. (*Beat.*) But he wasn't
around much.

Forrest (*to Ryder, smiling*) It appears this tour is to be in –.
What was the exact date? I forget. But I do remember it
was about three and a half weeks from today. (*Beat.*) Or a
week and a half before we finish our season here. (*Beat.*)
You haven't talked to Mr Hackett about joining this tour,
have you?

Fisher That wouldn't be right, Ned.

Pause.

Forrest I hear your brother hasn't been well.

Fisher What do you mean? I don't have a –.

Forrest So I'm sure there are a few unanticipated
expenses. (*Beat.*) For the remainder of our season, I have
decided to raise your pay by five dollars a performance.
(*Beat.*) Rather, let's call it a bonus – to be collected at the
end of our run.

Short pause.

Fisher Thank you. I can use it. (*Beat.*) Is there anything else, you . . .?

Forrest No.

Fisher nods, puts down his glass and goes. After he has closed the door.

You son of a bitch! (*to Ryder*) He's been in rehearsal for a week with Hackett. (*Beat.*) He's good though. Good with the sword.

Miss Bass enters, still in costume. She does not knock. In fact, throughout the rest of the scene, she undresses and changes into her normal clothes. Ryder takes notice of this, though for Forrest and Miss Bass it seems to be quite normal.

Miss Bass (*while entering*) Can Helen come with us to the party? (*Beat. She turns to Forrest.*) Mr Robert Jones is taking Miss Anne Holland to dinner tonight. So you can imagine how Helen is feeling.

Forrest I don't know how large the party's supposed to be.

Miss Bass I can't leave her alone. I just got her to stop crying.

Forrest Fine. (*Beat.*) Of course she can come. Maybe you, Mr Ryder, would like to join . . .

Ryder I'm having dinner with Mr Macready tonight. Otherwise . . . (*Short pause.*) I'll tell him I passed along his message. I should go. (*He goes to the door.*) By the way, thank you for last night. It was a pleasure to –. And I am pleased you like my Macduff. I'm a bit more critical of it than you though. (*Beat.*) I think I should try to, I don't know. I just think I could be subtler. After all, the play Shakespeare wrote isn't called *Macduff*, is it?

He forces himself to laugh, and he leaves. Long pause.
Forrest begins to get dressed.

Miss Bass I've heard that there are quite a few unsold
tickets for Mr Macready's *Macbeth*.

Forrest (*without looking up*) Is that true? (*He laughs to*
himself.)

Miss Bass Why is that . . .?

He looks up, shakes his head, suddenly sits and sighs.
She looks at him.

(*trying to be bright*) So where's the party?

Forrest New York Hotel.

Miss Bass You're sure they won't mind us bringing
Helen . . .?

Forrest I'm sure it's a big party. That's what I remember
my wife saying at least.

Miss Bass The bigger the better. For us.

Pause. Forrest slowly turns to her.

Miss Bass What? What?

Forrest My wife doesn't want you in our house any more.
She made this clear to me. This morning. (*Beat.*) Do you
mind?

Miss Bass Then – she's not welcome in mine either. (*Beat.*
She smiles.)

Forrest (*sigh of relief*) Thank you. You make this much
easier. (*He smiles but then nearly begins to cry.*)

Miss Bass Ned . . .?

Forrest I don't know what it is, Jane. (*Beat.*) For no reason my eyes start to well up. (*He wipes his tears, breathes*

deeply, sighs.) Life's not half as much fun as theatre. (*He continues to get dressed.*)

Blackout.

SCENE SIX

Projection: 8 P.M.

A private drawing room, New York Hotel.
   Macready, Ryder, Mrs Forrest, Dion Boucicault and his wife Agnes, in the middle of conversation.

Macready He said she was fifty if she was anything, and when she finished, she told Johnstone that her parts include not only Desdemona but also Juliet.

   He smiles and shakes his head, sips his drink. Others smile as well.

Then in Pittsburg – a town he said one should be lucky enough to avoid – he's to play Lear with a Goneril who never was sober – for four days, he swears – A Cordelia who not only talked nonsense, as if she had concluded that nonsense was Shakespeare's intention and she was only clarifying this point, but who also was a good three to four years older than him, and John Johnstone, well you've seen him.

Mrs Forrest Not for years, has he . . .?

Macready (*turning to Boucicault*) He's –. What? How would you describe . . .?

Boucicault No one would say he was too young for the part. Of Lear.

Macready It happened rather quickly as well.

Agnes His son died.

Macready Is that it? I didn't know.

Short pause.

Boucicault So his Cordelia was even older than –.

Macready Which he said actually made the relationship rather interesting.

Boucicault It's different.

Macready Anyway, he finally just felt that the performance he was giving was just too good for them. They cheered, of course, but he was convinced they didn't know what in the world they were cheering for.

Short pause.

Boucicault Hmmmm. (*He turns to look at Agnes for a moment, then turns to Ryder.*) Mr Ryder, has this been your experience of –?

Ryder No. (*Beat.*) Actually it hasn't. I think Americans –.

Macready (*interrupting*) Nor has it been mind, Mr Boucicault. American people are really rather charming and decent as well as intelligent in an instinctive sort of way. The actors I am working with, they may not know certain things, things you or I or your wife might take for granted, but that doesn't mean they aren't quick to learn.

Agnes Being married to an American, Mrs Forrest, you must have had experiences.

Mrs Forrest Oh yes. Very many.

Pause. They look to her to continue.

Macready (*finally*) Not only are they quick to learn, they are eager. They're more like children than us old jaded English actors. (*He laughs lightly, as do others.*) It's a fascinating country, it truly is!

Agnes Whatever it is, it at least sounds somewhat refreshing after the London theatre.

Ryder Absolutely nothing was happening there when we left.

Boucicault And it's got worse, hasn't it?

He turns to Agnes, who nods.

Kean's made a complete mess of the Princess.

Agnes (*to the others*) Not a complete –.

Boucicault He has, it's true. (*Beat.*) I gave him *The Corsican Brothers* – for nothing – for nearly nothing he has the play of the century. What is clearly my best play; what is going to be my most successful play that will make *London Assurance* seem like . . . Whatever. (*Beat.*) Crowds fight to get into my play. This play cannot lose money. (*He turns to Agnes.*) He ran it for what –?

Agnes Not long enough.

Boucicault I try to tell him. (*He shakes his head.*) What is in it for me? I don't get a pound more if he plays the play or not. Not there. At the Princess he can play it for ever and I don't get a farthing more. (*Beat.*) It's going to be done here. (*Beat.*) Last night Hackett agreed to take it.

Macready When did he say –?

Boucicault Some time after the new year. He didn't give me dates. (*Beat.*) But it's definite. (*Beat.*) We're going to work out a deal. (*Beat. He laughs.*) We're here one week and –! I love America.

Short pause.

Agnes (*smiling*) Hopefully we're saying the same thing next week. (*Beat.*) At first we were very happy with Kean.

Boucicault I never was, Agnes. It was the Princess Theatre that I loved. A beautiful theatre.

Macready This is true.

Boucicault What does Kean replace my play with? *Twelfth Night.* He insists on doing this play. (*Beat.*) It's not a bad play. (*Beat.*) But I tell him just run the goddamn *Corsican Brothers* until no one comes any more. Does this sound mad?!

Agnes Dion –.

Boucicault Let me finish! (*Beat.*) It's as if they don't want to make money. (*Beat.*) It is exactly as if they don't want to make money!

　Pause.

Ryder That is very good news about Hackett.

Agnes He's going to tell us for sure next week.

　Short pause.

Boucicault Have any of you been to Cincinnati?

Mrs Forrest Cincinnati? (*She looks at the others.*) No I haven't.

Macready No. (*Beat.*) Why? Is there something . . .?

Boucicault It's just that I always have loved that name: Cincinnati.

　Pause. They sip their drinks.

Macready Five Brits all in one room. In America. That doesn't happen very often.

Mrs Forrest Yes it does.

　Pause.

166

Agnes We've reserved a small table in the dining-room. As soon as Mr Forrest . . .

Mrs Forrest I think it might be dangerous to wait for my husband.

Short pause.

Boucicault Perhaps then we should go right to our table. We can bring our drinks.

They hesitate.

Agnes We should leave a message at the front desk.

Ryder He may have forgotten. Maybe there was something else.

Mrs Forrest Do you know if Mr Forrest has gone somewhere else?

Ryder No. (*Beat.*) I don't know anything.

Mrs Forrest I'll leave the note.

Boucicault We'll just be –.

Mrs Forrest Yes.

As the others move off towards the dining-room:

Boucicault So you're staying here as well?

Macready It's near the theatre.

Agnes They've been very nice to us.

Macready (*to Agnes*) Here, let me carry your drink.

Agnes Thank you.

They are gone. Mrs Forrest has watched them go; she sighs and sits. After a moment she stands again and turns to go off towards the front desk just as Forrest enters with Miss Bass and Miss Burton. Forrest stops.

Short pause.

Forrest Where's the party?

Mrs Forrest What party are you talking about? And where have you been?

Forrest Boucicault's party. You told me tonight was Boucicault's party. We've been looking all over the hotel . . .

Mrs Forrest It's not a party. It's a dinner, Mr Forrest. A small dinner.

Short pause.

Forrest Then I made a mistake.

Miss Bass If you want us to go, Ned . . .

Forrest Where's the dinner?

Mrs Forrest (*nodding*) Through there.

Beat.

Forrest What's a few more places? (*He tries to laugh.*) They're through there?

She does not respond. He hesitates, then leads the women in the direction of the dining-room.

Mrs Forrest Edwin.

He stops.

Forrest (*to Bass and Burton*) I'll join you in a minute. Just introduce yourselves. It'll be fine. (*Beat.*) It's fine.

They go. Short pause.

Mrs Forrest What have you been doing?

Forrest Rehearsing.

Mrs Forrest What have you been doing?

Forrest One of the girls, Miss Burton; she's upset because her boyfriend – the boy she thinks is her boyfriend . . . (*Beat.*) You know who I mean. (*Beat.*) My Banquo. Well, tonight he's taken another actress, Miss –.

Mrs Forrest Why do I care? How could you invite them?

Forrest They're actresses in my –! (*He stops himself. Short pause.*) I made a mistake. I am sorry. (*Beat.*) I invited them to what I thought was –. I can't tell them to leave. (*Beat.*) It would be profoundly embarrassing to just . . . (*Beat.*) Let's just get through this, Catherine.

The others all return from the dining-room.

Agnes (*entering*) No, it's my fault really for not reserving a larger table.

Mrs Forrest What's –?

Macready We don't all fit around the table.

Boucicault And they said they can't add on – The space in there, there's no –.

Beat.

Agnes They're seeing what they can do. They asked us to wait.

Awkward pause.

Forrest I'm sorry if I caused any trouble.

Agnes Of course not. We're very pleased and honoured you could come. And your guests. We're very anxious to get to know all sorts of Americans.

Forrest Thank you.

Agnes Aren't we?

Boucicault We are. (*Beat.*) We certainly are.

Another awkward pause.

Agnes I'll see if anything's been figured out yet.

She goes. Short pause.

Forrest Mr Boucicault, it is very nice to see you again. I hope your voyage was comfortable.

They shake hands.

Boucicault Very. Thank you. You of course know Mr Macready.

Forrest We've met before. How do you do?

Macready How do you do?

Boucicault And Mr Ryder.

Forrest Mr Ryder is my Macduff at the moment actually.

Boucicault Really? I didn't – You didn't say anything.

Macready I have an American Macduff for New York. I thought it a good thing. (*Beat.*) He's very good as well.

Short pause.

Ryder Funny, Mr Forrest, you asked me what I was doing this evening –. I guess you were going to invite me here. And here I am already. (*He laughs lightly.*) With Mr Macready. (*Beat.*) I told you I was having dinner with Mr Macready.

Mrs Forrest My husband invited you as well?

Pause.

Forrest (*to Miss Bass*) You've been introduced, I –.

Miss Bass Actually . . . (*She shakes her head.*)

Miss Burton No, we –.

Boucicault I'm terribly sorry.

Forrest Miss Burton. Miss Bass.

An exchange of polite greetings. Short pause.

They are two of my witches.

The others nod as if this explains something.

Miss Burton I'm the second.

Miss Bass I'm the first.

Agnes enters, followed by a maid and a servant carrying tables.

Agnes (*while entering*) They think we'll actually be more comfortable in here. We'll set up to eat in here. And we can add on as many tables as we wish. (*Beat.*) In case others should drop in. (*Beat.*) I do love it when people feel they can just drop in. (*Beat.*) For dinner.

During much of the scene, the tables are set up, then set with tablecloths, plates, glasses, etc.

Boucicault I hear wonderful things about your *Macbeth*, Mr Forrest. (*Beat.*) Or should I say, all of your *Macbeth*, as it seems half of your cast is with us tonight.

Forrest Thank you. (*Short pause.*) And let's not leave Mr Macready out. *His Macbeth* I have seen! Where was it? I was just today telling Mr Ryder. Baltimore? Cincinnati?

Boucicault Agnes – Cincinnati?

She nods and smiles.

Ryder It was Edinburgh.

Macready I hadn't know. Had I known –.

Forrest You were . . . Unforgettable. Even now I can close my eyes and see you there. (*Beat.*) As Macbeth. (*Beat.*) Unforgettable.

Boucicault Yes. And yours, it's on everyone's lips.

Forrest What brings you to New York, Mr Boucicault?

Macready He's sold his *Corsican Brothers* to Hackett. They're doing it next year.

Forrest I hope you got the money in your hand. He'll promise anything.

Boucicault looks at Agnes.

Agnes My husband has a new play.

Forrest What's the title –?

Boucicault I don't want to bother you two –. (*Beat.*) Actually, now that I think of it you both could be of some help to me. That's if you don't mind. I wouldn't want you to think you had to work for your dinner.

He laughs. No one else does.

Agnes I think we can sit down.

Boucicault Please, let's –. (*He gestures for all to go to the table.*) The play is called *Shakespeare in Love.*

Ryder Who's sitting where?

Agnes Dion should be at the head. Then Miss –.

Miss Burton Burton.

Agnes Burton to his left. And who –? Mr Forrest? Or would you rather sit by your wife?

Forrest I don't care where I sit.

Boucicault And it's about Shakespeare.

Agnes I'll sit at the other end. Mr Ryder, then . . . (*She* *points to where he should sit.*)

Mrs Forrest Then I'll sit there. (*She goes to her seat.*)

Boucicault And he is in love. Shakespeare.

Agnes Then Mr Macready.

Macready Where?

Agnes Right here, next to Dion and Mrs Forrest.

Boucicault He's in love with a neighbour.

Macready How old is he?

Boucicault He's in his late thirties I would say. Though that could be changed. (*Beat.*) He can be older. He can be younger.

Agnes And that leaves Miss Bass. Miss Bass on the other side of Mr Forrest. Who has Miss Burton on one side and Miss Bass on the other.

Mrs Forrest My husband will be in heaven.

Agnes Shall we sit?

They do. There is no food or drink on the table.

Boucicault It's a comedy. A rather fantastical comedy. Because, you see, various characters from his plays come back to him – to try to help him or they are just plain jealous of this love affair and are feeling neglected. They are very unhappy that this affair is upsetting their lives. (*Beat.*) It's a very good idea, isn't it?

Agnes Dion, they aren't serving the food. Maybe they've forgotten about us.

Boucicault Why would they? (*He gets up.*) I'll go and see. Excuse me. Remind me where I was.

He goes. Short pause.

Agnes It's nice in here. (*Beat.*) To have a whole room by yourself. (*Beat.*) Things do work out.

Forrest Mr Macready, Mr Ryder was telling me about some threats against . . . (*He turns to Ryder.*) Who exactly were they against?

Macready Threats?

Ryder About Monday. About the two *Macbeths*.

Macready Threats??

Ryder About being foreign. The letters you received.

Macready Threats???

Ryder You asked me to talk to Mr Forrest and –.

Macready Oh those. Silly ridiculous rumours. I'm sure the same must happen to you, Mr Forrest. Jealous people.

Forrest In England it happens to me all the time.

Beat.

Macready One learns to ignore such things.

Short pause.

Forrest You're selling very well, I hear.

Short pause.

Mrs Forrest They don't like English people.

Forrest Who are they?

She shrugs.

You don't know what you're talking about.

She looks down, puts her head in her hands.

Agnes Do you like English people, Miss . . .

Miss Burton Burton. Sure. (*She smiles.*) What's there not to like. (*Beat.*) What's *to* like? People are people. (*She shrugs.*) There are good and there are bad.

Miss Bass smiles.

What's funny?

Miss Bass Nothing.

Miss Burton You're laughing at me.

Miss Bass I'm not, Helen.

Agnes What you say is true.

Ryder Very true.

Beat.

Agnes Dion doesn't like English people, but then he's Irish.

Macready By the way, except for the accent, you'd hardly notice. He's very well groomed.

Agnes I don't think I will tell him that.

Miss Bass Why wouldn't I like you, Mrs Forrest? (*Beat.*) Just because you're English?

Pause.

Mrs Forrest I wasn't talking about you. I wasn't talking to you. (*She turns to Agnes.*) The women, you'll find, it will shock you, Agnes. No – subtlety. No – charm, that I can see. So of course they will do anything. Anything. (*She shakes her head.*) Sometimes for nothing, sometimes they want to be paid for it. (*She turns to Forrest.*) Isn't that right?

Forrest Catherine.

Mrs Forrest The men are much more subtle. No, perhaps subtle is the wrong word. (*Beat.*) Tricky. This is the word.

They can be very very . . . (*Short pause. Without looking at anyone*) My apologies. To all of you. Including Miss Burton and Miss Bass. (*Beat.*) I promise you I do not normally act in this manner.

Beat. Boucicault comes back in, followed by a servant with the food.

Boucicault I don't know what they were waiting for. Anyway, I was talking about my play. (*Beat.*) A very nice idea, isn't it? Shakespeare in love. So who should play Shakespeare? (*He has sat back down.*) That seems to be the question. (*Beat.*) You both know actors. On both sides of the ocean. Who would be good to play our greatest dramatist? (*Beat. To Miss Burton*) I'm having a reading next week. In the afternoon so all of you busy theatre actors can come. (*Beat.*) The reading isn't completely cast yet. (*Beat.*) Any ideas about who could play Shakespeare? Not in the reading. I'll play him in the reading. (*Beat.*) He'd have to be a major actor. Think about it. (*Suddenly he laughs.*) But as I said – I don't want you to think you have to work for your dinner. (*He laughs, stops, looks at the food.*) This looks good.

Blackout.

SCENE SEVEN

Projection: I A.M.

The same. The dinner is long over, though the dishes remain on the table, as well as wine bottles, glasses, etc.

Mrs Forrest and Agnes have left some time earlier. Forrest, with Miss Bass at his side, sits at the table and talks to Macready, who has his head on the table, and occasionally to Boucicault, who sits next to Miss Burton and at times turns and stares at her and smiles. Ryder is out for a pee.

Forrest I'm serious. I think what one must do –. What the
battle finally is about. For us. You need to –. With your
hands out – keeping it all away –. All out of the way.
(*Beat.*) Everything that is coming at you. The distractions
and everything. Everything like that. Out there. The
moment you go off the stage it is like – to me, I feel this –
it is like they are trying to take it all away from you.
(*Beat.*) Tell you it never happened. What you felt out
there on the stage! What you knew you had done out
there on the stage!

Short pause.

Miss Burton (*to Boucicault*) Will you stop smiling at me!

He smiles and takes a sip of wine.

Forrest They may mean well. These people. Well-wishers
mean well, but –. (*Beat.*) Sometimes I think it's all just
interference. And the test we are putting ourselves
through . . . Have been put through –. By whom? Where
does it come from? God? I don't know. But it's to push all
that away. Not let it break into the art of what we do.

Short pause.

Macready (*lifting up his head for a moment*) The world
should be left behind. In the dressing-room.

Forrest It certainly should not be brought on to the stage.
(*Beat. To Miss Bass*) You don't agree.

Miss Bass I didn't say any –.

Forrest Take an argument you might have. With –?
Anyone. A friend. (*Beat.*) A wife. You have this argument.
You're boiling over. Then you must play Hamlet. If you
try to bring that argument into –. On to –. (*Beat.*) You
have to push it all away. Become someone who has not
had an argument. In this case who does not have a wife.

Macready (*lifting head*) And into someone whose father just died.

Forrest Exactly.

Beat.

Macready Now if my father *had* just died and I *had* to play Hamlet that night –.

Forrest This I would love to see.

Macready That would be –. (*Beat.*) Yes. (*He smiles.*)

Forrest (*smiling*) But fathers don't die every time we play Hamlet. (*Beat.*) Instead, bills are sent that day which can be wrong. You step in horse shit on the street. Wives don't listen when you talk to them. You lose your favourite pen. Or hat. Or your right shoe. Or other stocking. (*Beat.*) Or you fall in love that day. Or hear a joke that you cannot forget and cannot stop smiling about. Your brother writes and says he's going to visit. The breakfast wasn't at all what you wanted. (*Beat.*) And then you play Hamlet. Then you become someone else. (*Beat.*) To do this you must learn to forget. (*He takes a sip of wine.*) Sometimes I think this is my favourite part of being an actor.

Pause. Ryder enters and sits.

Ryder What did I miss?

Macready, without picking up his head, just shakes his head.

Boucicault (*standing up, to Ryder*) Good idea. I have to go too.

He leans over and tries to kiss Miss Burton, who slaps him hard across the head. Others turn and see this. Boucicault smiles and leaves.

Macready (*with head down*) For me I think I like being able to –. It's not: forget. But I know what you mean.

Miss Burton (*standing*) I think I should be leaving, it's –.

Miss Bass Helen, it's only –.

Miss Burton He's climbing all over me. That's not what I came for!

Forrest Sit over here with us. We'll make room.

Miss Bass I'll move over.

Forrest Come on. Come on. We won't stay much longer.

She sits next to Miss Bass, protected from Boucicault by both Forrest and Ryder. They move a chair for her.

Macready (*finally*) As I was saying –.

Forrest (*to Miss Burton*) We're talking about why we act. What we –. Why do you act?

Miss Burton I don't know.

He looks at her and nods. He turns back to Macready.

Macready It's hard to explain really. Where shall I begin? (*Beat.*) You see – as Descartes has said – inside us all are these –. He called them animal spirits. (*Beat.*) Which are really, what other people call – passions.

Short pause. Forrest nods.

And they're all – these spirits – they're bordered, they're all sort of fenced in. (*suddenly remembering*) You could also call them *emotions*. (*Beat.*) Anyway, they're fenced in. But when one of them escapes from the others –. And is not quickly caught by –. I don't know, spirits who do the catching, like sheep-dogs catch –.

Beat.

Forrest Sheep.

Macready That's right. Like sheep-dogs catch sheep. Anyway, when one escapes and is not caught, then it becomes a very deep, a very –. A very passionate –. (*Beat.*) What?! (*Beat. He remembers.*) Feeling! Feeling. (*Short pause.*) So what an actor does – I believe – is this: philosophically speaking –. I haven't studied enough philosophy –. I'd like to study much much more, but –. Well –. People like us who are busy doing –! But, as I was saying, the art of the actor –. (*Beat.*) What was I going to say? I was about to say something that was very clear. I remember. The art of the actor is like ripping down the fences. (*Beat.*) And tying up the sheep-dogs. (*Beat.*) And letting the spirits loose. A few at a time. Or more! Depending on the part. Letting them roam for a while. (*Short pause.*) So, that's what I love about acting. (*Pause.*) I don't know how clear I've been.

Forrest No, no, you've been . . . (*He nods and shrugs.*)

Boucicault had entered while Macready was talking. He has noticed that Miss Burton has moved and has hesitated, not knowing where he should now sit. He brings a chair, trying to squeeze in next to Miss Burton.

Miss Burton There's no room here.

Macready Dion, stay over there.

Boucicault There's no one over there.

He stands behind her, making her very uncomfortable.

Forrest (*to Macready*) That was very interesting.

Macready I've only tried to explain it to one other person, and he laughed so –. (*He shrugs.*) You can see how I might be a little –. About talking about . . .

Forrest Please! (*Beat.*) Please, we are all actors here.

Miss Bass (*standing up*) I'll sit over there.

She moves to where Miss Burton had been sitting and Boucicault follows, going back to his seat.

Forrest (*to Macready*) No one would make fun . . .

Ryder (*to Macready*) What's that on your sleeve? Don't move, I'll kill it. (*He goes to get something off Macready's jacket.*) I got it! Oh my God, it's an escaped animal spirit! Quick, kill it! Kill it! Kill it!

He laughs at his joke, Macready and Forrest ignore him.

Macready It's a theory. A way of talking about something that is not easy to talk about.

Forrest nods.

Boucicault In my play, *Shakespeare in Love*, Shakespeare, by falling in love, can't write. Or doesn't want to write. (*Beat.*) His talent dies. This is why the characters from his plays –.

Macready I thought we finished talking about your play, Dion.

Boucicault Had we? I'm sorry, I didn't know. (*Short pause. He turns to Miss Bass.*) Which witch. (*Through his drunkenness he has trouble saying this.*) – Which witch do you play? May I ask? (*Beat.*) In *Macbeth*.

Miss Bass I'm the first witch.

Boucicault Ah, the first one. Mmmmmmm. Not the one I would have chosen for you, but a good one just the same.

Macready (*standing with difficulty*) I have no more to say. So I am going to bed.

Ryder stands, then Forrest.

Forrest (*to the women*) I shall take you two home.

Boucicault Wait a minute! What about my problem?
How shall I choose between you on Monday night?
Whose *Macbeth* do I attend?

Forrest It doesn't matter to –.

Boucicault Perhaps I shall have to flip a coin. Who has a
coin? I have a coin. (*Beat.*) Ready? Heads and I go to Mr –.
Forrest's. And tails to Mr Macready's. (*He flips and the
coin falls under the table.*) I will get it. No one move. I am
getting it.

>   The others stand and watch as Boucicault crawls under
>   the table.

I can't –. Did anyone see which way it rolled? (*He bumps
his head.*) Ow!

>   He grabs Miss Burton's ankle.

Miss Burton Stop that!

>   She kicks him, he laughs.

Get me out of here.

Miss Bass We're going. Ned?

Forrest It is late.

Boucicault I have it! I found it! (*He comes out from
under the table.*) Here it is. (*He looks at the coin.*) I forget. Who had tails and who had heads?

>   The others immediately move to leave, ignoring
>   Boucicault.

Forrest Mr Ryder, I shall see you on Monday.

Ryder I'll be there.

Miss Bass Can we drop you off somewhere?

Ryder I have rooms here in the hotel.

Miss Bass So you don't have far –.

Ryder No.

Miss Bass They're comfortable rooms I hope.

Forrest Do you want him to show you them?

Miss Bass Ned!

Forrest I didn't mean –. (*He turns to Boucicault.*) Mr Boucicault, I thank you for this evening.

Macready Yes, a lovely affair.

Boucicault Is everyone leaving?

Miss Burton We are.

Forrest Mr Macready, we have a cab.

Macready I'm staying in the hotel as well.

Forrest Ah. (*leaving*) Helen. Jane.

Macready (*leaving*) So – I'm home.

Boucicault (*leaving*) Thank you for coming. (*to Miss Burton*) It was charming to meet you.

> *In the distance, we hear them say 'goodnight' and they are gone. Blackout.*

SCENE EIGHT

Projection: THREE DAYS LATER, MONDAY 7 MAY. 7.30 P.M.

Backstage, Astor Place Opera House.
  A curtain, upstage of which is the stage and audience. On this stage, through the curtain, in silhouette, Act I

scene iii of Macbeth *is being performed by the Three Witches (Sefton, Chippindale and Bridges). Backstage someone makes the thunder-sound.*

Downstage of this curtain, actors in costume and not, listen, wait and mill around. After a moment, one actor with a drum bangs on it, and from 'the stage' one vaguely hears:

3rd Witch A drum! A drum!
Macbeth doth come.

All The Weird Sisters, hand in hand,
Posters of the sea and land,
Thus do go about, about:
Thrice to thine, and thrice to mine,
And thrice again, to make up nine.
Peace! – The charm's wound up.

Backstage, Macready dressed in costume has entered. He slaps Bradshaw (Banquo) on the back, and Bradshaw enters 'on stage'. From the audience, one hears cheers and yells. Macready smiles.

Macready (*to the actor with the drum*) They think he's me.

He makes his entrance.

So foul and fair day I have not seen.

Before he can even get the sentence out, boos and cries ring out from the audience, then screaming and yells and violent insults. The other actors look at each other. From the stage, Banquo is heard trying to go on, as do the Witches, but all is chaos. Finally, Macready can be heard screaming:

Stay, you imperfect speakers, tell me more!

But he is drowned out. Suddenly someone rips down the curtain, and Macready's face is seen to be com-

pletely bloodied; he staggers back, ducking the things being thrown at him. Other actors run for cover. Macready stumbles and turns to an actor.

Who are they? What do they want?!

The Witches hurry in (Sefton, Chippindale and Bridges).

Mrs Pope (*taking Macready*) Sit down. Over here. Let me get you a cloth.

She takes him to a chair.

Bridges He's bleeding.

Macready They tried to kill me! (*He grabs Chippindale.*) They want to kill me!

Chippindale (*taking the cloth from Mrs Pope*) Give me that. Let me wipe your face.

Macready screams.

Macready I haven't done anything to them. They have interrupted my performance! (*He stands.*)

Mrs Pope Sit down.

The yelling and screaming continue from the audience.

Bradshaw (*entering from the stage*) They're breaking the seats.

Chippindale Get them to stop!

Bradshaw And how am I supposed to do that?!

Macready Shoot them!

Bridges (*who has been listening to the crowd*) They're calling for Mr Macready.

Sefton Tell them he's left! Tell them he's gone!

He pushes Bridges to go on stage.

Macready I haven't left.

Bridges (*stopping and hesitating*) They'll tear down the theatre!

Macready I'm here.

Sefton Somebody tell them!

No one moves, then Sefton goes to the stage.

Macready I have a performance to give. People have paid to see me perform.

Bridges (*to Chippindale*) What are they screaming now?

Sefton (*repeating*) Kill the English bastard. We have our own actors now. Long live Ned Forrest.

Macready I have to finish!

Sefton (*off, to the audience, yelling*) Mr Macready has left the theatre!

Macready I need to finish!

Sefton (*off*) Mr Macready has left the theatre!

Yelling and screaming continues. Other actors find themselves watching Macready.

Macready I wish to continue my . . .

Sefton (*off*) Macready has left the theatre!!!

Beat. Screaming dies down and suddenly there is a deafening cheer from the audience. Blackout.

Act Two

Projection: THE NEXT DAY, TUESDAY 8 MAY. 9.45 P.M.

The stage of the Broadway Theatre during a performance of Metamora. *Forrest as the title character and Miss Holland as Metamora's wife, Nahmeokee. The last few minutes of the play.*

Metamora Nahmeokee, I look up through the long path of thin air, and I think I see our infant borne onward to the land of the happy, where the fair hunting grounds know no storms or snows, and where the immortal brave feast in the eyes of the giver of good. Look upwards, Nahmeokee, the spirit of thy murdered father beckons thee.

Nahmeokee I will go to him.

Metamora Embrace me, Nahmeokee – 'twas like the first you gave me in the days of our strength and joy – they are gone. (*He places his ear to the ground.*) Hark! In the distant wood I faintly hear the cautious tread of men! They are upon us, Nahmeokee – the home of the happy is made ready for thee.

He stabs her, she dies.

She felt no white man's bondage – free as the air she lived – pure as the snow she died! In smiles she died! Let me taste it, ere her lips are cold as the ice.

Loud shouts. Roll of drums. Kaweshine (Fisher) leads Church (Tilton) and soldiers.

Church He is found! Metamora is our prisoner.

Metamora No! He lives – last of his race – but still your enemy – lives to defy you still. Though numbers over-power me and treachery surrounds me, though friends desert me, I defy you still! Come to me – come singly to me! And this true knife that has tasted the foul blood of your nation and now is red with the purest of mine, will feel a gasp as strong as when it flashed in the blaze of your burning buildings, or was lifted terribly over the fallen in battle.

Church Fire upon him!

Metamora Do so, I am weary of the world for ye are dwellers in it; I would not turn upon my heel to save my life.

Church Your duty, soldiers.

They fire. Metamora falls.

Metamora My curses on you, white men! May the Great Spirit curse you when he speaks in his war voice from the clouds! Murderers! The last of the Wampanoags' curse be on you! May your graves and the graves of your children be in the path the red man shall trace! And may the wolf and panther howl o'er your fleshless bones, fit banquet for the destroyers! Spirits of the grave, I come! But the curse of Metamora stays with the white man! I die! My wife! My Queen! My Nahmeokee!

Falls and dies. A tableau is formed. Drums and trumpet sound a retreat. Slow curtain. Blackout.

SCENE TWO

Projection: WHILE AT THE SAME TIME:

Macready's rooms, New York Hotel.
The actors from the Astor Place Opera House produc-

tion of Macbeth – *including Clark, Mrs Pope, Wemyss,
Bridges, Bradshaw, Sefton, Chippindale, and Arnold – are
all shouting for explanations about what had happened.
They are shouting at an elderly man, Washington Irving,
who stands next to Macready, who now wears a bandage
on his head, and looks weary.*

Irving (*over the shouts*) Quiet, please! Please, let me
finish!

Macready Listen to him!

The actors quiet down.

Irving Mr Macready has been persuaded – to give tomorrow night a second performance of his glorious *Macbeth*.

*This upsets the actors again and all speak at once:
'Who's going to perform it?' 'Isn't once enough?' 'You
have to be joking!', etc.*

(*over the shouts*) We believe there is no significant risk!
For him. And for those of you who wish to join him on
the stage.

In shock they quiet down again.

Macready (*as if this makes everything clear*) Mr Forrest
has been spoken to –.

Irving Mr Forrest has agreed to perform only *Metamora*
for some time.

Macready So they'll be no more of this –.

Irving (*over him*) Not that he had anything to do with
last night. But we can thank him for his consideration.

Macready bites his tongue.

Clark (*to others*) It seems like a big risk to –.

Irving (*with sudden vehemence*) Of course it's a risk!

There's a risk in any important endeavour. And this is important!!!

Irving works to get a grip on himself.

Or maybe, sir, you wish to let these hooligans determine what can and cannot be presented on our stages? In our books? By our speakers. Is that what you want, sir?

Clark Of course, I don't want –.

Irving Then take some responsibility!!! That is what I am saying. What I've been asked to say – by a delegation of citizens. (*Beat.*) All leading citizens I hasten to add, who met together this morning. One conclusion of this meeting was the designation of a person to express for all a deep apology to Mr Macready.

He bows to Macready, who accepts the apology.

And to you other actors as well.

A shorter bow to them. Then he laughs to himself and explains.

I told them I was probably the worst person for this job. I told them – you probably had never even heard of me.

He laughs, no one else does.

Of Washington Irving.

Arnold I didn't realize that's who he –.

Mrs Pope Sh-sh.

Irving But I was assured. (*He takes out a letter.*) Together we signed a letter – with not only our apologies but also our word that should you agree to another performance, you shall be protected. You shall be safe.

He hands the letter to an actor.

Police will be stationed throughout the theatre and out-side.

This concerns the actors. They look at each other: 'Police???'

The Mayor has put the militia on notice.

The actors begin to panic again: 'The Militia?!' 'Soldiers? Why do we need soldiers?!'

Macready Quiet. Please.

They turn to Macready.

Not that it will affect anyone of you in making a decision. (*Beat.*) But you might like to know that our producers have offered us seventy-five per cent of the house. Fifty to me. Twenty-five to be split by you. (*Beat.*) It's generous. But I doubt if money alone would be enough to . . . To . . . But it's generous. (*Short pause.*) So think it over. Mr Irving had kindly arranged for food in the dining-room. So please – join us if you wish.

Silence as they put their hats and gloves on, etc. Preparing to leave. After a moment:

Mrs Pope (*to Mr Wemyss, under her breath*) An angel just passed.

Irving Mrs Pope?

She nervously turns to him.

Can Mr Macready count on you to attend rehearsal in the morning?

She hesitates, looks at the others, who watch her, then:

Mrs Pope In the morning? If it isn't an inconvenience – the afternoon would be a lot better for me. My sister's staying with me with her two children –.

Everyone starts smiling, trying not to laugh, which only makes her explain more.

– and she works in the mornings. But maybe I could ask Mrs Seymour, she lives just below –.

All the actors are laughing.

Macready Come when you can, Mrs Pope.

Mrs Pope I don't understand why you're laughing.

The mood has suddenly lightened.

Wemyss (*to Bradshaw*) Bradshaw maybe Banquo should enter with Macbeth – as it says, I think, in the text.

Macready It says that? I should read the text more carefully.

Laughter.

Arnold Perhaps Banquo should enter downstage of Macbeth!

Laughter.

Sefton (*kidding him*) Or even in front of him!

Big laugh.

Bradshaw Oh I don't think my character would ever do that.

Macready We should rehearse it and see.

Laughter. Nearly everyone slowly starts to head off to the dining-room and the promised food.

Macready (*to Wemyss as he passes*) And how is your lovely daughter, Mr Wemyss, does she still wish to become an actress?

Wemyss She's a thick one.

Mrs Pope (*behind him*) We never learn.

Irving is in another conversation with Bradshaw, etc.

Irving You actors are so full of – life.

Bradshaw (*to Bridges*) I'm glad he said 'life'.

Irving suddenly stops them from leaving.

Irving A story! During one of our amateur theatricals.
There were these soldiers running through a – 'wood'.
The trees about so far apart. And one actor with his gun
like this. (*horizontal*) And he gets caught on the trees and
he flips over and the whole army – all five or six of us –
we flip over too. (*He laughs and laughs. Then leading
them off*) Everyone of you must have stories like that.

All are gone except for Clark and Macready. Short pause.

Macready You're not joining us, Mr Clark? You're not
hungry?

Clark looks at Macready, then:

Clark Who ever heard of an actor who wasn't hungry, sir.

Macready Good for you, Mr Clark.

He slaps him on the back as they go.

Good for you.

Blackout.

SCENE THREE

Projection: 11 P.M.

The tavern.
 *Boucicault, Agnes and Fisher at one smallish table.
Fisher is reading Boucicault's play. At a table nearby,*

Tilton and Scott, who has a bandaged hand, sit and drink.

    As the scene begins Ryder has just entered; he has been stopped at Tilton's table to be introduced to Scott.

Tilton Mr Ryder played Macduff, when you –. The other night –.

Scott Oh yes. How do you do?

Tilton He was quite good.

Scott Oh how nice.

Ryder There wasn't much time to . . . (*He smiles.*) You understand.

Scott That's how the theatre often works. If one doesn't like it then one gets out. (*He turns to Tilton and laughs.*)

Ryder How is the finger? (*Beat.*) I hope . . . Everyone was hoping . . .

Scott The finger is gone, Mr –. (*He turns to Tilton.*)

Tilton Ryder.

Scott And at the moment I can't move my hand at all. (*Beat.*) They say that will change. Some time.

    Beat.

Ryder I heard you were a wonderful Macduff. That you are a –. I'm sure I didn't do justice . . . (*Beat.*) No doubt your public was profoundly disappointed with me last night.

Scott My public? (*He laughs and pours himself a drink.*)

Ryder Excuse me, I have friends . . .

    He nods towards Boucicault's table. Scott does not look at him.

Scott (*to Tilton*) Who's buying by the way? I don't have any money.

Ryder goes to Boucicault's table.

Tilton Don't worry about that.

Scott I wasn't worrying.

Ryder (*sitting at Boucicault's table*) Sorry. I dropped by backstage. I asked Ned to join us, but –. I don't know.

They nod. Beat.

Mind if I –?

Boucicault No, no, of course not.

Ryder pours himself a drink.

Ryder (*nodding toward Scott*) I took over for him in –. As Macduff. He –. There had been an accident with –.

Agnes We heard about that, didn't we?

Boucicault The finger?

Ryder That's right.

Short pause. Boucicault watches Fisher for a reaction as he reads.

Agnes (*turning to Tilton*) The performance tonight was terribly exciting. Thank you. I didn't know this play.

Tilton Which play are you –?

Agnes We were at *Metamora*. The three of us. (*Beat.*) Actually we were hoping that the rest of the company . . .

Tilton I don't think they're coming. Sometimes no one goes out. Sometimes it's only me.

Scott But if you're going out –.

Tilton It's the closest tavern. (*Short pause.*) Some of them have to go home. (*Beat.*) Scott here always had to go home. His wife made him.

Scott Now she's sick of me. (*He turns to Tilton.*) Still she doesn't give me any money. (*He shakes his head in disgust.*)

Tilton You saw it tonight? It was good tonight. I liked everything I did.

Ryder Forrest was extraordinary.

Agnes Wasn't he? There was a rawness, like some powerful animal –.

Ryder The nobleness of the character. That's what I was taken –.

Scott I play the Indian who betrays him.

Ryder That's a very interesting role.

Scott (*to Tilton*) Who played him tonight?

Tilton Jones.

Scott Jones? (*He smiles and shakes his head.*) I knew he wanted to play my character.

　Short pause.

Agnes Everyone was very good. Thank you. (*She turns back to her table. To Ryder*) It is a pity Mr Macready did not feel –.

Ryder I don't blame him. I wouldn't want to sit in a theatre of all places, not after last –.

Agnes He would have had a good time. He could have forgotten, at least for a short while –.

Ryder I only asked him once, I knew there was no –.

Boucicault But to see Mr Forrest in a native role. This is what he missed. (*Beat.*) Tonight you could really see his talent. Couldn't you Agnes.

Before she can answer.

The affect upon the women especially, this was most noticeable. I don't think an Englishman could ever play such an Indian. They wouldn't be able to create the affect – upon the women. An Irishman wouldn't have a problem, of course, but an English actor –.

Ryder I –. I don't know.

Boucicault With English actors, there's always a . . . (*He turns to Agnes.*) What am I trying to say, Agnes?

She doesn't respond; he smiles, she does not.

Tilton (*from the other table*) Shame about Mr Macready.

Boucicault I was there, you know. (*He shakes his head.*) Extraordinary. The look on Macready's face. He – I'm sure – thought they were going to kill him. (*He smiles.*)

Ryder I don't think it's funny.

Boucicault Of course it's not funny. I didn't say it was. (*Beat.*) Anyway, I thought he could have kept performing.

Agnes Dion –.

Boucicault It wasn't that many people for Christ's sake. But . . . (*Beat.*) Whatever, it's all part of a day for an actor. (*He laughs.*) Sometimes they love us, sometimes they –.

Scott I think they should have shot him. That's what I would have liked to see.

Fisher stops reading and looks up.

Tilton Come on, that's –.

Scott I mean it. (*Beat.*) He has no right to be here. People like him have no right. So he gets what he deserves. This is my opinion. (*Beat.*) I mean, why the hell did we fight a war? Why did we fight two wars?! They invade us! We threw them off! We don't need the goddamn English telling us –.

Fisher Stop it, Scott.

Scott American actors for America! I don't see what is so wrong with that?!

Ryder I doubt if the point of those hooligans was to support American actors.

Scott What hooligans? Who are you calling hooligans? You don't even know why they did what they did.

Ryder And you do?

Scott If they're like me, they're just fed up. You fight war after war –.

Tilton When did you fight a war? You didn't fight, Scott.

Scott I wanted to. But I had a job. I would have if I hadn't had the job.

Fisher Tilton is the only one of us who fought . . .

Tilton I fought and I didn't die. That's all that's worth remembering.

   Beat.

Scott (*suddenly standing and pointing to Ryder*) He took my job!

Fisher *You* cut off your finger!

Scott I slipped!

Fisher Blame Jones too then! He's got your role too!

Scott I do blame him! He was a friend. I was nice to him.

Fisher But he's not English.

Scott He's from Maryland. I've learned in my life never to trust someone from Maryland. I should have listened to myself.

Fisher So it's people from Maryland, people from England. You're talking nonsense.

Scott Is it nonsense that when we go to their country, they spit in our face?!

Tilton Are you talking Maryland or England now?

Scott (*pointing to Ryder*) Ask him, he knows what I'm talking about!

Ryder We have never spat in your –.

Tilton (*to Scott*) When have you ever even been to England?

Scott (*pointing to Boucicault and Ryder*) You make fun of us! (*He turns to Tilton.*) Don't be an idiot, Tilton, you know they do! We don't need them, that's all I want to say. (*Beat.*) Go home! Leave us alone! We don't want you! We don't need you taking our jobs!

Ryder (*to Agnes*) All this is about is my playing Macduff –.

Tilton It's his accident. Excuse him.

Scott Don't apologize –.

Tilton You're grouchy, Scott. (*Beat.*) He's grouchy. (*Beat.*) Ask his wife. Why do you think she let him out? Because he's been so grouchy. (*He tries to laugh. To Scott*) If your wife heard you talk like that . . .

Scott Shut up.

Fisher Don't embarrass yourself!

Pause.

Tilton Just a few months ago he was saying how much he wanted to visit England. (*to Scott*) Weren't you? (*Beat.*) To visit London. (*Beat.*) It must be very nice.

Awkward pause.

Fisher (*starting a new conversation, he slaps the manuscript he has been reading*) I like this play. I think I could be very interested in appearing in this play.

Boucicault smiles at Agnes, then:

Boucicault We're just talking about the reading at this point. There's no pay of course. For a reading. I understand this is the practice.

Fisher But Hackett you say is interested. Has he mentioned dates?

Boucicault (*shrugging and looking at Agnes*) November?

Fisher I might have a problem with that. I might be doing a play in Philadelphia in November. Nothing's set. But they want me, I know they want me.

Boucicault But you're available for the reading.

Fisher The part is Hamlet, am I right?

Boucicault None other than – Hamlet. Who doesn't want to play Hamlet?

Fisher Right. (*Beat.*) But it appears that in your play – Hamlet, as far as I can tell, has only about five lines.

Boucicault This is true. He comes into Shakespeare's

study and tries to help him figure out what he should do about being in love with his neighbour.

Fisher And he does this in five lines.

Boucicault The part is Hamlet for God's sake. (*to Agnes*) I don't think I've ever met an actor who didn't want to play Hamlet. (*He moves to take the manuscript away.*) Maybe you'd rather play Romeo.

Fisher (*taking the script back*) How big is Romeo?

Boucicault Five, six lines, same as Hamlet.

Fisher Maybe I can play them both.

Boucicault It's an interesting thought but they appear in the same scene. (*He opens the script.*) Here. Romeo arrives in Stratford while Hamlet is still there and tries to find out why Shakespeare isn't writing any more. Hamlet of course already knows but he can't make up his mind whether to tell someone.

Ryder (*holding up a pitcher of beer, to Scott and Tilton*) We have some beer.

Scott turns away, ignoring him.

Tilton No, thank you.

Fisher (*continuing*) Who played Hamlet in the London production?

Boucicault What was his name? A very good actor. The next Kean everyone was saying. He found a lot to do with the part. There's a lot there.

Fisher The next Kean? And he just played Hamlet?

Boucicault Just Hamlet. He seemed satisfied.

Fisher And Hackett's definitely interested?

Boucicault I'm just talking about a reading.

Fisher (*no longer listening*) I like Hackett. And he likes me. (*Beat.*) Still I never thought he'd ever hire me for Hamlet.

> *He starts to look through the script again. Boucicault looks to Agnes, and rolls his eyes – all this to cast a small role in a reading.*
> *Forrest enters.*

Ryder There he is! It's Ned.

Agnes (*to Boucicault*) He came.

Forrest Forgive me, I forgot where John said you were going to go.

Boucicault Sit down, sit down. Here's a glass.

> *Forrest sits; Boucicault pours him a glass.*

Agnes I can't tell you how much we loved the performance –.

Scott (*calling out*) Ned!

> *Forrest turns.*

Ned? (*He suddenly gets up.*)

Forrest Mr Scott, what a surprise! You weren't in the audience tonight –.

Scott No, no. I wasn't.

Tilton I dragged him out of the house –.

Scott My wife threw me out –. (*Beat.*) For the night.

Tilton He'd been driving her –.

Forrest How's the finger?

Scott I'm getting better. They say in a few days, I'll . . .

Forrest That's good to hear. (*Beat.*) You'd be proud of young Jones. He's doing his best.

Scott Good. *That's* very good to hear. (*Beat.*) They really say that in a few days –.

Forrest Let me buy you a drink.

Scott No, no, please, it's I who should –.

Forrest What are you drinking? Here. (*He puts money on the table.*) You're looking great. (*He smiles and goes back to his table. Short pause.*)

Boucicault I enjoyed tonight a great deal.

Forrest nods.

It made me think perhaps I should try my hand at an American theme. (*He turns to Ryder.*) Maybe an Indian play as well.

Agnes It seemed very authentic.

Forrest turns and looks at Fisher, who looks up.

Fisher Mr Boucicault's play. He wants me to play Hamlet.

Boucicault (*quickly*) In the reading. This Saturday. You'll be there, I hope.

Fisher I don't know yet if I'm available for the full production.

Boucicault (*to Forrest*) So we'll have to hold our breath for a while.

Short pause.

Forrest (*distracted, pointing to a glass*) Is this mine?

Agnes That one there. Yes.

Forrest drinks.

Forrest The house was full tonight I gather. It felt that way.

Boucicault Packed.

Agnes Thank you for the seats.

Ryder The couple next to us was sobbing at the end.

Beat.

Agnes I was sobbing at the end.

Beat.

Boucicault If I *were* to attempt an Indian play, Mr Forrest, I don't imagine you'd be interested in seeing –.

Forrest (*not listening*) Sometimes you can feel an audience giving back as much as you are trying to give them. (*Beat.*) It felt like that. You were a good audience.

Boucicault I know exactly what you mean.

Forrest And sometimes –. (*He turns to Ryder.*) How is Mr Macready? I meant to write him today.

Ryder He's –. In shock? (*He shrugs.*) How should he be?

Boucicault I was there, you know. We were. It was unbelievable.

Forrest (*to Ryder*) What about his wounds? I heard –. He was cut?

Boucicault There was blood all over the stage. When he walked off, Macready's face was covered. You couldn't see his –.

Ryder It was cut. On his forehead. (*He turns to Boucicault.*) It looked worse than it was.

Short pause.

Forrest (*without looking at anyone*) I've heard someone –. Someone was saying – I forget who it was – they were saying that people think I'm somehow . . . (*Beat.*) That I bear a responsibility.

Boucicault For last night?

Forrest This is what I've heard.

Fisher People are nervous, all kinds of things are being said.

Ryder I have heard this as well, Mr Forrest. You try to tell people that –.

Agnes No one can –.

Forrest As if attacking Macready's *Macbeth* was somehow praising mine. This is thinking I do not grasp myself. (*He smiles.*) It's ridiculous. It's unfair. If they knew –. If only someone had come to me and said there could be trouble. I now understand there were threats made days ago.

Ryder Mr Forrest –.

Forrest Let me finish. Where was Mr Macready? Why did he not confide in me? We had dinner only the other day. He said nothing, isn't that right, Mr Ryder? You were there.

Ryder That's correct.

Forrest Just the other day, we had dinner. My wife and I did. (*Beat. He sighs.*) As if I don't have enough to worry about. (*Beat.*) We don't know who these thugs were, do we? Or even what they wanted. (*He shakes his head.*) It seems so unnecessary. (*Beat.*) How many were there? I've heard at least ten different accounts.

Boucicault They were in the balcony. Most of them were in the balcony, weren't they?

Forrest I've even heard . . . (*Beat.*) I'm sure this is not true. You were there. I'm sure he did the right thing. (*Beat.*) But someone was saying –. Who was it? (*He shrugs.*) They were saying that if Macready had only stayed on the stage and shouted back at them.

Agnes He tried this. (*He turns to Boucicault.*) Have you –.

Forrest Oh. Then he tried.

Boucicault Not for that long though.

Forrest Really? (*Beat.*) I mean we've all had audiences that –. I don't know. Can't be pleased, I suppose. Nothing will please them. (*Beat.*) We get such audiences here. Maybe not in England, but –.

Boucicault You get them in England. You really get them in Scotland.

Agnes Scotland can be bad, this is true.

Forrest Then you know what I'm talking about. How sometimes one needs to fight back. To assert oneself. You let a crowd have their way . . . (*He shrugs.*) If you don't lead . . . (*Beat.*) I'm sure it's not true, but it is possible that Mr Macready – for whatever reason – was simply unable to lead. Unable to do his job. (*Beat.*) And so – he ran away.

Ryder I don't think that's fair.

Forrest Is it fair to blame me?

Short pause.

Ryder No. That isn't fair either.

Forrest Because some unhappy people decide to rip up

some seats while shouting out my name?

Ryder They shouted your name? That I hadn't heard. (*to Boucicault*) Did you –?

Boucicault They did. That's true.

Forrest I'm an actor. What can I do? (*Beat.*) People sit in their seats and dream about you, until what they dream isn't you. (*Beat.*) What people shout . . . (*He shrugs.*) I have enough things . . . (*Pause. He looks to Agnes and Boucicault.*) My wife, Catherine – she left me today. This morning.

Agnes Oh God, I'm sorry –.

Forrest She'd – had enough, she said. So she walked out. (*Beat.*) I don't need this other –. I did nothing wrong?!! He should have just yelled them down. Had the guts to yell them down. And then all of . . .

Macready has entered with Clark and Bradshaw.

Macready Mr Forrest.

Forrest turns and stands.

Forrest You don't look any worse for wear. Please, won't you –.

Macready We just took a table in the next room. I heard you were here and . . . (*Beat.*) I want to thank you for changing to *Metamora*.

Forrest nods.

It will help to –. This so-called rivalry.

Forrest What rivalry? (*Beat.*) I heard that in some quarters we are both being blamed for what happened last night.

Macready I had not heard that we both were being blamed.

Ryder Mr Forrest was just saying that they were shouting out his name.

Macready I remember hearing it very distinctly.

Forrest It will all calm down.

Macready Of course it will. (*Beat.*) It has nothing to do with us, does it?

Forrest No. Nothing.

Beat.

Macready (*suddenly turning to Ryder*) Where have you been, John? I expected to see you this evening.

Ryder I went to Mr Forrest's *Metamora*. I told you I was going. I asked you to go.

Macready Did you? (*Beat.*) I suppose it is all very – original. My loss, no doubt. Get us some liquor, will you? Different kinds. You choose. (*He turns to go, stops, goes back.*) Oh. I forgot. You need my money, don't you? (*He puts money on the table.*) Don't be too long.

He and Clark and Bradshaw – who have stayed at some distance – now leave. Pause.

Ryder I better . . . (*He stands.*) Perhaps, first I'll finish my wine. (*He sits.*) I just have a sip left. (*He drinks it.*)

Forrest Let me fill up your glass.

After some hesitation, Ryder hands him his glass. Forrest pours him another drink.

On tour, a few years ago, in a small southern town, I happened to cast as my Ophelia, the daughter of a preacher. (*Beat.*) I had not known this. And the true extent of his rage had been kept from me. (*Beat.*) But as I made my first entrance, I heard the clicks of many revolvers being cocked. (*Beat.*) You know, it never occurred to me to leave that stage.

Pause, then blackout.

SCENE FOUR

Projection: 2 A.M.

A small attic apartment.
Forrest and Ryder come up the stairs (up through a trap); they carry lanterns.

Forrest I'm surprised you're even interested. Watch your step.

Ryder I'm interested in talking about anything. And everything.

Forrest (*holding up the lantern and looking around the room*) I told you it was small. But it is convenient. Put it over there.

Ryder sets down his lantern.

Sit down, sit down. (*Beat.*) One block from the theatre. (*He lights another lantern.*) It is a place to get away.

Ryder I'm sure –.

Forrest Sit down, please Mr Ryder. And when they throw you out of the tavern, it is a place to get a drink. Let me get you that drink. (*He goes to a cabinet and takes out a bottle, glasses, etc. Pause.*) It's cold tonight. Cold for May. (*Beat.*) Feels like it's going to rain. But that I am sure is something you are used to.

Ryder Rain? (*He smiles.*) I don't miss it.

Forrest Do you miss anything? (*Beat.*) Won't you miss –?

Ryder I haven't agreed to anything, Mr –. Ned. I thought we were just . . . (*Beat.*) I'd probably be interested in a season. (*Beat.*) A four- or five-month season. Depending on where it is. Where you are going. There's much more of this country I'd like to see. I'm not homesick yet. (*He looks at him.*) I admired your performance tonight enormously.

The door opens and Miss Bass enters, a blanket around her shoulders. Underneath she is naked, having just been woken up.

Miss Bass What time is it –? (*She sees Ryder.*) Oh, I'll . . . I didn't know you'd . . .

Forrest Have a drink with us, Jane. You know John, of course.

Miss Bass Yes, of course. Let me get some clothes on.

She goes. Pause.

Forrest She lives here. (*Beat.*) She looks after it for me. (*Beat.*) I'm pleased you enjoyed *Metamora* tonight. I paid for that play, you know. Had a contest. The best play on an American topic. (*Beat.*) That came in. It was a mess. Wrote three-quarters of it myself. (*Beat.*) Fits like a glove now. Could play some of it in my sleep. And they can't get enough of it. Anywhere I go. (*Beat.*) You'll see yourself. (*Beat.*) I don't need anyone for *Metamora*.

Ryder I wasn't suggesting –. That's not why I –.

Forrest I need a Buckingham. (*Beat.*) A Mercutio. An Edgar, son of Gloucester. As well as Macduff of course.

Ryder That's very generous.

Forrest Between you and me . . . We can talk about Iago another time.

Ryder I've played Iago.

Forrest That's good to know. (*Short pause.*) In my production he's very subtle. The man who plays him now is very good.

Ryder I'll come and see –.

Forrest We do New Orleans, St Louis, Cincinnati, then to Baltimore and Philadelphia. Then back here for a month for Hackett. (*Beat.*) This is November.

Ryder I thought Boucicault's play was to be done by Hackett in –.

Forrest The problem of course is can I afford you. (*Beat.*) You are probably very expensive.

Ryder You know what you paid for one Macduff.

Forrest You are very expensive.

Miss Bass enters, having quickly dressed.

(*getting up*) Let me get you a –.

Miss Bass I can get a drink myself.

Forrest sits back down. Short pause.

Ryder I should probably be –. (*He starts to stand.*)

Forrest Don't be silly. Sit down. We don't have that many guests, do we?

He sits. Short pause.

Miss Bass I'm sorry I couldn't join you at the tavern tonight. I was exhausted. (*Beat.*) Did I miss anything?

Forrest Did you miss –? Did she, John?

Ryder I . . . (*He shrugs. He has been fiddling with a manuscript that is in front of him.*)

Forrest Boucicault's play. Take a look if you want. (*Beat.*)

I'm supposed to be reading it. (*Beat.*) He asked me to –.
(*He turns to Miss Bass.*) I've read most of it. I've read some
of it. He says Macready's interested if you can believe that.

Ryder I doubt if –. (*Beat.*) I don't know.

Miss Bass I've tried to read it tonight. (*She rolls her eyes
and laughs. Short pause.*)

Forrest John loved *Metamora*.

Miss Bass Ned wrote most of that.

Pause.

Ryder It's a lovely apartment. (*to Miss Bass*) It's yours?

She turns to Forrest, then back.

Miss Bass Yeah. (*Beat.*) It's mine.

Ryder It's very convenient.

Miss Bass Isn't it?

Forrest John has asked to join us for a season.

Ryder I haven't actually –. (*He stops himself and smiles.*)
If Ned can find a place for me. (*Short pause. Suddenly he
stands.*) Really, it is late. I must go.

No one gets ups.

Thank you for the drink.

Forrest (*gesturing that he could stand*) Let me.

Ryder I think I can let myself out. (*He takes the lantern.*)
Miss Bass. (*Beat.*) Ned.

He goes. Long pause.

Miss Bass (*finally*) Do you want to go to bed?

He doesn't respond.

It was nice having company. It was nice to –. Entertain. This way. (*Beat.*) He's a nice man. Why he wants to work in America when –.

Forrest He liked my performance. He wants to work with me.

Miss Bass I didn't mean . . . (*Beat.*) He must have many reasons. Maybe things in England weren't working out so . . . I don't know, Ned. I'm sorry I brought it up.

He sips his drink. Short pause.

I ran into our landlord this morning. (*Beat.*) The rent's due. (*Beat.*) I know I reminded you already, but –. I didn't know if you'd forgotten. (*Beat.*) Sometimes you do forget. (*She laughs. He doesn't seem to hear her.*) Ned? (*Beat.*) My –. (*She opens her mouth.*) I broke a tooth.

He looks at her.

I'm sorry to bring it up now. I know you're tired but –. (*Beat.*) This is the only chance we seem to have, so . . .

He takes out some money and sets it down.

I don't like to beg.

Forrest You're not begging.

Short pause.

Miss Bass My mother wrote. She's finally coming to visit. I don't believe it, I've asked her a hundred times. (*Beat.*) I guess she finally accepts my being an actress. (*She laughs to herself.*) She wants to stay here. She thinks it's –. Mine. (*Beat.*) She'll stay for three weeks.

Short pause. Forrest just sits there.

Do you mind? (*Beat.*) Do you mind? (*Short pause.*)

Blackout.

213

SCENE FIVE

Projection: LATER THAT NIGHT.

Macready's room, New York Hotel.
  Macready asleep, drunk, in a chair. Ryder sits in another chair, reading Boucicault's manuscript. Pause. Suddenly Macready screams – he's having a nightmare.

Ryder It's all right. Calm down. It's me. It's me.

  Macready opens his eyes, he breathes heavily; looks around him.

You had a dream.

  Pause. Heavy breathing; rubs his eyes.

Macready How long have I –. When did you . . .?

Ryder You asked me in, remember? We were talking. You were telling me about the meeting. (*Beat.*) With Irving. (*Beat.*) You fell asleep.

Macready What time is it?

Ryder Nearly half past four.

Macready I can't sleep in my bed.

Ryder That's what you'd been saying . . . That's why –. (*He gestures 'I am here'.*) Let me get you a drink. It helped before.

Macready I'm going to smell for days. (*He smiles.*) My spit will intoxicate at least the first three rows.

  Wider smile. Ryder brings him a drink. He sips.

It was an actor's dream, John.

Ryder Not surprising.

Macready The actor's dream. (*Beat.*) Do cobblers and coat-makers have their dreams? One wonders. Though mine was an interesting variation. It wasn't that I could not remember my lines or what part I was playing or which play I was in, rather – it was the reverse. (*Beat.*) In my dream, I was speaking all the parts. One second I was –. Whatever. I can't remember. Then the next, I was speaking back to me. Then entering to tell me something. Then telling me to leave so I could be alone and have my soliloquy. (*Beat.*) Rather exhausting this was. And rather unnerving to the other actors whose parts I was obviously usurping. Thus one by one they – my fellow actors – retreated from the stage and allowed me to be alone with various other me's. (*Beat.*) One or two left quite angrily too. This I could not understand. After all I was much better than they could ever hope to be. They should have appreciated this. (*Short pause.*) When it came time for Macduff to kill Macbeth – so obviously this was *Macbeth* – I found myself in a quandary, of course. (*He laughs to himself.*) The audience was cheering. They screamed. Were they praising my performing? Were they after my death? I did not understand the effect I was having. (*Beat.*) And then – as the script calls for it – I killed myself, or rather my Macduff killed my Macbeth. And the pain, it was horrific. (*Short pause. He looks at Ryder.*) I knew every part and was good. (*He laughs. Beat.*) I shall be afraid now to go to sleep again. The sun should be up when?

Ryder shrugs.

What time did you come here?

Ryder It was a little after two.

Macready And I was up then?

Ryder I think you had been asleep, but . . .

Short pause.

Macready (*suddenly starts*) Had I written to my wife?! I always write to my wife!

Ryder Yes. You had. It's . . . (*He nods to the table. Short pause.*)

Macready (*suddenly starts again*) And when you came, there were crowds in the streets. Angry crowds!

Ryder No. (*Beat.*) The streets were . . . A few carts. A few people. (*Beat.*) That must have been another dream.

Macready notices the manuscript in Ryder's hands.

Boucicault's play. I see he gave you a copy. (*Beat.*) Did you read it?

Macready I looked at it. (*Beat.*) Forrest is interested. That's what one hears.

Ryder I wouldn't know. I don't –. (*Beat.*) Maybe.

Pause.

Macready They say I will be safe. Besides the police they may even circle the entire theatre with soldiers. Nothing can happen. (*Beat.*) Soldiers. (*Beat.*) What a country. And now you want to stay here. This is what you were telling me, wasn't it? (*Beat.*) See, I was awake.

Ryder I didn't think –.

Macready I was even listening.

Beat.

Ryder Then you know, and that is that.

Macready Is it? (*Beat.*) I paid your way here *and* back, Mr Ryder.

Ryder I have done everything you've asked.

Macready You were brought here to work for me, not for Mr Forrest!

Ryder I shall make sure you are safely on a ship and very comfortable. That's where my responsibility ends!

Pause.

Macready (*to himself*) Alone on the stage. The actors are deserting me. Dreams and life. Life and dreams. How can you stomach such a country where soldiers stand around theatres?! (*Beat.*) When audiences –. But of course you didn't see this. You were busy playing for Mr Forrest.

Ryder You agreed that I could.

Macready How could I say no? (*Beat.*) This does not mean I approved, John. I had hoped you'd have recognized your own responsibility. Your own duty. But . . . (*Beat.*) This is how one learns about one's friends. (*Short pause.*) I will never employ you again. (*Beat.*) Never.

Pause. Ryder says nothing.

I may change my mind, but that is how I feel at this time, John. (*Beat.*) I'm planning a season at the Drury Lane. Nothing has been cast. Except the leads, of course. We can talk about anything you wish. (*Beat.*) We can talk now.

Ryder I will be back in a few months. It's only for a few months.

Macready Oh. You didn't say that. (*Beat.*) Then we will talk in those few months. (*Beat.*) How many is a 'few'?

Ryder Three.

Short pause.

Macready In two months, I begin to cast. (*Pause.*) Forrest has parts for you?

Ryder If he didn't, he wouldn't be asking –.

Macready Make him give you excellent parts, John! In America you deserve excellent parts, remember that.

Ryder I saw his *Metamora* tonight.

Macready I have seen this performance. (*Beat.*) Years ago. Seven years or so ago. (*Beat.*) Somewhere. He has power. In this role.

Ryder Absolutely. When he kills his wife –.

Macready Ah. Yes. True. (*Beat.*) And that must have been quite heartfelt tonight.

Ryder looks at Macready.

His wife has left him, you know. Just today. Everyone was talking about it. (*Beat.*) She's staying with a friend. Just left him a note. (*Pause.*) *Metamora* is a very good role for him. I would never attempt it myself. (*Beat.*) Audiences love it. (*He shakes his head.*) He's made a fortune from it. (*Beat.*) I understand he's building a castle of some sort just up the Hudson. All from the money he's made from . . . (*Beat.*) Lucky him. (*Beat.*) Every actor is staying. I don't have to replace anyone. I take my hat off to all of them. Not one is deserting. (*Beat. To himself*) Actors. By and large we are good and decent people. (*Beat.*) So they left the stage and there I am trying to kill myself! (*He laughs.*) I can see myself as Macduff. I'd be a very good Macduff. If the part were larger. Mmmmm-mmmm. (*He smiles to himself.*) Mmmmmmmmmm. I'm waking up. (*Beat.*) Let's wait for the sun to rise. Which, like stage light, will keep us out of the dark. (*He takes a sip of the drink.*)

Short pause. Blackout.

SCENE SIX

Projection: 10 MAY 1849. 8.30 P.M.

*The wings of a stage, first representing the wings of the
Broadway Theatre, later the wings of the Astor Place
Opera House. The 'stage' is just off, where the end of Act
II of* Metamora *is in progress.*

*A number of actors in soldier and Indian costume wait
and watch; they include Fisher and Miss Holland.*

*From the stage: the council chamber scene. Errington
(Blakeley), Metamora (Forrest), Goodenough (Miss
Burton) and Annawandah (Jones).*

Tilton enters the wings from the dressing rooms.

In the wings:	*On stage:*
Tilton How's it going?	**Metamora** You believe his words.
Miss Holland Fine. It's going fine.	**Goodenough** We do, and will reward his honesty.
Tilton Either of you been outside tonight? I just stepped out. It's crazy out tonight. A bunch of drunks nearly knocked me down.	**Metamora** Red man, say unto these people they have bought thy tongue, and thou hast uttered a lie!
	Errington He does not answer.
	Metamora I am Metamora, thy father and thy king.
Fisher It's fine in here. It's a good house.	**Errington** Metamora o'erawes him – send the witness home.
Tilton Is it? (*He checks out the audi-*	**Metamora** I will do that! Slave of the white man, go follow Sassamond.

ence.) I was thinking I might even skip the tavern tonight . . .

They listen to the silence from the stage.

Fisher Ned's dried. He's dried.

Miss Bass (*entering from the stage*) Do something! Help him!

Tilton Get a script!

Miss Holland (*at the same time*) Give him a line!

Miss Bass (*to Fisher*) Bang the –!

They listen.

Tilton He never dries.

Miss Bass (*to Miss Holland*) Every time Ned comes off stage he says he sees his wife out there. She's not. I checked.

Errington Seize and bind him.

Metamora Come! My knife has drunk the blood of the false one, yet it is not satisfied.

Silence from the stage.

Miss Burton (*from the stage*) Prompt! Prompt!

Metamora From the east to the west, in the north and in the south shall cry of vengeance burst, till the lands you have stolen groan under your feet.

Errington Secure him!

Metamora Thus do I smite your nation and defy your power!

Errington Fire upon him.

*Metamora/Forrest
runs into the
wings. Fisher gives
a drum roll. Huge
applause is heard
coming from the
theatre. Forrest
gets a hold of him-
self and returns to
the stage for a
bow. Others fol-
low.*

Soldiers fire on stage.

Tilton (*the last to
go*) It is a good house
tonight.

*The applause fades away and from the stage one hears
Macbeth and we are in the wings of The Astor Place
Opera House.*
    *Numerous actors in costume wait and watch. From
the stage:*

Macbeth . . . there, the murderers,
Steeped in the colours of their trade, their daggers
Unmannerly breeched with gore. Who could refrain
That had a heart to love, and in that heart
Courage to make's love known?

Lady Macbeth   Help me hence, ho!

Macduff Look to the Lady.

*Scene continues 'on stage'. Lady Macbeth (Mrs Pope) is
carried from the stage. As she enters the wings:*

Bridges How is it out there?

Mrs Pope A couple of people in the balcony. A couple of
boos nothing else.

Bridges Then that's not too bad, is it?

Mrs Pope No. It'll all be fine.

On stage, continuing:

Macduff And so do I.

All   So all.

Macbeth Let's briefly put on manly readiness
And meet i' th' hall together.

All   Well contented.

*Macbeth (Macready), Macduff (Clark), Banquo
(Bradshaw) enter from the stage. Scene between
Malcolm and Donalbain continues off.*

Macready (*entering*) I've played to better houses.

Bradshaw They're nervous.

Clark That is true.

Macready The soldiers still outside?

Bridges There seem to be even more.

Macready Don't complain.

Bridges I wasn't –.

*Malcolm (Arnold) and Donalbain (Sefton) enter from
the stage and Bridges (Ross) and Wemyss (Old Man)
leave the wings and enter on the stage for Act II. iv – a
heavily cut version.*

Sefton (*to Macready, as a joke*) As soon as you get off
they settle down and listen.

Macready Very funny, Mr Sefton.

*He smiles. Suddenly from above, the sound of a win-
dow being smashed by a rock. Everyone stops. The*

scene on stage has stopped as well.

Bridges *(from the stage)* What was that?!

Macready Keep playing, Mr Bridges! Everyone, do not stop, please!

The scene continues on stage.

Mrs Pope They're putting in a new sewer across the street. Did you notice? They've got stones piled all over the place.

Arnold I guess some boy couldn't resist.

Mrs Pope That's just what I was thinking.

Clark (Macduff) leaves the wings and joins the scene on stage. From the stage:

Ross How goes the world, sir, now?

Macduff   Why, see you not?

Etc. The scene continues.

Macready *(to Mrs Pope)* How's your sister?

Mrs Pope Who?

Macready Didn't the other day you say something about your sister visiting?

Mrs Pope Did I? She's good. Very good.

Bradshaw (Banquo) leaves the wings for the stage as Clark, Wemyss, and Bridges come into the wings.

Bridges *(entering, to Macready)* I'm sorry, it's just when I heard –.

Arnold Some boys – with stones.

Bridges Oh. Oh that's what it was.

Clark What is it about that audience? There's something –.

Macready As someone was saying – they're nervous. (*He turns to Bridges and smiles.*) As some of us are.

He smiles, laughs, others laugh.

Clark There's something else. I can't put my finger on it.

Macready (*to Mrs Pope*) We're on.

Clark Wait a minute! I got it. They're all men! The audience! There aren't any women!

Actor Let me see. (*He goes to look.*)

Macready We're on!

Macready and Mrs Pope enter the stage, followed by Bridges and others. Trumpet fanfare.

Arnold Maybe we should have a few police back here with –. I'll go see if . . . (*He moves toward off.*)

Macbeth (*at the same time, from the stage*) Here's our chief guest.

Lady Macbeth If he had been forgotten,
It had been a gap in our great feast –.

A scream from the audience. Arnold stops. The acting on stage stops. Clark turns back to Arnold.

Arnold What's –?

Clark Someone's tried to jump –. From the balcony. Police are trying to –.

Chippindale (*entering from the dressing rooms*) They're bolting the doors!

Macready (*on stage, at the same time, to his actors*) Do not stop! Keep speaking!!

Chippindale They are bolting the doors! We're being locked in!

Arnold goes off to see.

Clark They caught the man. The police have him.

A cheer from the audience.

Lady Macbeth   . . . in our great feast,
And all-thing unbecoming.

Macbeth Tonight we hold a solemn supper, sir,
And I'll request your presence.

Banquo   Let your Highness
Command upon me, to the which my duties –.

*Suddenly a number of windows are broken, large rocks
crash against the door of the theatre. On stage the play
tries to continue but is hardly audible.*

Chippindale Jesus Christ.

Then there is a single gunshot from outside the theatre.

Clark What was that?

Sefton I heard it.

Clark Who's firing?

Bridges hurries in from the stage.

Bridges What was that? We heard a gunshot.

Clark It was from –.

*Suddenly tens of gunshots ring out, and screams. Then
the full-fledged sounds of riot from outside.*

Bridges They're storming the doors. They want to kill us.

*Panic from the house and stage, Macready and the
other actors hurry into the wings.*

Macready What's going on? Where are the police? Why aren't the police back here?!

Mrs Pope They're setting fires in the balcony.

Chippindale (*yelling*) The balcony's on fire!!

Bradshaw Open the doors and get the soldiers in here.

Panic. No one knows where to go. The battles being waged in the house get closer; Arnold appears from above and hoists a ladder down.

Arnold Up here! Climb up! They're coming on stage!

Mrs Pope screams.

Macready (*pulling out his sword*) Fight them off! Fight!

Banging on the doors continues. Bridges begins to climb up the ladder.

Wemyss The doors are breaking in.

Bradshaw (*grabbing others*) Quick through the house. Come on. Through the house. Take off your costumes!

Actors start ripping off their costumes. One starts to head toward the stage.

Not across the stage! That way! That way! There's a door! (*grabbing an actor who is taking off his costume*) There's no time! Go! Run!

Actors run off. Ryder appears from the stage after having obviously battled his way there. He sees Macready.

Ryder Mr Macready!

Macready (*dazed*) Stand back! Stand back! Or die!!!

Ryder It's John. (*Beat.*) John Ryder. (*Beat.*) It's me.

Macready finally lets Ryder near him. Ryder puts a coat over his shoulders.

Bradshaw Hurry!

They all go off. The riot continues off.
  Blackout.

SCENE SEVEN

Projection: 11.30 P.M.

Forrest's dressing-room; the Broadway Theatre. Forrest, half-changed out of his costume for Metamora, *and Ryder and Macready, both dishevelled and out of breath.*
  Outside, in the distance, the occasional gunshot and whoops from a roving mob.

Ryder There were some rocks thrown. Some boys, they –. At first the soldiers fired into the air. But then one or two . . . (*Beat.*) I suppose . . . (*Short pause.*) I figured the last place anyone would think of looking for –.

He looks at Macready, who is very upset, trying desperately to get his breath.

I need to find some horses. I need to contact friends. My guess is that they would kill him, it's a riot. No one's in control. (*Beat.*) The soldiers are running through the streets firing. The police refused to leave the theatre. (*He laughs to himself.*) We left with the audience. We just got out and ran. (*Beat.*) Inside, I don't think there's . . . By now. The seats were being ripped apart. Someone set a fire under the balcony. (*Beat.*) From the parquette. (*Beat.*) They just suddenly were crawling over the seats, over people in the audience – from the parquette. How they got there . . . It could all be on fire now.

Short pause.

Forrest Are people hurt? Someone must have been hurt.

Ryder looks to Macready, who doesn't answer, then turns back.

Ryder We saw ourselves –. What? (*He covers his eyes for a moment.*) People are dead.

Forrest I don't believe this.

Ryder Who knows how many. Five, ten, at least. (*to Macready*) Right? (*Beat.*) And a lot wounded. Seriously wounded. Twenty, thirty, fifty? I don't know.

Pause.

Forrest (*suddenly turning to Macready*) You goaded them! Why did you perform?!

Ryder That's not fair.

Short pause.

Macready (*quietly*) I didn't *goad* anyone. Could I get a drink, please? The opposite is true.

Forrest doesn't move.

Forrest Ten people dead, Mr Macready!

Ryder I don't know for sure how –.

Macready Could I get a drink, please?!

Ryder looks at Forrest, then goes to a cabinet and pours the drink.

Forrest You should not have played.

Macready They begged me. Irving promised me it'd be –. He had a petition. Everyone said –. (*Beat.*) I wasn't to worry. I wasn't to . . .

Macready starts to sob. Short pause. Ryder hands Macready the drink.

Forrest (*to Ryder*) People killed for what?

Macready (*suddenly turning*) They were shouting your name again!

Forrest turns to Ryder, who nods.

'Kill Macready! Three Cheers for Ned Forrest!'

Forrest Why would they do that? That doesn't make sense.

Macready 'Ned Forrest – an American!'

Forrest I have made it very clear that I –.

Macready I didn't want this! (*Beat.*) After the other night, I . . .

Forrest When you should have shouted them down. That's your mistake. You should have had the guts to shout them down! All of this could have been –!

Ryder You don't know what you're talking about.

Pause.

Macready I was told – if I didn't perform – I'd be hurting American . . . American what? They made it sound like I had to . . .

Forrest For 75 per cent of the house! I heard about this!

Macready That had nothing to do with –. (*Beat.*) Money has nothing to do with this. (*Beat. Attacking*) 'Three cheers for Ned Forrest. Hurray for Forrest!' As they try to burn down a theatre!

Forrest Those people have nothing to do with me! (*Forrest walks away. Pause. Finally:*) You want him to stay here.

Ryder I shouldn't be too long. We can't go back to the hotel.

Macready No.

Ryder I'll take him to Boston. We have friends. (*Beat.*) He can get a boat home from there. (*Beat.*) But if you don't want to . . .

Forrest He can stay.

Short pause.

Ryder He'll need some clothes.

Forrest He can stay. Don't be long.

Ryder hesitates, then hurries out. Pause.

Macready He didn't know where else to bring me. Could I have another? (*He holds out his glass.*)

Forrest Listen.

Pause. From outside the noise of the mob. After a moment Forrest goes and gets the bottle and pours Macready a drink.

Forrest Were they really shouting my name again?

Macready nods.

What the hell did they think they were doing?

Macready You obviously –. For them. For some of them. Represent –. (*He shrugs.*)

Forrest I'm an actor!

Macready shrugs again. Pause.

Macready Any money I do receive I shall give away. I did not perform for . . . (*Beat.*) I'm not a greedy man. (*Beat.*) The charities I support, I should give you a list, I also give anonymously to –.

Forrest Shut up. (*Short pause.*) Please. Your generosity is well known.

Macready Is it? (*Beat.*) Good. (*He looks towards a clothes trunk, hesitates, then goes to look in it.*)

Forrest Take whatever you need. Whatever might fit. A cape maybe . . .

He shrugs. Pause. Macready begins to look through the costume trunk. From outside closer gunshots, and shouts.

(*suddenly he turns to the noise, screaming*) Leave us alone in here!!!!!

Pause.

Macready (*pulling something out of the trunk; quietly*) Is this your Lear?

Forrest nods.

It's funny how we rarely get a chance to see each other's . . .

Forrest I've seen your Lear. (*Beat.*) I found the time to see your Lear.

Short pause.

Macready Is that it? You've just seen it? You don't want to say –?

Forrest (*quickly*) I enjoyed it.

Short pause.

Macready You've got an interesting costume.

Forrest So did you.

Macready Actually this sort of looks like mine. (*Short pause. Without looking up*) How was *your* play tonight?

Forrest Fine. (*He laughs to himself.*) There was no riot. A large section of my audience did not try to murder me. The theatre is not burning. Not a bad night. (*Beat.*) They love *Metamora*, the noble savage. (*Beat.*) Who has the decency to die. (*He smiles.*) So they cheered as always. I was not very good tonight, I thought. (*He shrugs.*)

Macready As we get older . . . It's funny, isn't it? When we begin – when I began – I thought always about what they would think about me. (*Beat.*) You want so much to please them. (*Beat.*) But you get older – and that's still there – but . . . Well, it's us who start to judge them, isn't it?

Forrest I'm not that old yet.

Short pause.

Macready (*choosing to ignore him*) Sometimes you stand on that stage and know you are achieving a level of excellence few before you have ever achieved. And you watch an audience watching you as if on some river bank staring at the natural flow of water. (*Beat.*) And then on other nights – probably like you felt tonight – you hate what you've done, perhaps even embarrassed –.

Forrest I didn't say I was –.

Macready And your audience receives you with rapturous attention and applause. (*Beat.*) There seems to be no rhyme or reason. (*Beat.*) The older you get, the more confusing it all becomes. The reaction. Like tonight, what you were telling me about your performance. Where's the logic.

Forrest looks at him.

And I'll tell you what makes it all even worse. It's going to see another perform – especially a part that you know like your own soul – and then witnessing grotesque exaggeration, which one could forgive perhaps in a novice, but

232

when it's an actor of some note, some ambition. And then when the crowd – the mob, one should call them in this case – greets this fraud with its misplaced adulation, I find myself in an almost state of total fevered despair.

Short pause.

Forrest I enjoy watching other actors –.

Macready When they are excellent! Which is so rare, as we both know so well.

Short pause.

Forrest I enjoy watching other actors even when they're bad, even when they're silly.

Macready But then when an audience praises –.

Forrest I enjoyed your Hamlet a great deal. (*Beat.*) When I was in London. I enjoyed it. (*Short pause.*) That dance you did – Hamlet's little dance before the Gertrude scene. I'd never seen anything like it. I will never forget it.

Macready You're not the first to –.

Forrest A fancy dance? I asked myself. Where does this come from in the play? I knew no reference to it. I had never before seen an actor –.

Macready An expression of his madness. A colour. A texture of the performance.

Forrest And a costume for this dance which, if I remember correctly, had a dress with a waist up to about the armpits, huge overlarge black gloves –.

Macready True, I –.

Forrest A great big hat with a gigantic plume –.

Macready The character is mad!

Forrest Is this Hamlet or Malvolio, I remember saying to myself. But still, I enjoyed it. (*He suddenly turns to Macready.*) It's true, Hamlet is mad. And in preparation for my own performance I became a student of the mind's disease, visiting asylums and talking not only with the doctors, but also with the ill. And the result of this study, Mr Macready, was the knowledge that true madness is expressed through the heart, not the costume. Madness is not funny clothes, but a funny soul.

Macready We are different actors.

Forrest This is very true.

Macready You study asylums and I study the play.

Forrest That's not –.

Macready Perhaps I am old-fashioned, but I continue to believe that all one needs is to be found in the play. Mr Shakespeare knew what –.

Forrest I don't disagree.

Beat.

Macready Then perhaps all I am saying is – from one actor to another – a little more time with the text and a little less in asylums might do a world of good.

Forrest You haven't even seen –.

Macready One hears, Mr Forrest, one hears! It is a small business we're in.

Forrest In that case, as we are talking text, perhaps – as one actor to another – I can make a suggestion as I have also seen your Othello.

Macready You *are* a fan, I'm flattered.

Forrest As I've said, I enjoy watching other actors –

234

whatever they do. Anyway, *Othello*. (*He begins to recite:*)
  'Rude am I in my speech,
  And little blessed with the soft phrase of peace;
  For since these arms of mine had seven years' pith'

Macready joins in.

Both 'Till now some nine moons wasted, they have used
  Their dearest action in the tented field;
  And little of this great world can I speak
  More than pertains to feats of broil and battle;'

Forrest drops out.

Macready 'And therefore little shall I grace my cause
  In speaking for *myself*.'

Forrest 'For *myself*'! That's just how you said it when I saw you.

Macready And that is the line.

Forrest That's not the meaning though. (*He laughs.*) Othello starts by saying he is rude in speech, how there is little he can speak about except battles. So what he is saying here is that he's bad at *speaking*, not that he doesn't want to talk or have people talk about him. He's not being humble, for Christ's sake, he's saying that he's awkward and out of place where he is! So the line should be!:
  'And therefore little shall I grace my cause
  In *speaking* for myself.'

Beat.

Macready That's a different reading. It's interesting. But it's just a different reading.

Forrest It's the right reading!

Macready That's your opinion.

Forrest And when I go and see your Othello again that's how you'll be saying the line, I'm sure. (*He smiles.*) Here, you want another one! The same scene:

> 'Which I observing,
> Took once a pliant hour, and found *good* means
> To draw from her a prayer of earnest heart
> That I would all my pilgrimage dilate'

And so on. (*Beat.*) 'Good means'! Not 'Good *means*'!

Macready I don't hear the difference.

Forrest He was after a *good* reason, a *good* way, a just way to get his promise. As opposed to a successful means to –.

From outside sudden gunshots which are closer. Short pause.

Macready The other reading maybe. But not this . . .

Forrest Fine. Fine. At least I got you to agree about one. (*Short pause.*) I only brought it up because –. What you said, about reading the . . .

Crowd noise off. Macready looks through the trunk. Long pause. Macready pulls out a costume.

Macready Richard?

Forrest nods. Macready pulls out an identical costume.

Why two?

Forrest I started with the hump on my left and my left hand curled –. Then I broke my right wrist, so I had to change, put the hump on the right.

Macready nods.

Now I keep them both. I've found that if I've got three or four Richards close together, I switch back and forth. It helps the back.

Macready Kean I think did that too.

Forrest Did he?

Pause.

Macready Kemble too. I think. (*Beat.*) Ever see
Kemble's . . .

*He mimics Kemble's walk as Richard III. Forrest
laughs.*

I don't know what it was about him. Every time he tried –.
Hamlet. Richard. Macbeth. (*Beat.*) But did you see his
Cassio?

Forrest No, I –. No.

Macready Brilliant. (*Beat.*) He was a first-rate actor, but
only in second-rate parts.

Forrest I've known other –.

Macready An incomparable Cassio. (*Beat.*) You've never
played –.

Forrest No.

Macready Neither have I. (*Pause.*) There are so many
great supporting parts in Shakespeare. When I was young
we'd fight for them.

Forrest They still –.

Macready Not in England any more. You used to have to
constantly look over your shoulder. People had ambition!
Now no one wants to work. No one wants to begin. But
they work in my productions. (*He laughs.*) And so they
hate me. (*He laughs.*) You want to know what it's like in
London today? I tried to correct this actor. He works for
me. And he's a nothing. All I say to him is, 'Please do not
speak your speech in that drawling way, sir.' I'm very

polite. 'Here,' I tell him, 'speak it like this: "To ransom home revolted Mortimer!" That's how you speak it!' (*Beat.*) He turns to me, in front of the whole company, and says, 'I know that, sir – that is the way, but you'll please remember you get one hundred pounds a week for speaking it in your way, and I only get thirty shillings for mine! Give me one hundred pounds and I'll speak it your way; but I'm not going to do for thirty shillings what you get paid one hundred pounds for.'

   Macready laughs, Forrest smiles.

Actors. (*He shakes his head. Short pause.*)

Forrest What I hate is when they come late for rehearsal.

Macready Which happens more and –.

Forrest Once, a rehearsal of mine was being delayed by this actor; he only had a small part, but it was quite an important part in the first scene. So we were all waiting. (*Beat.*) I became visibly upset. Everyone knew enough to stay away from me. And when finally the truant – a quiet gentlemanly man, who had never before been late for one second – once he arrived I knew I needed to make an example of him. (*Beat. He smiles.*) So I said, 'Sir, you have kept these ladies and gentlemen waiting for a full half hour.'

   Macready nods and smiles.

'You cannot be ignorant, sir, of the importance of a rehearsal in which every member of the company is to take part!' (*Beat.*) At that moment, this actor looked at me. I could see there were tears now in his eyes.

   Macready smiles and shakes his head.

And then he spoke. 'Mr Forrest, sir,' he said, 'I beg your pardon. I could not come sooner.'

   Forrest looks at Macready, who snickers.

'My son – my only son – died last night. I hurried here as soon as I could.'

Macready suddenly stops smiling. Short pause. Forrest looks at Macready and shakes his head.

Actors.

Long pause. Macready goes back and looks into the costume trunk.
Slow fade to blackout.

The bare stage of the Broadway Theatre. Macready and Forrest enter – each having thrown on pieces of different costumes. As they enter, they are giggling and carrying swords.

Forrest Who taught you fencing?

Macready Angelo?

Forrest shakes his head.

You haven't heard of him? He's wonderful. He's dead now. But he was wonderful when I was young.

They are centre stage looking out at the house.

Forrest It's paradise. Even without an audience.

Macready Especially without an –.

Both Audience.

Forrest tips Macready's sword, he smiles and they begin to fence. After some time:

Forrest Come for a third, Laertes.

Macready I thought *I* was Hamlet.

Forrest You should have spoken sooner.

They fence.

'You but dally.
I pray you pass with your best violence;
I am afeard you make a wanton of me.'

Macready I don't know his lines.

Forrest (*stopping*) You don't know Laertes . . .

Macready I'm never listening at this point. (*Beat.*) What is it?

Forrest thought he heard something, but now shakes his head.

Forrest Should we go back into my –? Ryder shouldn't be much longer.

Macready I don't care.

Forrest I suppose he will find us here.

Macready (*looking out*) How many seats?

Forrest Nine hundred and seventy-eight. (*Beat.*) I added those seats over there.

Macready Can they see –?

Forrest No one's complained. I've been waiting for someone to complain, but . . . (*He shrugs.*)

Macready I wouldn't want to sit there.

Forrest No.

Macready walks to the apron to get a closer look, then turns to see the particular sight line. He shakes his head.

Macready No, I wouldn't.

Forrest I do play to them at times. I try to. (*Beat.*) I try to remember to, but they are way over there. Added fifty-three seats.

Macready suddenly turns, thinks he hears something.

Forrest It's outside.

Macready nods.

I have it for another five weeks. The sound is very good. Much better than a lot of . . . I hate your theatre.

Macready It's not my . . .

Forrest They should tear the Astor Place down, if you want my opinion.

Macready That may in fact be being done.

Forrest walks to the apron and speaks into the house, at first to show off the acoustics.

Forrest (*as he speaks Othello he gains in passion*)
'It is the cause, it is the cause, my soul.
Let me not name it to you, you chaste stars!
It is the cause. Yet I'll not shed her blood,
Nor scar that whiter skin of hers than snow,
And smooth as monumental alabaster.
Yet she must die, else she'll betray more men.
Put out the light, and then put out the light.

He chokes up.

If I quench thee, thou flaming minister,
I can again thy former light restore,
Should I repent me; but once put out thy light,
Thou cunning'st pattern of excelling nature,
I know not where is that Promethean heat
That can thy light relume. When I have plucked the rose,
I cannot give it vital growth again;
It needs must wither. I'll smell thee on the tree . . .'

He cannot go on. He covers his face, hiding his tears,
Pause.

Macready (*without looking at him*) You should add a
few *Othello*s next week. (*Beat.*) I'm sorry about your wife
leaving.

Forrest turns to him. Short pause.

Play it out. (*Beat.*) You are certainly right about the
sound.

Forrest Go ahead and . . . (*He tries to get a hold of him-*
self.) Really, go ahead . . .

Short pause. Macready walks to the apron.

Macready You'll be hard to follow.

Forrest Modesty? You're acting already, Mr Macready.
And acting well.

He smiles, Macready turns to the house.

Macready 'Rumble thy bellyful. Spit, fire. Spout, rain.
Nor rain, wind, thunder, fire are my daughters.
I tax not you, you elements –.

From outside, quite near, gunfire and shouts.

Forrest (*screaming*) I told you before, to just leave us
alone!!!!!

Pause.

Macready (*continuing*)   you elements, with unkindness.
I never gave you kingdom, called you children;
You owe me no subscription. Then let fall
Your horrible pleasure. Here I stand your slave.
A poor, infirm, weak, and despised old man.'

He stops. Continues to stare out. Ryder has entered
upstage, he carries a cape. Pause.

Ryder Mr Macready?

Forrest (*turning without seeing who it is*) Leave us in peace!!!

Macready turns, Forrest sees who it is.

Ryder I have the horses. (*Beat.*) We must go. Put on this. (*He goes to give him the cape.*) Why are you dressed like . . .?

Macready looks at Forrest.

Forrest We were rehearsing –.

Ryder Rehearsing –?

Macready Give me the cape. What's it like out there?

Ryder It's gotten worse. (*Beat.*) Reports are that there are nearly thirty-five people now dead. And hundreds seriously . . . (*Beat.*) Hundreds wounded. (*Beat.*) We should hurry. There are people who are running through the streets looking for that English actor 'Macreilly or whatever his name is'. (*Beat.*) Buses have been stopped, turned on their side and set afire, on just the rumour that you were aboard. (*Beat.*) Our hotel –. I had to go past. That too has been torched.

Forrest Go.

Ryder Put up the hood.

Ryder pulls up the hood of the cape on Macready.

We have a safe house for tonight in New Rochelle. We'll go to Boston in the morning. Come on.

As they start to leave, Macready stops and looks back at the theatre.

There's talk that they'll close the theatres.

Pause.

Macready You should come to England again, Mr Forrest. (*Beat.*) And get away from all these troubles. .

Short pause.

Forrest I'm away from all these troubles here.

Macready nods and leaves with Ryder. Pause. Forrest starts to go, stops and comes back. He looks around the theatre. With sword in hand, he stands, not knowing where else on earth he wants to go.

NEW ENGLAND

for Patricia Macnaughton and Peter Franklin

*This play was commissioned by the
Royal Shakespeare Company*

Characters

Harry Baker, *sixties, professor of music at Dutchess Community College, New York State*
Alfred Baker, *sixties, Harry's brother*
Gemma Baker, *39, Harry's oldest child*
Elizabeth Baker, *37, Harry's other daughter*
Paul Baker, *32, Harry's son*
Sophie, *41, Paul's wife*
Alice Berry, *54, Harry's girlfriend*
Tom Berry, *40, Alice's ex-brother-in-law*

All the characters are English except for Sophie, who was born in France.
The play takes place in a farmhouse in Western Connecticut, just across the border from New York State. The time is the present.

New England was first performed by The Royal Shakespeare Company on 23 November 1994 at the Pit in the Barbican, London. The cast was as follows:

Alice Berry Angela Thorne
Alfred/Harry Baker David Burke
Tom Berry Mick Ford
Elizabeth Baker Selina Cadell
Paul Baker Duncan Bell
Gemma Baker Diana Hardcastle
Sophie Baker Annie Corbier

Directed by Peter Gill
Designed by Hayden Griffin
Music directed by Terry Davis
Produced by Lynda Farran
Stage Manager Jane Pole
Deputy Stage Manager Caroline Beale
Assistant Stage Manager Lynda Snowden

New England was subsequently produced by The Manhattan Theatre Club (Lynne Meadow, Artistic Director, Barry Grove, Executive Director) on 17 October 1995. The cast was as follows:

Alice Berry Penny Fuller
Alfred/Harry Baker Larry Bryggman
Tom Berry Tom Irwin
Elizabeth Baker Mia Dillon
Paul Baker T. Scott Cunningham
Gemma Baker Allison Janney
Sophie Baker Margaret Whitton

Directed by Howard Davies
Set designed by Santo Loquasto
Costumes designed by Jennifer von Mayrhauser
Lighting designed by Richard Nelson
Sound designed by Mark Bennett
Stage managed by Franklin Keysar

SCENE ONE

A small room on the ground floor, which serves as a study. Late afternoon; a Friday.

    Harry Baker, sixties, sits at a desk. On the desk is a CD player and a row of CDs – all classical; Harry is a professor of music at the local community college. He reads or looks through a book as he listens to music – Debussy's The Girl with the Flaxen Hair *(played on the violin), begins with the scene.*

    After a moment, Alice Berry, fifty-four, enters from the hall; she is Harry's girlfriend and she shares the house with him. She stops, looks at Harry for a moment; he is absorbed in thought or in the book or the music, and does not at first see her.

    Harry suddenly lets out a large sigh.

Alice Harry?

    Harry turns, startled.

How's the – headache? I'm sorry, I didn't mean to –. You had a headache. You took some aspirin?

    It has taken him this long to realize who has startled him. Finally, he nods and turns back to his book. The Debussy continues.

Tom's here.

    No response.

I just picked him up. His bus was even on time, if you can believe that. A miracle! (*She tries to smile.*) He's very excited. A weekend out of New York . . .

Harry (*without picking his head up from his book*)
Who's Tom?

Alice Harry, I told you about –. You said it was –. We
talked about –!!

Harry (*over this*) It's fine, Alice, I just forget who Tom is!

Short pause.

Alice He's my –. Bill's brother. He was my brother-in-law.
So he's my ex –.

Harry (*over the last part of this, turning to Alice*) He was
good to you, wasn't he? During your divorce. He was
very helpful to you.

Alice He was, Harry. If you didn't want –.

Harry I think that is wonderful! That Tom's here.
Someone you like. Someone who has been – helpful.

Alice I hadn't seen him for –.

Harry (*over this*) Someone like that doesn't change.
Someone – helpful. Good.

*He turns back to his desk. She looks at him, confused.
He pushes a button on the CD and the Debussy begins
again. Alice turns to leave and there in the door, having
just arrived, is Tom Berry, forty. Alice is startled.*

Tom (*smiling*) Sorry. I couldn't find the –. In the
bathroom – which towels should I . . .?

Alice Tom – this is Harry.

Tom goes to Harry with his hand out to shake.

Tom How do you do? I can't thank you enough for –.
Sometimes the city –. It gets so depressing. Most times!
(*He laughs.*)

Harry (*at the same time, shaking hands*) Welcome, to our humble –. Alice has told me all about you –. She's been looking forward to –.

Alice (*over this*) Tom said the bus ride up –.

Tom It was beautiful!

Harry It's supposed to be a nice weekend. Weather-wise.

Alice I heard it might rain, but –.

Tom Whatever. It's – great to be in the country.

He smiles. No one knows what to say.

Alice (*finally*) I'll show you where we keep the towels, so if you need . . .

Tom (*to Harry*) Thank you for inviting me. I'll see you later.

Alice and Tom leave. Pause.
Harry pushes the button on the CD player and the Debussy begins again.
He opens the drawer of the desk and takes out a revolver. Without hesitation he cocks it, sets it on the desk, takes off his glasses. As he does he notices that they are dirty. With a handkerchief he begins to clean them, then realizes what he is doing, laughs to himself and stops. He puts down the glasses, picks up the gun and puts the barrel to his head.
Alice enters from the hallway.

Alice (*entering*) Tom's so happy to be –. (*She sees what Harry is doing. She screams.*) Nooooooo!!!!!!!!!!!

He pulls the trigger, gunshot. And he is dead.

SCENE TWO

Much later that evening.

Part of the kitchen of the house. There is a large rustic wooden table, which has been used both for eating and as a sort of desk. Piles of papers, bills, catalogues, etc.; a phone, whose cord extends to the wall, making a kind of obstacle for anyone going around the table. There is a transistor radio on the table.

The Debussy continues from the last scene, though over the theatre's speakers now.

Tom enters from the pantry; he carries a bowl, a spoon, a box of cereal. He does not hear the music. He sets his things down on the table and goes off again. From off, we hear the opening and closing of a refrigerator. Tom returns with a carton of milk. He sits, pours the cereal, the milk, he reaches across the table for the sugar. He spoons on the sugar and begins to eat. He stops and turns on the transistor radio. The Debussy is gone and from the radio we first hear: a pop tune with a lot of static. Tom fiddles with the knob; tries another station, then another. He hits upon a religious programme. He listens for a moment to the minister on the programme as he eats.

The phone rings. Tom doesn't know what to do. He looks in the direction of the door. It rings again. And again. He puts down his spoon, begins to reach for the phone, when the ring stops – someone has picked up the phone on another extension.

Tom changes the channel again, then again, then again – everything is junk: pop tunes, commercials. After about the twelfth station, he turns off the radio.

In silence he eats.

Alice enters from the living-room. She has a drink in her hand. At first she says nothing; Tom just eats. Then finally:

Alice That was Elizabeth on the phone. She'll be here in a minute. She's just down the road at the gas station. She couldn't remember the turnoff.

Tom (*eating*) Which one is –?

Alice She's the middle child. She lives in the city too. (*She smiles.*) She's in publishing.

Tom In the same –?

Alice She's with a different house. (*For the first time she notices that he is eating.*)

Tom I found some cereal, I hope that wasn't –.

Alice You haven't eaten anything have you?

Tom I didn't expect –.

Alice You come out for the weekend and – and you don't even get fed! What could I have been thinking –.

Tom Alice, I'm –.

Alice (*looking for food*) I'm not normally like –

Tom I am fine, Alice! Please.

   Beat. She stops looking around.

I don't expect anything. Not now.

   Pause. Tom eats. Alice sips her drink.

Alice You want a drink? I . . .

Tom If I do, I'll find it.

   Neither knows what to say. Alice sighs.

Alice I've been in his study – cleaning up.

Tom I thought that's what that woman –.

Alice (*over this*) She missed some places. Look at this.

(*She holds out the small photo album she's been carrying.*) They're already in the album. I didn't even know he'd got the photos back yet. And they're already in his . . .

Tom And that is unlike him?

Alice Very. (*She looks at the photos.*) From Bermuda. We were there in –. Last month.

Pause. They look at the photos and say nothing.

(*hearing something*) Was that a car? (*She listens.*) No.

Tom It looks like you had a really nice time.

Alice (*not hearing him*) He's got papers . . . It'll take weeks to go through everything. I thought the priority seemed to be the cleaning. I didn't think his family should see –. (*To herself, running through a list.*) I called the school. I did that.

Tom What school?

Alice Harry teaches at Dutchess –. I didn't tell you this?

Tom Maybe you did.

Alice (*over this*) How could I not tell you this?! What could I have been thinking?!

Tom Alice!

Alice You're staying, right?

Tom If that's what you want.

Alice (*sighing*) I can't face his family.

Tom (*taking her hand*) If I'm not in the way.

He pats her hand. Alice, not listening to Tom, turns again toward the door, as if hearing something.

Alice She doesn't like me. We've only met five, six times –.

Harry kept us apart. I asked him to. She's also in publishing.

Tom So you said.

Alice So we know a lot of the same people. (*hearing Tom*) Did I? (*Beat.*) She's going to walk into here and start telling us all what to do. In my own home. There's her car.

Sound of car in the driveway.

I think I've done everything. I like that man at the funeral home. I thought funeral home people were supposed to be –. I don't know.

Tom I guess not all of them are. There are exceptions.

Alice (*smiling*) And he is one.

Tom I guess so.

Alice So – we're lucky. (*She sighs.*) I feel like I haven't stopped.

Tom You haven't.

Elizabeth Baker enters. She is one of Harry's three children. She is thirty-seven.

Elizabeth Alice!

Alice Elizabeth!

They hug.

Elizabeth I don't know what to say. I don't know what to say.

Alice begins to cry. Elizabeth hugs her. Tom tries to be inconspicuous.

Alice (*crying*) So – you couldn't remember the turnoff.

Elizabeth I knew it was –. I should have just followed my instinct. Anyway.

Alice gets a hold of herself and they part. Elizabeth looks at Tom; Alice sees this.

Alice This is Tom. Berry. He was my ex-husband's brother.

Tom I still am. (*He tries to laugh.*)

Alice Right. That's true.

Tom I always liked Alice. And when she left my brother I liked her even more. (*He smiles at his joke; no one else does. To Elizabeth*) How do you do?

Alice (*to Elizabeth*) Do you want something to eat? To drink?

Elizabeth (*shaking her head*) There was no traffic.

Alice It's late.

Elizabeth That's why then. (*She looks at Tom again.*)

Tom I came up on the bus. This afternoon. I also live in the city.

Elizabeth (*to Alice*) This afternoon? I thought, it only happened –.

Alice It did. I called you right away, Liz. Tom – happened to be here for the weekend.

Beat.

Tom I needed to get out of the city and Alice was nice enough to . . .

Pause.

Elizabeth Do you have a coke or something?

Alice I have some seltzer.

Elizabeth Seltzer's fine.

Alice hurries off into the pantry. Tom and Elizabeth are left alone. Short pause.

Tom I'm sorry about your –.

Elizabeth (*interrupting*) I have a bag in the car. Excuse me.

Tom Let me –.

Elizabeth It's not heavy, please. (*She goes out.*)

Alone, Tom doesn't know what to do, he sits again, begins to take another bite of cereal, notices the photo album open on the table and begins to look at the open page.

Alice (*entering with the seltzer and a glass*) Where's –?

Tom She's getting her bag.

Alice sees that Tom has been looking at the album and she goes and looks over his shoulder.

Alice (*pointing to a photo*) Harry bought that bathing suit for me in Hamilton. That was so unlike him. He was scared to buy me anything. Afraid, he said, I'd just take it back. (*She smiles.*) It took me about two days to get the nerve to wear it in public. Finally – I did. (*Short pause.*) After your brother –.

Tom looks at her.

I'd convinced myself I'd never meet another man. You see other women, my age and –. You see yourself in their shoes. I expected nothing. Then I met Harry.

Elizabeth enters with her bag. Pause. For a moment no one knows what to say. Finally:

Alice Here's your seltzer.

Elizabeth finally takes it and drinks it.

Elizabeth (*as she drinks*) I had lunch with Dick Riley last week. Your name came up, Alice. He said you were the best managing editor they'd ever had. (*She finishes drinking.*) What a shame it was when you left. (*Beat.*) So – know that even after a couple of years, you're still missed.

Alice (*to Tom*) I was cheap. I didn't know any better. That's all he means. (*She turns to Elizabeth.*) The man at the funeral home – he's not bad. He's not what you'd expect.

Elizabeth Good.

Beat.

Alice Gemma and Alfred have made it as far as Denver. They have to wait 'til morning for the next flight. They called.

Elizabeth Good. (*Beat.*) I mean good that they called, not that they have to wait –.

Alice I understood. And Paul and Sophie – they'll get a flight in the morning as well. (*She turns to Tom.*) From L.A.

Tom (*to Elizabeth*) I was amazed when she told me everyone lives in the States.

Elizabeth Why?

Tom That's rare, isn't it?

Elizabeth (*to Alice*) He wouldn't say that if he worked in publishing –.

Alice (*over this*) You wouldn't.

Elizabeth (*to Alice*) Have you worked out where everyone will sleep? It isn't a very big house.

Tom I can move –.

Alice (*to Tom*) There's the pullout couch –.

Tom The floor is fine –.

Alice I meant for Paul and Sophie –.

Elizabeth (*picking up her suitcase*) Let's figure it all out.

Alice I think I have. Harry's brother can have my room. It'll work out. I'm going to the grocery store in the morning –.

Elizabeth You're not going to cook! There are too many people! I won't let you, Alice. Gemma and I can share a bed. We shared a room as kids.

Alice That's what I thought.

Elizabeth What about Chinese?

Alice There's a terrific Chinese –. Just in our village. Harry loves their dumplings. (*She stops and corrects herself.*) He loved them. (*Short pause. Alice tries not to cry; she turns to Elizabeth.*) He did it in front of me. I think that's what I can't forgive him for. (*Beat.*) But I don't think he meant to hurt me.

Elizabeth No –.

Alice Because, he loved me. (*She takes Elizabeth's hand.*) Your Father was a very – tired man.

Elizabeth I know. And he'd been tired for years – long before he'd met you, Alice.

Alice (*looking up at her*) Thank you.

  Beat.

Elizabeth This isn't a surprise. (*Then to change the subject:*) So – it's Chinese! (*She turns to Tom.*) Do you like Chinese?

Tom Anything is fine with –.

Elizabeth (*not listening to him, turning to Alice*) I knew I'd have at least one good idea. I think Father once even mentioned the restaurant –.

Alice Usually the Chinese food you get up here in the sticks, but this place –.

Elizabeth I know what you mean. But I'll bet this place is great. Father always had good taste.

Alice takes Elizabeth's hand.

Alice Thank you.

Elizabeth realizes that Alice has taken this as a compliment.

Elizabeth I didn't mean . . . But – of course that too. With you too. That's obvious. Father had impeccable taste.

Alice He was a refined and cultured man.

Elizabeth I always thought so. Come on. (*She helps Alice up.*) Let's you and I figure out where to put everyone.

They go. Pause. Tom is alone. He takes another spoonful of cereal and –.

SCENE THREE

The same. The kitchen, early evening of the next day.
[Note: a few hours ago, Paul (the son) and his wife, Sophie, arrived by rental car from Kennedy Airport. Just a few minutes ago, Gemma (the oldest daughter) and Alfred (Harry's brother) arrived also by rental car from the same airport.]
Paul, 32, sits at the kitchen table, surrounded by his two sisters, Gemma, 39, and Elizabeth. Alice is taking

silverware out of a drawer in the table, to set the table for dinner. As the scene begins, Tom has just entered with bags of Chinese food.

Paul (*to Gemma*) If we'd known you were arriving at Kennedy –.

Gemma (*over this*) We didn't know ourselves. We had tickets to Bradley –.

Paul (*over this*) We'd have waited.

Elizabeth (*over this*) You could have shared the car rental.

Paul Still it'll be useful to have another car up here.

Gemma The drive was wonderful. Very relaxing.

Paul (*over the end of this*) This is my first autumn in three years. You forget what it's like.

Alice (*over this*) Someone said it was supposed to rain.

Gemma How's L.A.?

Paul Warm and sunny.

Alice (*to Gemma*) And Albuquerque?

Gemma Sunny and warm!

They laugh.

Tom (*who has been holding up the Chinese food, trying to get someone's attention*) I have the . . .!

Alice Let me help, Tom. That was quick. We're all here! Alfred and Gemma just arrived –.

Gemma (*to Elizabeth, over this*) I love New England. You're lucky to be so close.

The phone rings.

Alice (*same time*) Excuse me. (*She goes to pick up the phone.*)

Elizabeth (*same time, to Gemma*) I never get up here. Father had me up twice, maybe three times. I hardly could remember the way.

Alice (*with her hand on the receiver, as it rings*) I've told everyone it's the best Chinese I've ever had! Even in the city. And in all places –. (*She picks up the phone.*) Hello?

Tom (*to the others*) Actually, the place she sent me to –. It appears to have closed. They'd gone out of business, I suspect. (*Beat.*) There was another place. Just down the road. (*He holds up the bag of food.*) There was hardly a wait. I don't know how they cook it so fast.

The others look at Tom.

Alice (*into the phone*) Yes. At eleven. Here in the garden. Yes. Harry would have liked that. (*Beat.*) Thank you so much. See you tomorrow. (*She hangs up.*)

Pause.

Tom I hope it's good. The food! (*He smells a bag.*) It smells good.

Alice It's always good at that place. 'Harry's Place' was what we called it. Because Harry . . .

Elizabeth (*getting up*) We'll need some serving spoons.

Alice (*pointing to the drawer in the table*) In that drawer. Elizabeth.

Gemma (*to Tom*) We haven't met.

Alice This is Tom. He's my –. A relative of mine. Gemma. Harry's eldest.

Tom How do you do?

They shake hands.

My sympathies. To all of you.

Gemma Uncle Alfred will be down in a –.

Alice Harry's brother.

Gemma (*to Tom*) Were you very close to our father?

Beat.

Tom Close? To tell the truth, I only just met him –.

Alice (*interrupting*) Where are we going to eat? There's the dining-room.

Elizabeth Won't that be too formal? It's just Chinese –.

Gemma And we're a family.

Elizabeth The kitchen's fine.

Gemma Let's eat here. I always eat in my kitchen.

Elizabeth Move a few things out of the way –. (*She begins to pick up the papers on the table.*)

Alice Smell how good that smells.

Gemma (*over this*) We'll need large bowls or do we just serve it out of the boxes? At home I just serve it out of the boxes.

Elizabeth (*to Alice, over this*) Is it OK if I just pile these papers together?

Paul (*interrupting*) Sophie's still taking a nap! Shouldn't we wait for her?

Beat.

Gemma (*to Elizabeth*) I forgot she was here. I hadn't seen her so –.

Elizabeth She's taking a nap.

Paul I just think she might feel –. I don't know – to come down and find us all eating dinner . . .

Beat.

Elizabeth Couldn't you wake her up, Paul? I wouldn't want people waiting to eat because of me.

Gemma The food'll get cold.

Paul She didn't sleep at all last night. Or on the plane.

Beat.

Elizabeth We can reheat it for her later then.

Alice Maybe she's reading, I'll go and see if –. (*She starts to go.*)

Paul Let her sleep! Please. I want her to get some sleep.

Beat.

Gemma So we're to – what? The food's here. This makes no sense.

Paul I told her we wouldn't be eating for a while. That's what Alice told me –.

Alice Because I thought there'd be a wait –.

Tom There wasn't any wait at the restaurant.

Alice On a Saturday night?! That's incredible. It's such a popular place.

Short pause.

Gemma So what are we going to –?

Elizabeth (*over this*) What if we don't sit down? What if we – say, put out the food and whenever anyone wants to –. Buffet-style. So no one's missing anything. How's that, Paul? We can keep reheating it, so it's always ready.

Gemma Sophie can't get upset about that.

Paul It wasn't because she'd get upset –.

Gemma I mean, it sounds fair.

Paul (*continuing*) She's not the one upset, I am. I told her –. She doesn't care. Why should she care? Whatever we want to do is fine with –.

Elizabeth Fine! Then we'll need some plates –.

Alice I'll get them.

Paul How would you feel if you walked in on –. And there was your husband surrounded by his sisters, having dinner and you'd been told –.

Elizabeth We understand, Paul. Forget it.

Alice starts to leave, stops, notices the drinks in her hand.

Alice Who else wants a drink? I forgot to ask. I'll open one of Harry's good bottles of wine. I think he'd have liked that.

Beat.

Gemma (*after looking at her brother and sister*) I don't think any of us drink.

The others shake their heads.

I suppose we'd seen enough of what that can do – growing up. But please . . . Don't let us stop you, Alice.

Beat.

Alice Tom? What about you?

Tom A –. Small glass. Very small.

Alice (*to herself as she leaves*) More for me. (*She goes.*)

Pause. Tom begins to take the food out of the bags. Elizabeth and Gemma straighten up the table.

Gemma (*to Paul*) You were right to stick up for your wife.

Paul I wasn't sticking up for –.

Gemma That was a good thing to do, Paul.

Short pause. They continue to get the table straightened.

(*to Elizabeth*) Where's the body?

Paul Gemma, please!

Gemma Don't stop us from talking!

Elizabeth Some funeral home. Alice says he ought to be cremated.

Paul Oh God.

Elizabeth What do you think?

Gemma What did father want?

Paul Does it matter?

Elizabeth Alice has this idea which –. I don't know, it's not what I'd have expected from her. She seems so – matter-of-fact. That's her reputation in the city – very matter-of-fact.

She looks at Tom, who smiles.

Tom I'll find some glasses. (*He goes.*)

Elizabeth Alice has this idea in her head about standing in the garden and throwing his ashes into the air.

Gemma That's what she meant on the phone. Is that legal?

Paul What harm could –?

Gemma When mother died, she was buried.

Elizabeth I know that. But I do not think father would have wanted to be buried next to mother.

Gemma Or vice versa.

Elizabeth (*shrugging*) I don't know that. Do we know that? (*Short pause.*) What did you feel when you heard, Gemma?

Paul sighs.

Ignore him. (*She turns to Gemma, then quickly, suddenly back to Paul to shut him up.*) I wish to talk to my sister!

Short pause.

Gemma I – was angry. I don't think I have ever been so angry with anyone – ever. (*Beat.*) I'd told Father – if he ever did do it – I'd hate him for the rest of my life.

Elizabeth You were angry, but you weren't shocked? I wasn't shocked. Was anyone shocked?

No one says anything.
   Alice enters with the plates; Tom is behind her with a bottle of wine, a bottle of seltzer, glasses and a corkscrew.
   There is silence for a long time. Tom opens the wine bottle; Alice sets out the plates. When she finishes:

Alice Since we're eating in the kitchen, I thought we wouldn't use our fancy plates. These aren't our good plates. We have much nicer plates than these. (*Short pause.*) Do any of you smoke?

Paul, Gemma and Elizabeth look incredulously at her at this question.

I didn't think so. (*She picks up her purse and takes out a pack of cigarettes. She taps one out, then lights it.*)

Gemma Neither did father. He hated smoke.

Alice Which is why he made me smoke outside. Even in the rain. The snow. (*Beat.*) But from today – I can smoke where I please. As they say, every cloud has its silver lining.

Elizabeth Oh my God!

Alice I'm joking, Elizabeth! That was a joke! (*Beat.*) Not the smoking – the silver lining. (*Beat.*) I'm terribly sorry if it wasn't funny. (*She exhales, then takes a sip of her drink – the ice cubes clanking against the glass. Awkward pause.*)

Tom I'll just dish out the rice into a bowl –.

Alice (*as she exhales*) Look at that rice. I told you the place was good.

Paul I think I heard a creak –. Maybe Sophie's . . . (*He gets up.*) I'll go see if she's awake. I'll tell her we're waiting for her.

Gemma I thought we weren't waiting for Sophie.

Alfred, Harry's twin brother, enters. Tom sees him and nearly cries out in shock – irrationally thinking this is Harry's ghost. As he sees him he nearly knocks over the wine bottle; glasses tip over, rice spills. Others cry out: 'Careful!' 'Watch out!' 'Catch it!' as they scramble to save the glasses, bottle, etc.

Alice (*to Alfred*) Are you unpacked?

Alfred Alice, I feel awful kicking you out of your room –.

Alice That's silly. Did you look through Harry's clothes?

Alfred I haven't had –.

Alice If there's anything that –.

Alfred Later, Alice.

Alice Of course.

Paul (*explaining the table*) We're waiting for Sophie. When she's awake –.

Elizabeth I thought we were setting out the plates –.

Alfred She's in the bathroom. She's using the bathroom.

Paul (*to everyone*) Sophie's in the bathroom.

Tom has been staring at Alfred; Alfred now stares back at him.

Alice This is Tom. You haven't met him. He was out getting the food when you arrived. (*Introducing*) Tom – Alfred, Harry's brother. Alfred – Tom. He's a relative of mine. Sort of.

Alfred And obviously a good friend of Harry's. Thank you for coming.

Paul If Sophie's awake –.

Alfred She's in the bathroom.

Paul (*over this*) Then we can set the table. Go ahead and set the table. We'll eat together at the table. (*He goes out.*)

Gemma (*to Elizabeth*) What happened to buffet-style?

Alice (*half-whispering to Tom*) They were twins.

Tom (*still in some shock*) When I saw him I thought –.

Alice I know. It's odd for me too.

Alfred Could I have a glass of that? I haven't had a drink for months.

271

Gemma You had two on the plane.

Alfred (*taking the bottle, ignoring Gemma; to Alice*) I've been taking care of myself, Alice.

Alice It shows, Alfred.

Elizabeth Are we setting the table or not?

Alfred Is that the famous Chinese Harry was always going on about?

Tom I'm not sure it's exactly the same –.

Alfred He used to say, Alfred, we have the best Chinese take-out in this hick village than anywhere in New York City, San Francisco, Seattle. You name it. In this village, for Christ sake.

Tom Actually, I don't think it's from the place he –.

Alfred It smells good. Harry always loved food.

Tom Did he?

Alfred Loved it. Talked about nothing else.

Alice That's not true, Alfred. He rarely –.

Alfred Who cares? Now we can say anything we want about the bastard.

Short pause. Alfred stands at the table; and suddenly he nearly collapses. Everyone hurries to him, to grab him, as they do they shout: 'What's wrong?' 'Sit down!' 'Get him some water!' 'Are you all right?', etc.

Alice (*with a glass of seltzer*) Here drink this.

Alfred drinks. He holds up his hands – to show that he will be fine. He drinks some more, then finally:

Alfred You said – in the study? Down the hall. (*Beat.*) That's where it was?

Alice nods.

I just looked in. I didn't see anything. Have you been cleaning, Alice? (*Beat.*) Get someone in. Do yourself a favour. (*He sips, then:*) I threw up – in the study. I couldn't get anything to clean it up with. Sophie was in the bathroom.

Beat.

Gemma We'll clean it up, Uncle Alfred.

Pause. No one knows what to say.

Alfred We're eating in here?

Elizabeth Maybe you'd like to get some air. The air on airplanes –.

Alfred I'm hungry. I want to try some of my brother's famous Chinese take-out.

Gemma Give Alfred a plate –.

Elizabeth (*at the same time*) Are we sitting down? I'm confused.

Alfred Pull up some chairs. (*realizing:*) I'm at the head. I suppose that is where I should be now.

Elizabeth We thought it'd be nicer – less formal in the kitchen.

Alfred I don't care where I eat.

Elizabeth I like it in here. We were all saying – how relaxed it is in here. Let's set out plates.

Paul enters with Sophie, 41; she is French though has lived in the States for many years.

Paul Look who's awake!

Everyone greets her: 'Sophie!' 'How was your nap?' 'Sit

273

down.' Gemma and Sophie hug as they have not greeted each other yet.

Alice (*pointing to Tom*) Tom you've met.

During this, the phone rings and Alice picks it up.

Sophie (*over this*) Why are you eating in here when there's such a lovely dining-room?!

Paul She's right. We could eat in the dining-room. It'll be much nicer there.

Elizabeth You agreed that the kitchen –.

Sophie Alfred?

Alfred I don't care.

Elizabeth We're all set up in –. Gemma?

Gemma It is a nice dining-room.

Elizabeth It's just so much less formal in here.

Paul (*over this*) Everyone grab something. I'll take the glasses.

Elizabeth I like it in here.

Sophie I didn't mean –. (*to everyone*) If Elizabeth wants us to eat in the kitchen –.

Paul Of course, if Elizabeth insists . . .

Elizabeth I'm not insisting.

Paul Then Tom, could you bring the rice? You be in charge of the rice.

Elizabeth (*over this*) It just seems silly. We're already in the kitchen –.

Alice (*putting her hand over the receiver; to the others*)

They want to know – should they send flowers or is there some charity . . .?

Beat.

Sophie Flowers are such a waste. Don't you think? They just die.

Paul A charity then. Did father have a charity –?

Gemma Maybe the school –.

Alice He hated the school.

Paul Was there anything he . . .? (*He looks at the others.*) I don't know.

Beat.

Gemma Who'd father want to give money to??

Pause.

Elizabeth I think flowers would be nice, myself.

Alice Then we'll have them send flowers!

She returns to the phone, relays that flowers would be fine.
Everyone is standing, carrying something on their way to the dining-room.

Sophie (*to Paul*) I hope this isn't just because I said –.

Paul Of course it isn't. It's just a good idea.

Alfred (*to Gemma*) What about the study? Who's going to clean –?

Gemma There's probably a sponge under the sink in the bathroom. Don't worry about it.

Elizabeth (*to Gemma*) Don't you think flowers will be nice?

Alice puts down the phone.

Alice (*to Tom who is balancing a few things*) There's a tray in the pantry. (*She calls out to everyone as they head off towards the dining-room:*) Why are we moving? Why can't we stay where we are? (*She gets up and follows them out.*)

SCENE FOUR

The kitchen, a short time later.
  Alice, Tom, Alfred, Gemma, Elizabeth, Paul and Sophie sit around the table, half-way through their Chinese meal. The papers, phone, etc. have been pushed to one side, giving the table a very cluttered look.

Paul (*as he eats*) I think we actually like L.A. And I know that sounds crazy.

Alice No one's eating the moo-shoo.

Gemma I tried it.

Paul (*continuing, over some of this*) And I don't mean the weather. I like the people. I like my work.

Elizabeth Isn't it nicer in here than in that stuffy old dining-room?

Alice It's not stuffy.

Elizabeth Don't you agree, Sophie?

Sophie I didn't mean it to become a thing. I'm sorry.

Elizabeth It hasn't become a – 'thing' as you call it. (*She smiles and eats.*)

Tom (*to Paul, changing the subject*) What work do you –?

Paul I read. I'm a reader.

Alfred Is that now a professional position in Los Angeles? (*He laughs.*)

Paul For films. I read scripts and . . .

Sophie Tell him.

Paul I give my opinions. About how to develop those scripts.

Beat.

Alfred (*sipping his drink*) And what is your opinion?

Gemma We've had this conversation before. (*to Alfred*) You know what Paul does –.

Paul (*over this*) Depends upon the script, of course.

Alfred I would have thought they'd all be rubbish.

Paul Some are and some –.

Alfred (*interrupting*) I can understand liking the weather. Even some of the people. But even you can't keep a straight face when you talk about their movies –.

Paul (*over this*) My face's completely straight!

Sophie It is!

Alfred My mind would go to mush if I had to –!

Sophie It's a good job! A way to learn the business!

Paul (*over this*) I'm learning what people want!

Alfred (*yelling back*) They don't know what people want!

Paul And in England they do?! (*Beat.*) In London today there aren't three people who know how to make a successful movie. That's my opinion.

Short pause. No one knows what to say.

Sophie And if Paul hadn't moved to L.A., we never would have met.

Short pause, as Paul's family bite their tongues.

Elizabeth Uncle Alfred, you're here. I wouldn't criticize.

Alfred They pay me twice what I got at Hull. Full stop. *I* didn't come for the culture.

Tom (*to Alice, referring to Alfred*) What does he do –?

Alice He teaches English. (*Short pause. To everyone*) Tom *teaches* – acting.

Everyone politely nods or mumbles, 'Oh really.'

(*to Paul*) So he's in the performing arts as well.

Tom Not in L.A. In New York.

Paul For theatre?

Tom Some.

Paul I'd have thought you couldn't make a living from the theatre –.

Tom Students of mind – they do television, films, plays. I mostly do accents. (*Beat.*) For Americans trying to be –. (*He shrugs.*) English? As well as the other way around.

Elizabeth There's a lot of need for –?

Tom I survive. (*Beat.*) I do the best I can. It's a living. (*to Paul*) I like Los Angeles too.

Gemma For me – New Mexico is paradise. Isn't it, Uncle Alfred? I sit on my porch, brush in hand and paint and before me –. I don't even have to put on shoes! Before me is a landscape that is not only the most extraordinary I've ever seen, but it also *changes*. Totally, completely remakes itself, I don't know, five hundred times a day! Because of the light, the clouds, even the density of the air. I don't mean just shadows, I mean one minute it's yellow and the next it's blue! (*She smiles and shakes her head.*) It's so different from England. Or the Alps or Provence where everything's fixed. Some mornings what gets me out of bed is the thought that if I weren't out there to paint it all, it'd be lost for good.

Beat.

Alfred (*to Tom*) She came to visit and she stayed. Every day, I blame myself.

Gemma An amazingly beautiful place. Even you say that sometimes. I can't imagine living anywhere else now.

Alice (*to Tom*) Gemma's a painter.

Tom I'd guessed that.

Gemma I've wondered what Turner would have made of it. Where instead of just a sea or sky or horizon, there was a landscape that was constantly changing, that was all – movement. (*Beat. She smiles.*) I try. But I'm no Turner, am I?

She turns to Elizabeth, who says nothing.

Elizabeth's bought four of my paintings. She said she bought them as an investment, but I think she just wanted to give me some money.

She laughs to herself; Elizabeth does not correct her. No one is really eating the Chinese food, which is awful; so they sort of move it around their plates.

Paul Could you pass me the seltzer?

Alice (*at the same time*) New England's very beautiful as well.

Sophie The drive up –.

Paul I haven't seen autumn for years.

Gemma (*to Alice*) There must be –. You must have all

sorts of special places where you go. Natural – I don't know, you tell me.

Alice There's a waterfall that's supposed to be –. I haven't seen it. I haven't actually driven around very much. Mostly it's just been to and from the city.

Paul It's a nice drive.

Alice I've wanted to see more, but . . .

Beat.

Tom (*to Alice*) How long have you lived here? Maybe you told me . . .

Alice Harry's had the place for –.

Alfred Years and years.

Elizabeth (*at the same time*) Fifteen, twenty years.

Alice I moved in two years ago, next month. The six months before that, I came up every weekend. (*Beat. She smiles.*) First it was – 'come on, Alice, stay over Sunday night, take the early bus back.' Then I was taking Fridays off. Then I quite my job. Sublet my apartment – then sold it.

Silence. No one has anything to say.

Elizabeth (*finally*) Two years? It was that long ago? I hadn't even heard about you until . . . (*to her siblings*) When did Father tell about Alice?

No response.

Gemma (*to Tom*) And New York is nice as well.

Tom (*to Elizabeth*) You're in the city –.

Elizabeth East Eighty-first.

Tom I'm on the West Side. A Hundred and Third.

Elizabeth It's gotten better there.

Tom It has.

Elizabeth I love New York. I wouldn't want to live anywhere else. Nothing closes. You can stay out all night.

Sophie sighs, wipes her forehead with her napkin.

Paul What is it?

Sophie I'm fine, I just –.

Paul She's sweating.

Gemma Maybe the food, it does taste sort of –.

Elizabeth I stopped eating it –.

Paul She's hot.

Sophie I'll be OK. It feels stuffy in here.

Elizabeth It would have been a lot stuffier in the dining-room.

Alice The stove is on. We can turn that off; I don't think we need to keep reheating the –.

Sophie (*standing*) Maybe I'm just tired. Would it be impolite if I –. Maybe if I just lie down.

Everyone adds: 'Of course.' 'Please.' 'Get some rest.' 'Relax.'

Gemma (*over this*) It's been an exhausting day for all of us.

Sophie I'll come back down later. Maybe if I read. (*She touches her head.*) There's aspirin or something in the bathroom?

Alice nods. Sophie turns to go, then turns back:

Paul, can you help me look for the aspirin?

Paul (*standing*) I'm sure it's in the –.

Sophie Paul. Help me look.

She goes. Paul hesitates, then hurries after her. Short pause.

Elizabeth The dining-room is stuffier. She always seems sick, doesn't she?

Gemma I hadn't noticed. Paul's never said –.

Elizabeth Every time we're together, she's sick. (*to Tom*) She's nine years older than Paul. And I say that to flatter her – she looks great. When she's not sick. (*Beat.*) She's even older than Gemma.

Alice Is anyone going to eat anymore . . .?

No response.

Alfred How long has she been away from France? I don't think I know that.

Elizabeth Sophie hasn't lived anywhere but West Hollywood since she was eight. She puts that accent on.

Tom It's a good accent.

Elizabeth Remember her mother? We met her at their wedding last December – she now sounds like she comes from Texas.

Alfred Isn't that where she lives –?

Elizabeth Sophie's no more French any more than I am!

Alice Maybe she puts the accent on to please Paul.

Beat.

Elizabeth How do you mean?

Alice says nothing; Elizabeth considers this, then:

I'll bet you're right. (*And she laughs at the thought.*)

Alfred She's a nice girl.

Tom (*changing the subject*) Funny, isn't it, all of us –
we're living all over *America*. What does that say?

Alfred What?

Tom It's strange. How did it happen? How did *you* –?

Elizabeth I think we all came for different reasons.

Alfred Harry was first. He led us all here. Blame him!
(*He laughs.*)

Elizabeth (*continuing*) You can't generalize, I think. For
me. London had become so . . . (*She makes a face.*)

Gemma (*over this*) I followed Alfred. He kept sending
postcards of the desert.

Alice (*half over this*) I was brought over years ago by my
publishing company.

   *This question has definitely animated the table – they
   talk almost at the same time.*

Alfred (*continuing*) Harry left about – twenty years ago
was it?

Gemma We were kids.

Elizabeth I was seventeen. Exactly.

Gemma (*to Tom*) What about you? You asked the
question.

Tom I was offered a job. As a stage manager. I started as
a stage manager. I guess you're right, we shouldn't
generalize.

Alice (*over this*) And as for why Harry – Harry's wife,
right? She'd just died. Their mother.

Everyone is now listening to this.

You children were all in schools. He wanted to . . . (*She shrugs.*) Get away from some memories, I suppose. Clear his head. That's how I've always . . . (*Beat.*) He didn't plan on staying. I don't know how many times he told me that.

Alfred His wife died? Twenty years ago?

Alice You must have known that.

Alfred looks at his nieces.

He came for –?! I don't know. A semester. That's all he said he was hired for. Then one thing led to another. And he stayed. (*Beat.*) And one by one – you came. (*Beat.*) What's wrong?

Elizabeth Mother died – two months ago.

Pause.

Alice What do you mean?

Elizabeth We were all at the funeral. Father was there. (*Beat.*) He said you'd felt it wasn't appropriate for you to come. We understood, didn't we?

She looks to Gemma who nods.

Alice Two months ago? Where was the –?

Gemma Brighton. Where mother lived.

Alice Harry was in England two months ago?? (*Then suddenly:*) Oh that's right. Now I remember. Yes, I couldn't come. I hope Harry sent my condolences. I think I sent flowers.

Pause. Paul enters.

Paul A delicate flower! That is what I tell her she is.

Sorry. Sophie'll be fine; she's tucked in, reading a magazine. (*Noticing the faces:*) What's . . .?

Alfred We were telling Tom how Harry came to the States.

Paul You've told him that Mother just threw him out?

Alice Did she?

Paul She'd had enough of him. She used to say that marrying Father was like buying a boat; your happiest times are when you get it, and when you get rid of it.

He laughs, no one else does.

Alice What exactly had your father done for your mother to throw him out?

Beat.

Elizabeth (*after checking with her siblings*) She never said. I don't think we ever asked.

Gemma There's a lot we don't know. Why didn't they ever divorce –. (*She is about to continue a list.*)

Alice (*interrupting*) Harry was still married to your mother?

Gemma Didn't you know that?

Pause.

Tom (*to Paul*) So your wife is just tired.

Elizabeth She looked tired.

Tom I gather you've only been married –.

Paul Not even a year. It's made a big difference in my life.

Tom Something like –.

Alice (*standing*) Excuse me. (*She takes the bottle of wine* *and fills up Alfred's glass.*) I should get more.

Tom I can go if –.

Alice I know where Harry's best stuff is hidden. (*She goes.*)

   Beat.

Elizabeth Father never told her he was still married.

Gemma (*picking up plates*) Is anyone still eating?

Tom (*taking a last bite*) I've had a lot worse in New York.

Elizabeth Father didn't tell her. What does that say?

Alfred Harry once talked to me – about Alice.

   Beat.

Elizabeth And . . .?

Alfred He said he'd met this woman. Alice. And, I think
he said, that their relationship was – the word he used
was – 'comfortable'. (*He looks to Tom.*)

Tom She's a nice woman. I'm not going to repeat
anything that could hurt her.

Elizabeth 'Comfortable.' (*Beat.*) What are we going to do
about this cremating-idea? Alice said she thought that's
what Harry would have –.

Paul Alice said.

   Beat.

Gemma Do we know what Father –.

Paul Mother was buried.

Gemma And he certainly would not have wanted to be
buried with –.

Paul Do we know that for sure?!!

Beat. Phone rings. In the middle of the second ring, it stops. Someone else in the house has picked it up.

I'm still hungry. Maybe there's some peanut butter or something.

Elizabeth What are we going to do? Don't you think it's a mistake? I think we tell Alice that we want our father buried. If she gives us any flack we tell her that's what he'd told us he wanted.

Gemma We should tell her now.

Paul What about the service tomorrow in the garden –.

Elizabeth We'll make it a memorial. People can still come, whatever. (*Beat.*) Is it agreed?

The others nod.

Then we'll tell her.

Alfred (*turning to Tom*) How well *did* you know my brother?

Tom I didn't know him at –.

Alfred I think that's how most of his friends felt. Let me tell you the truth. Harry wasn't a very nice man. He wasn't very nice to me and I wasn't alone. And I got a job at the University of New Mexico and he was working in a bloody community college! And he said this country would eat me alive! (*He laughs.*) You know what they say about twins? That there's always a good one and a bad one.

Tom I can't believe that's –.

Alfred Guess which he was. (*Beat.*) Go ahead and guess.

Beat.

Tom The bad one?

Alfred You knew him well! Still, I think his friends – like yourself – were too hard on him. He used to say that to me. He had a lot of sides to him – Harry. Be fair, Tom. Don't be too quick to judge.

Tom (*confused*) I wasn't –.

Alfred Give the man the benefit of the doubt, for Christ sake.

Alice enters with a bottle of wine. The others look to Elizabeth to begin a conversation, but before she can begin:

Alice (*opening the wine*) That was the funeral home – we can pick up the ashes anytime now.

She pours herself a glass of wine, sits down and opens the photograph album. No one says anything for a moment, then, holding up the album:

Our photo album. (*Pointing to a picture:*) Bermuda. (*to Elizabeth*) Harry bought me the bathing-suit.

Pause. She continues to look. No one knows what to say, when finally:

Tom (*to Paul*) Read any good film scripts lately?

Alfred (*almost chokes on his wine, laughing*) Right!

Paul The funny thing about living in America as a foreigner is the way you see other foreigners act.

Gemma (*trying to stop him*) Paul.

Paul They love to criticize. Everything's – what? Rubbish, Uncle Alfred? Some things are and some things aren't. That's how I see things, but . . . I had a friend from London visiting – to him everything was either stupid or plastic or barbaric. Then you couldn't get him out of the damn sun. At night you couldn't get him away from the damn TV. (*He sips his water.*) But I know why this is. I've thought about this a lot. It's all so – threatening. It's too much for some people to handle. The size of everything. The importance of everything. So they're actually being defensive. They're scared. (*Beat.*) I try to avoid people from home now. They're so predictable. (*to Tom*) To answer your question: I have read a couple of nice scripts this week. We'll see. I've been reading long enough to know that you can never know. You do your best. And try to have an impact where you can. (*He sips his water.*) The other day, I had a thought. You get these kinds of thoughts reading scripts. Let's say there are maybe ten thousand film scripts in circulation in L.A. on any given day.

Elizabeth That many –?

Paul I think I'm being conservative. And each script will have at least twenty copies. Probably more, but let's say twenty. And each script – the rule is about 110 pages. That's –. I did the maths before, something like twenty-two million pages of film script just – on any given day. (*Beat.*) Now if each writer were to say just decrease the margins – both left and right – by say three spaces. Three spaces – no more. It would mean each script would be about five pages shorter – or a total savings of about one million pages, which I'm told roughly equals 200 trees. (*Short pause.*) I wrote a memo. (*He shrugs.*) Who knows?

Pause.

Alice I did – know about Harry being married. (*Short pause. She goes back to looking at the album.*)

Alfred (*looking at Alice, then*) He talked to me about you, Alice. Harry.

Alice looks up.

He said the nicest things. He told me how much he loved you. This new 'gal' he called you. He said – you were everything to him.

Alice nods and goes back to the album.

Elizabeth (*to Paul*) There are so many Brits in publishing here. I have friends – Americans who say the only way to advance is to go first to England – or fake a British accent. (*She laughs.*)

Gemma (*to Tom*) Work for you!

Laughter.

Tom (*over this*) So that's why they take my classes!

More laughter. Short pause.

Gemma All of my English friends – such as they are in New Mexico – make fun. It's an easy place to make fun. On the one hand I suppose Paul is right – they're scared. We are. But on the other, you can't help yourself – there's so much that's crazy.

Elizabeth Father used to make fun – lest we forget.

Paul Father was scared too.

Gemma He didn't make fun, he hated. The last time I called him – he just started ranting.

Paul About?

Gemma He hated this country and everything it tries to be. Or doesn't try to be.

Paul He loved looking down his nose –.

Elizabeth I never took him seriously when he talked like that. It was just talk. I laughed at him, Paul.

Paul You encouraged him.

Elizabeth He made me laugh, as I've just said. And he wasn't scared, Paul – he was angry.

Paul (*erupting*) If the man wasn't scared then why the hell are we here?!! And he hated all right! But the only thing he really hated was himself!! (*Beat.*) Isn't that now obvious?

  Pause.

Alice (*holding up the album*) You all might be interested in this. The photos go back years. You're all in here.

Elizabeth Pass it around.

Alice In a minute, when I'm done. (*She continues to look through the album as she lights a cigarette.*)

Alfred I'm all in favour of keeping your sense of humour about things. Sometimes I think it's the only thing of any value that we have left. And if Americans wish to make fools of themselves in front of us – day after day after day after day after day – what are we supposed to do, cover our eyes? Well I don't. (*He shrugs.*) So shoot me, Paul.

Gemma (*to Paul*) And I don't know what you're talking about. (*to Elizabeth*) Have you heard him do his American accent?

Tom American accent –??

Paul (*at the same time*) Once. I did it once!

Gemma (*over this*) Get off! Let's hear it, Paul!

Elizabeth When did he –?

Gemma At his wedding!

Paul I only do it in England!

Alfred Come on, Paul.

Gemma (*over this*) Tom here can help you improve it!

Elizabeth, Gemma, Alfred and Tom are now all shouting to Paul to do his American accent. He is resisting – all in good humour, with a lot of sisterly pushing and nudging. 'Please, Paul!' 'We want to hear, Paul!' 'I'll bet you can't do one!', etc.

    As the noise reaches its peak, with people banging on the table and hitting glasses with knives, urging Paul to do his 'American' – Sophie enters in a nightgown and robe.

Sophie What's . . .?

They see her and stop. Short pause.

I'm sorry, I didn't mean to . . . You were making so much noise, I didn't know what . . . I see – you were just having fun. (*Beat.*) Good for you. I'm sure it's not easy to find much to laugh about on a day like today. I'm sorry if I interrupted. (*She turns to go.*)

Paul Sophie, sit down if you –.

Sophie (*interrupting*) I don't think I'm dressed for a party. (*Beat.*) Come up when you feel like it, Paul. When you're ready. I'll wait up. (*She goes.*)

    Pause. Paul stands, looks at his sisters, then picks up a knife, and says in his best 'Brando' or 'Pacino':

Paul Hey woman, how come you just don't cut the whole thing off!

    He turns back to his sisters, smiles and they burst out laughing. Through the laughter they shout 'He's good!' 'That was very good.'

    Alice continues to look through the album. As the sisters laugh, Sophie returns.

Sophie Perhaps I will join you. (*She goes and sits next to Paul.*) I can't sleep anyway. I told Claire I'd call at seven – her time.

Gemma How is Claire, you haven't said a word –.

Elizabeth (*over this*) I meant to ask . . .

Sophie She's very upset, of course. She adored Harry. Even though they'd only met the one time at the wedding. Still, we always put her on the phone when we called. She said, when we told her – of course we didn't say how – she said, 'So how many grandparents do I have now?' (*She smiles.*) She's going to write you each a note.

Beat.

Elizabeth (*to Tom*) Claire is Sophie's nine-year-old –.

Tom I guessed.

Sophie She's devoted to Paul. Worships him, doesn't she? (*Beat.*) I'm jealous. (*She smiles.*)

Gemma (*to Elizabeth*) What time is it?

Elizabeth Too early to go to bed.

Short pause, then:

SCENE FIVE

The kitchen. An hour or so later.
   [Alice, Alfred and Elizabeth are out for a walk.]
   Sophie sits at the table, talking on the phone to her daughter in California: what they are saying cannot be heard. Gemma is beginning to clean up the table, piling dishes, scraping plates, etc. and carrying them (off) to the sink and garbage. Tom and Paul sit across from each other, talking.

Tom (*in the middle of a story*) 'What are you up for, dear?' I ask. (*in American:*) 'It's a play by Oscar Wilder. Do you know him?' (*own voice:*) 'Not for years. Have

293

you done English accents before on stage?' (*American:*) 'I was in a show by George Bernard Shaw once.' 'Funny, I hadn't realized he'd written – shows. And what part did you play?' (*American:*) 'I was one of those dancers, you know, in the ballroom scene.'

Paul What ballroom –??

Tom *My Fair Lady*.

Paul Of course!

Tom (*over this*) Last year in her prep school. (*American:*) 'I wore the pink dress?' 'I should have guessed just by looking at you. What else could you have played?' (*He sips his drink*.)

Paul Once –.

Tom Just a second. (*He continues:*) I reply, after listening to her act – I use the term loosely – for a few moments: 'I can see there is nothing I can teach you.' (*American:*) 'Oh, but there must be!' She had your typical American sense of irony. Anyway, to make a long story short, I tried. Her mother paid me fifty bucks to go and see her Gwendolen or (*American:*) 'Gwendolen' is how her fellow actors – again the term is used with freedom bordering on abandonment – referred to her character on stage. In the end I would hazard to say she was the most authentic thing in the whole evening. (*Beat.*) I met the director after the 'show', which by the way is the appropriate term for what I saw, they, the Americans, have that right – he was, I would say, the most tired human being I have ever been exposed to. He literally fell asleep while *he* was talking to me. But then I'd learned that this was something like the ninth prep-school production of *Importance of Being Earnest* he'd directed in – I think he said – the last three weeks. But maybe I didn't hear him right.

Gemma returns from the sink and picks up more dishes.

Paul Where in England was he from?

Tom He was from England, you knew! Bristol, he said. But he may have only been mumbling that in his sleep – a memory? Of something else perhaps?

Sophie suddenly laughs at something her daughter has told her on the phone. Paul looks at her then back at Tom, who pours himself more wine from the bottle.

He perked up after a couple of drinks though. His 'Gwendolen's' Mum was paying. Then after we were in this bar for a while, the Mum says (*American:*) 'So what did you really think?' To me. I look at the director, and he says, could I wait a minute, he's really interested in what I have to say, but he has to go to the loo. He gets up, goes – and we never see him again. (*He sips his drink.*) I suppose he had another show to direct. He did say, sometime during the evening, that the highpoint of a busy artistic year was being allowed – by someplace somewhere – to do a production of a Chekhov play. He couldn't recall which one.

Gemma laughs at this.

Paul My favourite –.

Tom I haven't quite –.

Paul (*at the same time*) I'm sorry, I didn't mean –.

Tom (*at the same time*) But go ahead, please . . .

Beat.

Paul My favourite's . . .

Gemma stops to listen.

I'm in line at the grocery store. I obviously must have said something, because this fellow behind me, hearing the accent I suppose, says (*American:*) 'What the fuck is going on with that Queen of yours? Why she letting 'em push her around! If I was Queen I wouldn't let nobody push me around. That lady needs some balls!' (*He smiles.*) They say whatever comes into their heads, I swear. There's no – editing.

Beat.

Tom That's funny. (*He continues with his story:*) So – the Mum, she says 'I thought every penny I'd laid out for those lessons was worth it.' (*He looks at Paul and shrugs.*) I suppose I must have done some good. I don't know. (*Beat.*) I can't work miracles. But sometimes I guess I do OK.

Paul nods.

Paul It can be a strange place.

Gemma (*as she picks up dishes*) Sometimes – I pretend, when I'm sitting out on my porch, painting – I look out across the landscape and I say: this is Africa. Like a hundred, hundred and fifty years ago. Africa. (*She starts to leave with the dishes.*) Or India. It makes me feel better for some reason. (*She goes.*)

Sophie holds out the phone.

Sophie Paul, talk to Claire. I have to get a book to read to her.

Paul I'll get it for you –.

Sophie (*over this*) It's in my bag. You'll never find it. And besides, Claire's dying to talk to you. (*into the phone*) Here's Paul, dear. He's grabbing the phone from me, he wants that much to talk to you.

He obviously has not been grabbing the phone; she now hands it to him. As she does, to Tom:

I always read to Claire at night. (*She goes.*)

Paul (*into the phone*) Hi! What did you do today? I'm sure you already have, I'll ask her to tell me. What's the weather like?

Gemma returns from the sink.

Tom (*to Gemma*) I had one student. This was when I'd only been here a few years. My wife couldn't believe this.

Gemma (*interrupting*) Your wife? I didn't know you were –.

Tom We're divorced. (*He continues with the story.*) He comes in. His shirt's unbuttoned down to –. And it's goddamn winter. (*He laughs.*)

Gemma Was she English?

Tom My wife? Yes. She's back in London now. (*Beat.*) When we were breaking up, I used to say to her (*in American:*) 'What's the matter, can't you take it?' (*He smiles.*) She couldn't.

Beat.

Gemma I didn't mean to be –.

Tom That's –.

Gemma I just suddenly realized. I don't know anything about you. Here you are at . . .

Tom Alice wanted me to stay –.

Gemma I wasn't saying –. Of course you're . . . (*She stops herself.*) Kids?

Tom Six and nine. Boys. In London.

Beat. Then, changing the subject before it becomes too personal:

Gemma Anyway, you were saying about a student . . .

Tom He comes into my class, this kid really, and he says to me, in front of everyone, (*American:*) 'I want to try some of that British bullshit acting, you know – with the funny voice.'

He laughs, then she laughs, not quite understanding.

Paul (*covering the phone*) I missed that.

Tom pours himself more to drink.

Gemma (*to Paul*) A student of Tom's – he wanted to learn the way the British act.

Paul doesn't understand.

Tom Another story! A young woman – she's been a model, now she wants to act. So I've asked her to prepare something. Not that I'm going to reject anyone. God forbid that we have standards.

Paul sets the phone on the table.

So she recites. (*American:*) 'Thus do I ever make my fool my purse.' I ask her if she knows what she's saying. She says that *for her* it means – how she shouldn't spend so much money on clothes. She says, (*American:*) 'That may not be what it means to others, but that's what it means to me.' (*Beat.*) I ask her: does she know what character she is acting? She says (*American:*) 'Iago.' Very good. I ask her: did she know that Iago was a – man? She says (*American:*) 'So what? My last drama teacher –.' 'Drama. Drama.' My favourite American word. 'My last drama teacher said there were no male or female parts anymore – only people parts.' I want to say, I think your teacher could have chosen a better word than 'parts', but I bite my tongue. (*He opens his mouth.*) See? Seven years in this country and there's permanent teeth marks there. (*He*

298

continues.) 'Only people parts.' Interesting. Why not? I say to myself, she's paid in advance. Then about a half hour later, for the hell of it or maybe I'm just wanting to get into the swing of this 'people-part' notion, I say, 'Now that you've done your Iago, what about trying Othello?' (*Beat*.) You'd have thought I'd hit her in the face. (*American:*) 'Othello,' she says in her lovely American, 'I couldn't do Othello.' 'Why is that, my dear?' 'Othello is a black man.' Or is it 'African-American' now? I don't know and I don't give a fuck. Anyway, 'A black man. And only a black man can play a black man.' (*Beat*.) I asked if she felt that was in any way contradictory to what she'd said about 'people-parts'? And she said, she didn't see why it was. (*Pause*.) They don't see themselves. They don't question themselves.

Paul And the things you can't say. Sometimes I think a decent English comic would be in prison in a wink in this country.

Gemma (*entering from the sink*) I thought you loved America?

Paul You can love something and still find fault with it.

Sophie enters with the book.

Sophie I'd put it in your bag for some reason. (*She notices the phone on the table*.)

Paul We had a nice talk.

Sophie picks up the phone and begins to read from Charlie and the Chocolate Factory *to her daughter.*

Tom If they weren't so thin-skinned. Sometimes you just want to scream: 'RELAX!'

Noise outside.

Gemma They're back from their walk.

Tom Anyway, why did you let me go on like that? It must have been very boring, you should have stopped me.

Alfred, Alice and Elizabeth enter from their walk; Alice and Alfred wear wellingtons.

Alice What a beautiful night. You should have come with us, Gemma.

Paul You've been gone for ages. Where was there to walk? I thought father only had a half acre.

Elizabeth We walked through other people's. They don't have fences.

She looks to Gemma, who picks up more plates.

Gemma I've been picking up.

Elizabeth You shouldn't have to do it all.

Gemma I was hoping I wouldn't have to.

Sophie (*to everyone*) Would you mind –? Please. Sh-sh. (*She continues to read on the phone.*)

Paul Sophie, I don't think you can ask everyone –. It's the kitchen –.

Sophie Fine! I'm sorry I'm in the way.

Paul No one said –.

Sophie I'll go upstairs. If it isn't a big bother could someone hang up the receiver when I get to the phone upstairs? (*She goes, carrying her book.*)

Elizabeth Is that the same call she was making –?

Alfred (*sitting taking off his wellingtons; reads the bottom of the boots. American:*) 'Made with pride in the U.S. of A.' (*to the others*) Are we still doing our American?

Alice (*over this, to Elizabeth*) I'll look for that stomach medicine –.

Elizabeth You said it was in the medicine chest. I'm not stupid.

Gemma Is something . . .?

Alfred Her stomach.

Elizabeth (*as she leaves the kitchen*) And you could help Gemma, Paul. You're not home. (*She goes.*)

Tom (*standing*) Let me, I –.

Gemma You're a guest. (*She turns to Alice.*) Her stomach?

Alice It's the emotion. She holds everything in.

Alfred She said it was the Chinese food. I better open another bottle. (*He starts to leave for the pantry. American:*) 'What should it be? Red or white – or blush?' (*He laughs to himself and goes.*)

> *Gemma and Paul start to head for the sink, carrying the glasses, plates, etc.*

Gemma (*as they go*) I can't believe Sophie wanted us to be quiet –.

Paul She didn't mean –. Sometimes she says things without thinking. Who doesn't?

> *They are gone. Alice and Tom are alone. Alice suddenly sighs.*

Tom Are you all –?

Alice It's late. (*Beat.*) And no one wants to go to sleep.

Tom Alice –.

> *She turns to him.*

301

Take care of yourself. This can't be easy.

She smiles, takes his hand and pats it.

Alice When we were walking –. Elizabeth spent most of the time on a bench –. So Alfred . . . (*Beat.*) He asked me to go to bed with him.

Tom He's drunk. He's been drinking all –.

Alice Thank you.

Tom I mean –. I meant, don't be too angry with him. Harry's death . . . Everyone in this house. You can see how emotional it all is.

Alice Thank you, again.

Tom What do you want me to say?

Alice 'Do you want to go to bed with him, Alice?' (*Beat.*) And the answer to that is . . . (*She shrugs. Beat.*) It was very beautiful out tonight. I love the fall. There was nearly a full moon. Maybe by tomorrow night. I'm going to have a cigarette. I don't give a shit. (*She takes out a cigarette and lights it.*)

Gemma (*off; calling*) My God, Paul's washing a dish!

Tom Don't do anything that . . . You might regret tomorrow, Alice.

Alice What a bullshit thing to say to me!

Tom (*over this*) Then don't ask me for my –!

Alice Who asked you?! (*Beat.*) Don't worry, I'm not stupid. I'm not going to bed with him. It's nice being asked though.

Alfred enters with the wine. Short pause. He looks at both of them.

Alfred Did I interrupt something? What were you talking about?

Beat.

Alice Harry. Of course.

Elizabeth enters with the medicine.

Elizabeth (*entering*) None of this kind of stuff ever works for me. I don't know why I'm bothering. Could you hand me a spoon?

Tom takes a spoon out of the drawer and hands it to her.

Gemma (*off*) Elizabeth, look what our brother's doing? Have you ever seen him wash a dish in his life?

Elizabeth I'll get a camera! (*to the others*) Who's paying for that phone call by the way? She's still on the phone. Is she going to read the whole book to her?

Alice I assumed it was a credit card call.

Elizabeth I think we better ask Paul. (*She goes off to the sink.*)

Alfred So you were talking about Harry. There were times when we'd be together, Harry and me, and I'd look at him, sipping his Scotch, and it was like I didn't know that man at all. I had no idea what he was thinking. What he was feeling. Which is a weird feeling, when the guy looks just like you.

Paul (*entering and heading for the upstairs*) I'll talk to her. I didn't realize it was bothering everyone!

Elizabeth (*following him in*) Alice shouldn't be asked to pay –.

Paul (*over this*) Get off my back!

He goes. Gemma also enters from the sink, wiping her

hands. Pause. Elizabeth pours the medicine and drinks it. Finally:

Gemma You know we've hardly talked about the service.

Alice Alfred and I were talking about it on our walk. He was saying he thought Paul wanted – to sing something.

Gemma Paul said that?

Alfred He hinted to me, when we were –.

Elizabeth What does he want to sing?

Beat.

Gemma Father hated Paul's singing. It offended him.

Alice Perhaps that is why Paul wants to sing. Maybe each of us – something. Before we throw the ashes into the garden. I was going to read a poem.

Tom Maybe it's none of my business, but what I would suggest is that you make a list. Put what you're going to do in the order you plan to do it in. You can always change, of course, but . . . It's a good thing to have written down. That's been my experience. In front of people. (*He looks at each one of them.*) I can be secretary if you'd like. If that'd make it easier. Is there a piece of paper?

Everyone ignores him. Short pause.

Alfred (*sitting and leaning over, he takes Alice's hand*) I wasn't lying. He told me that he loved you.

Alice I know he did.

Beat.

Alfred (*to everyone*) I noticed a pile of jigsaws in the closet. Anyone else like to do jigsaws? I'll choose one. (*He goes.*)

*No one has anything to say. Elizabeth turns on the
radio for a moment – pop music – she turns it right off
again. Alfred enters with a puzzle.*

(*holding up the front of the box*) The Grand Canyon!

*Elizabeth suddenly grabs stomach in pain, and cries
out.*

Gemma Elizabeth!

*Gemma and Alice go to her, as she doubles over and
nearly collapses to the floor.*

Alice Oh my God!

Elizabeth I'll be fine. Give me some water. I'm fine.

*Alice gives her some water. Elizabeth sits back in her
chair, breathing heavily now. She wipes the sweat from
her brow.*

(*faintly*) Do the jigsaw. I like jigsaws.

*Alfred opens the box and pours out the pieces on to the
table. Paul storms into the kitchen from upstairs. He is
very upset.*

Paul (*entering*) I'll pay for the goddamn call!!! What do
you want – a cheque?! Cash?!!! Whatever you want!! Just
get off my back!! She's trying to talk to her daughter!! Is
that so bad?! Can't you leave her alone?!!! She's up there
crying now. She thinks you hate her! I can't stand it
anymore!! Grow up!!!

*He suddenly becomes aware that Sophie is behind him.
She has been crying.*

Sophie Paul, your sisters meant well. You shouldn't talk
to them like that. (*Beat.*) Apologize. (*Beat.*) You heard
me. Apologize.

Beat.

Paul I'm sorry.

Sophie tries to smile.

Sophie I'm going to bed now – everyone. Goodnight.

Everyone except Paul says 'Goodnight' or 'Goodnight, Sophie.' Sophie turns to go, then turns back.

Paul, stay up as late as you want. And visit. (*She leaves.*)

Alfred (*over the puzzle*) Anyone else ever been to the Grand Canyon? I know you have Gemma. Elizabeth?

She nods. He looks at the others, and one by one they nod as well.

Everyone?

Gemma (*to Elizabeth*) You should go to bed. I'll take you up. Come on. (*She helps Elizabeth up.*) Goodnight. Say goodnight.

Elizabeth (*to the others*) Goodnight.

The others say 'Goodnight.'

Alice Sleep well.

Gemma I'll come back down and help.

They go.

Paul I'll finish with the dishes.

Tom Why can't I –.

Paul I'm used to it. It's my job at home. (*He goes to the sink.*)

Tom now sits between Alfred and Alice. Alfred continues to work on the puzzle – turning over pieces, occasionally matching two. He continues this

306

*throughout the rest of the scene. Tom begins to feel a
little uncomfortable between these two.*

Alice About a year ago, Alfred –. (*She ignores Tom.*)
Harry started going on and on about this new student of
his. A young woman. Said she was –. Amazing. I ran into
the two of them one afternoon in the parking lot of the
college, chatting. She's beautiful. (*Beat.*) You may see her
here tomorrow. I think she's invited herself. (*Beat.*) After
seeing her, I said to Harry, what the hell did he take me
for? I didn't want any of that. My last husband –. (*She
turns to Tom and pats his hand.*) Tom's brother. (*She
turns back to Alfred.*) I'd had it with that. I can live alone.
I don't mind. (*Beat.*) He smiled – the way he smiled. The
way you smile. He was a handsome man.

Alfred looks up.

And he kissed me on the lips or tried to. And he said, I
don't believe what I'm hearing, Alice. That girl is
probably the best violin student I've ever had in America.
Her potential is limitless. Finally I feel my talents as a
teacher can be fulfilled. You can't know how lucky I feel.
Though of course I'm trying to convince her to transfer to
Julliard. (*Beat.*) I felt like shit. (*She looks at Tom, then
back at Alfred.*) He spent a lot of time with her. He loved
teaching. (*Short pause.*) Then one day, I happened by his
office door. It was opened a crack. There's also a little
window. And there she was with him. She had her violin.
I saw her put it under her chin. Raise her bow. And I
don't know what I was prepared for, Alfred, but – she was
the worst violinist I have ever heard. (*She smiles without
looking up.*) I mean it was painful. (*Beat.*) He screwed
around all the time. Though after hearing the girl play I
realized that there was some suffering on his part as well.
It wasn't all . . . (*She shrugs.*) Maybe even more suffering
than pleasure. (*She smiles.*) We can hope. (*Short pause.*

She reaches over and takes Alfred's drink and takes a sip.)
So – a few months ago Harry was in England? At his –
wife's funeral? What did she die of? Do we know?

   Beat.

Alfred Her liver. She was a drinker.

   Alice takes another sip of Alfred's drink.

Alice It was a nice walk. Harry never wanted to take a
walk with me after supper. Except – when we were
courting. For that one week – he would.

   *She looks at Alfred. He looks up. They look into each
   other's eyes. Tom turns away and tries to be invisible.*

SCENE SIX

The kitchen. One o'clock in the morning.
   *Tom and Paul sit at the table, working on the puzzle –
the frame is now completed. From above, there is a
banging/pounding sound.*
   Beat.

Paul (*looking up, after listening for a moment*)
Unbelievable. Don't you find it –? (*He stops himself.*)
What were we talking about?

Tom (*without looking up from the puzzle; American
accent*) 'What you don't understand . . .'

Paul (*remembering where he was; American*) 'What you
don't understand about America is . . .' Fill in the blank.
I don't know how many times I have been told that. 'You
don't understand –' that there was – 'all these different
races.' That America is – 'soooo big.' That 'we actually
vote for our leaders.'

More banging from above interrupts him. He stops.
Gemma enters from the sink and stove area; she has
just made herself of cup of tea. She wears a nightgown
and a robe.

Gemma (*listening to the noise above*) I hope to God I
have Uncle Alfred's genes.

Paul It's been going on for like an hour now. (*Beat.*) Am I
the only one offended by this? By our – recently deceased
father's girlfriend and our recently deceased father's
brother screwing like a couple of bloody rabbits up there
in his own goddamn bedroom?!!

He looks at Gemma, who sips her tea.

No one else is even a little troubled by this turn of events?
No? Fine. Then it must be me. (*He turns to Tom.*) What
were we talking about? I keep forgetting.

Tom I heard this once (*American:*) 'I love England. It's
my favourite of those countries.' (*Beat.*) I should have
said – by 'those countries' do you happen to mean
Europe? Europe the home for the past three millennia to
what we humbly call – Western Civilization?!! (*He smiles
and shakes his head.*)

Gemma Don't you two get tired of complaining?

*More banging upstairs. Gemma sits down at the table
and picks up a puzzle piece.*

Paul (*pushing her hand away from his pieces*) I'm doing
the sky. (*He turns to Tom.*) Alfred once was telling –. This
must have been at my wedding. I'm not sure. He's
teaching a class. (*He turns to Gemma.*) What's his field
again?

Gemma The Romantics.

Paul So – say he was teaching – Shelley? Whatever. And a student stands up in the class and says (*American:*) 'What the hell does any of this have to do with my life? Why do I even have to listen to you? You worthless Englishman!! Don't you know you are nothing now? That you count for nothing in this world! This is our world! Get it?! So why don't you just shut up and listen!!' (*He laughs to himself.*)

Tom He really –?

Paul Something like that. I don't remember the exact words.

Tom What did Alfred do?

Paul looks to Gemma who ignores him and continues to look over the puzzle.

Paul He didn't do anything. The students here grade their teachers, so Alfred says – you just have to take it.

The banging seems to have reached its climax upstairs. They listen, then it stops. Pause.

(*looking up at the ceiling*) Silence. Dare we hope. (*standing, arms outstretched*) Thank you God! Maybe someone's finally come!!

Elizabeth enters from the hallway in her robe.

Elizabeth (*entering*) Have you been hearing what's been going on upstairs? You can hear everything!

Paul They've stopped.

Gemma (*under her breath*) I wouldn't bet on it.

Tom (*to Elizabeth*) How's the . . . (*He touches his stomach.*)

Elizabeth The medicine helped. Also the sleep, I think. I didn't know how tired I was.

Paul (*looking at his watch*) You only slept for –.

Elizabeth (*interrupting, to Gemma*) Is that tea?

Gemma The water's still –.

Elizabeth (*on her way to the stove*) Anyone else? (*She is gone.*)

Beat.

Gemma Who can sleep?

Paul (*over the puzzle*) As long as Sophie can –.

Gemma The light was on in your room. When I came down.

Beat.

Paul (*without looking up from the puzzle*) Then I better go. (*He doesn't move. Beat.*) I've got one (*American:*) 'The farther east you go – the more dead they are.' I swear I heard this. In California.

Silence. They work on the puzzle. Suddenly both Tom and Gemma speak at the same time.

Tom (*to Paul*) I hear that you –.

Gemma (*same time, to Tom*) I wanted to ask –.

They stop themselves.

Tom Go ahead, what were you –?

Gemma (*over this*) No, please. It was just –. What were you going to say?

Beat.

Tom Remember your thought. I was only going to say that I understand you're going to sing tomorrow, Paul.

Paul looks up.

311

What are you going to sing?

Paul Who said that?

Tom Alfred thought –.

Paul I haven't sung in front of people in years.

Tom You were a professional singer –?

Paul I took classes. I wasn't bad. But it was clear I was destined for the chorus, so . . . I hadn't even thought of singing. (*Beat. To Gemma*) Think I should? What would father have thought – such a mediocre voice sending him off.

Gemma I think he's already gone. Do what you want.

Elizabeth enters with her tea and a cookie which she has found and now eats.

Elizabeth (*eating the cookie*) I think it's sick. Up there. How do they get the nerve? And do they think we're deaf?

Paul (*over the puzzle*) So I'm not alone.

Tom (*to Gemma*) What were you going to say –. Before –.

Gemma Oh right. It wasn't . . . I was going to ask –. (*She looks at her brother and sister.*) Don't get angry with me. (*to Tom*) Since you were here – I'd like to know what happened yesterday.

Elizabeth Gemma, it's one in the morning –!

Paul You don't have to Tom, I apologize for my sister.

Gemma (*over this*) I mean – after. I understand what he did. (*Beat.*) Were there police? I feel like I'd like to know. Should know. But if you don't want to –. It's not that important. (*Pause. She goes back to the puzzle.*)

Tom (*remembering*) The police did come. An ambulance.

An officer talked to me. (*to Alice*) He was pretty nice.
Younger than me.

He smiles. No one is looking at him. They are doing the
puzzle.

Alice was able to say she wasn't all that surprised, he'd
been depressed, and so . . . That made things – quicker.
(*Beat. Trying to recall more:*) Some people from the
ambulance cleaned up the study a little bit. I don't know
how much you want to know?

Elizabeth (*sitting down now, to get closer to the puzzle;*
to Gemma) Move over a little.

Paul (*to Elizabeth*) The sky is mine. Do all that pink
rock. (*Beat.*)

Tom Before the police came, Alice and I just sat in the
hall outside the study. I wouldn't allow her to go back in.
Once I'd seen . . . (*Beat.*) I helped her wash her face. She
had some blood . . . She'd seen him do it – you knew
that. So everything she does –. I think we should
remember that. (*Beat.*) I came in and she was just
sobbing. I pulled her into the hall. I called the police.
They took out the body in a body bag; on a stretcher. I
drove Alice in her car to the hospital behind the
ambulance. I don't even have my license with me. (*Beat.*)
A funeral director was called. We met him in a room of
the hospital. Alice liked him right away. He's about my
age. Maybe a little younger. (*Beat.*) I'm just trying to
recall if there's anything . . . It was the funeral director
who gave us the name of the woman who did most of the
cleaning up. Alice – Elizabeth knows this – found a few
places she'd missed. You couldn't stop her. I couldn't
have done it. There was a stain on the floorboards she
couldn't get out or she didn't have the stuff in the house
to get out. So Elizabeth –.

Elizabeth (*doing the puzzle*) I moved the carpet from one of the bedrooms. It's in the study now.

Tom Where I'm supposed to sleep. (*He laughs.*)

Paul (*looking up*) Tom shouldn't have to –.

Gemma (*at the same time*) We can't let him sleep –.

Tom (*over this*) I can't sleep anyway, please! (*He pats the puzzle.*) I'll just stay up all night. I often do.

More 'banging' from upstairs.

Paul (*looking up*) Now – the other one has to come! Jesus Christ . . .

They all look back at the puzzle.

Tom (*to Gemma*) Is that enough? Is there a specific thing . . .?

Elizabeth (*changing the subject*) Who is this Alice anyway?

Gemma I thought you knew her from publishing –.

Elizabeth I'm asking Tom.

Tom is surprised by this.

He's her relative.

Gemma I think we've imposed upon Tom enough for –.

Tom I don't mind. Let's see. Alice was married to my brother. I knew her then. I always thought she was one of the more alive people that I knew.

More banging from upstairs.

They seemed happy. My brother and –. One of those couples who seem to get along. Then he found someone else. I thought he acted in a real shitty way. I told her so. Is this the sort of thing –?

Elizabeth It'll do.

Tom We hadn't seen each other for a few years. We ran into each other a couple of weeks ago on Fifth Avenue, agreed to have lunch, had lunch. I'd just broken up with a girl.

Gemma Your wife?

Tom (*shaking his head*) This was just a few weeks –.

Gemma Right. American? The girl.

Tom That's right. Anyway Alice took pity on me, invited me up here for a weekend in the country. (*Beat.*) So I could relax.

The noise from above has stopped.

She's a good person. She's gone through a lot.

Paul Sh-sh!

Everyone listens.

Dare we hope that this unpleasant experience is now behind us?

Elizabeth I'd only met Alice a few times. I think it's the same with all of us. I don't know – there's my father's house. My father's funeral service. Calling my father's friends. She's everywhere, isn't she? That's what I was thinking about upstairs. That I don't know who she is. Or what she wants.

Paul What are you talking about?

Elizabeth Father has a lot of things in this house. That were his. Open your eyes, Paul. Just look at the situation we're in: she decides about the cremation. She tells us where to sleep.

Gemma I thought you helped with that.

Elizabeth I did my best. Look, I don't want to make a big deal about this. I don't mean it to be a big deal. It's just something I've been thinking about.

Paul What is? I don't understand.

Elizabeth holds her stomach.

What's wrong?

Elizabeth I'm sure it was the eggroll. That's what I've been burping up. Forget it, Paul. Do your jigsaw. That's what you're interested in.

Paul I'm not interested in the jigsaw!

Sophie now enters from the hall. She wears a thin, translucent nightgown.

Sophie Is no one going to sleep in this house? What night owls you Bakers are.

Elizabeth We got woken up by –.

Sophie Me too. (*She yawns.*) What was that noise? Sounded like a tree limb banging on the roof. Must have gotten windy all of a sudden. Is that tea?

Elizabeth There's still water in the kettle.

Sophie (*yawning*) I'm half asleep. (*She puts her arms around Paul's neck.*) How's the puzzle coming? I love puzzles. They're a complete waste of time. I like that. (*She kisses him on the head.*) What are you going to do, make me sleep alone all night? Your sisters can't be that interesting. (*She laughs.*) Just joking. I'll make myself some tea. Anyone else? (*As she leaves for the stove:*) I'm upstairs thinking: what do I have to do to get my husband to go to bed? (*She smiles, then as if another thought – she fans herself for a second with her nightgown.*) I put on a cooler nightgown. It was hot in the room. (*She goes.*)

Elizabeth You're not going to shut me up, Paul.

Paul (*over this*) Leave me alone. This is all I ask.

Elizabeth (*over this*) You never change!

Gemma (*over this*) I don't want to talk about this! I don't want to talk about this! I don't want to talk about this!

Alice has entered in a robe and bare feet. She stands, startled to see everyone. Short pause.

Alice What's everyone . . .? Do you know what time it is? I think it's –.

Elizabeth We're having tea.

No one knows what to say. Sophie comes in, having put on the kettle.

Sophie The kettle's on.

Alice You too? What's going on?

Sophie I was just telling everyone – there was a tree limb, banging against the roof. Did you hear it? (*Beat.*) You must have, Alice. It woke me up.

Beat.

Alice I did hear it. Thank you. (*She goes to the table and picks up a bottle.*) Alfred wants a . . . drink. I ran into him – in the hall. I'd been asleep. And then I suppose the tree limb . . .

Paul Sounded like a very big limb.

Alice yawns.

Alice I promised to bring this . . . He's waiting. Goodnight. Remember, tomorrow is going to be a long day as well. (*She turns to leave.*)

Elizabeth Alice, when do we decide who gets what?

Paul This is not the time –.

Gemma It's the middle of the night, Elizabeth!

Elizabeth I want to know!!

Beat.

Alice What's there to get?

Elizabeth There are chairs. Silverware. Plates. Photographs and frames. Books. Table.

Alice (*turning away*) Take what you want, Elizabeth.

Elizabeth (*irrational now*) How dare you speak to me like that!

Gemma Stop it, Elizabeth!

Paul (*same time*) Leave her alone!

Elizabeth I only want what is fair!! This was my father!! Do you understand that, woman?! So how are we going to divide his things?! What is so wrong with that question?! Do we divide into three? In four . . .?

Alice Is that what you want to ask me?!! Is it?!!! Or do you want to know why I –. Do you think I didn't know you could hear?! I've lived in this house for two years and I know what can be heard!! But I didn't care! Why? Because I don't give one fuck what you – kids – think of me!! Why should I?!

Elizabeth (*nearly in tears*) I don't know why I'm listening to this. What have I done?

Tom I think we should stop before –.

Elizabeth (*to Alice*) What you don't understand is I'm not interested in you, Alice. My question had to do with chairs, tables, there are lamps, rugs . . .

318

Alice He was so disappointed in all of you!!

Elizabeth (*desperately trying to stay calm*) Books, there's his car, garden equipment –.

Tom (*putting his hand on Elizabeth's arm*) I think you should talk about all this in the morning.

Elizabeth (*suddenly all of her anger comes out, directed at Tom*) Who the hell are you?! You little son-of-a-bitch, you don't even belong here. This has nothing to do with you!! Shut up! Shut up! Shut up! (*She starts to sob. No one knows what to do. Pause.*)

Tom I think I'll take a walk.

Paul Tom, she didn't mean –.

Tom I know. I didn't take it personally. But I could use some air.

He goes out. Elizabeth cries.

Alice I'm sorry. We'll discuss everything. The house – that was your father's. It's yours. I have a few things . . . I'll make a list of what they are. (*She sits and pours herself a drink.*)

Sophie goes to Elizabeth and puts her arm around her.

Sophie It's all right.

She pats Elizabeth. Short pause.

Elizabeth I'm sorry about . . . (*She gestures toward where Tom exited.*) But it really is none of his business. What is he doing here anyway? (*She blows her nose.*)

Tom returns, unseen by anyone.

Alice said on our walk that she can't get rid of him. She doesn't know why he stayed. He didn't even know father. You'd think he'd know he didn't belong.

Alice I put him in the study for Christ sake. You'd think he'd have taken the hint.

She laughs, as does Elizabeth. Then slowly they realize Tom is there and heard all this. No one knows what to say. Short pause.

Tom It's – raining. Outside. Just started. (*Beat.*) I think I'll go to bed now. Goodnight. (*He goes.*)

Elizabeth sniffles. Alice takes a sip of her drink.

Alice I'm drunk.

SCENE SEVEN

The kitchen. An hour later.
Gemma sits at the table, staring into space. Elizabeth sits, going through Harry's photo album which Alice had left on the table. From upstairs, we hear Alice screaming; the realisation of what Harry did has hit her and she sounds like a wounded animal.
Gemma and Elizabeth pretend to ignore the screams.
Alfred enters from the hallway, obviously upset. He wears only his underpants.

Alfred (*entering*) Where's Alice's purse? Have you seen –? (*He grabs the purse.*) Is this it? (*He opens it, digs around and pulls out a bottle of prescription pills.*)

Alice screams again.

Elizabeth (*looking through the album*) Can't you do something?

Alfred It's all just hit her. She needs to sleep.

He goes back into the hall with the pills. Alice screams again. Pause.

Elizabeth (*holding the album*) Look at this. I tell you
there are pictures of us I've never even seen before. You
must be no more than six.

Gemma, distracted, nods.

Here's one of Paul. (*Beat.*) I'm thinking of keeping this.
The whole thing.

Gemma Oh God, Liz –!

Elizabeth I want it. She can't know who half the people
are.

Gemma She'll make you copies. It's Alice's! (*She reaches
over the table for the album.*)

Elizabeth (*pushing her off; over this*) She can't appreciate
it like we can!

Gemma (*over this*) It's not yours to take!

They struggle over the album.

Elizabeth (*over this*) Let go! I want to take it!

Gemma (*over this*) Give it to me!!

*Finally Gemma gets the album. Tom has entered to see
the end of this fight. He wears pyjamas now. Elizabeth
and Gemma breathe heavily for a moment.*

Elizabeth (*to Gemma*) I don't understand you.

They notice Tom for the first time. Beat.

Tom (*to Elizabeth*) I'm still here. Sorry. There's no bus
service at two o'clock in the morning.

*He crosses the room and goes off to the sink. Gemma
sighs.*

Gemma What that man must think of us.

Elizabeth Who cares? (*She gets up and leaves.*)

Beat.

Gemma (*after her*) Goodnight, Liz! Goodnight.

Beat. Tom enters, on his way back to the hall. He carries a roll of paper towels.

(*as he passes her*) So – you teach acting.

He stops.

That must be very interesting. I love the theatre. In London I used to go all the time. I remember when I first came to the States –.

Tom Gemma. I'm tired.

Gemma (*over this*) Uncle Alfred had invited me –. I grabbed at the chance. I needed to get away. Perhaps like you needed to get away from New York and come up here –.

Tom (*turning*) Alice invited me for this weekend. I didn't ask to come.

Gemma I'm sure she did, I didn't mean –.

Tom I had to get out of quite a few other commitments. It wasn't easy.

Gemma No.

Tom I had other places I could have gone to. And then when – your father . . . What the hell was I supposed to do?! I would have felt like I was abandoning –.

Gemma (*over this*) You don't have to explain.

Tom (*continuing*) I couldn't even get to the bus station. Alice wasn't going to take me. How could I ask –? I told her I'd only be in the way. With all of you coming –. I asked her to let me leave. You think I'd want to put myself through –?! (*He stops himself.*)

Short pause.

Gemma Thank God you stayed. You've been such a help.

Tom I'm not hurt. I'm fine. You don't have to say anything. (*Beat.*) There's a bus at nine. I found a schedule in your father's desk.

Pause.

Gemma What were we –? The theatre.

Tom Gemma.

Gemma Anyway, I arrived here and I saw a show in New York. And there was this actor, long hair down to –, almost growling, spitting as he talked. I remember thinking, is this acting? The growling, I mean. Then after about a year of living in the States, I began to realize I could not imagine there was anything else. Why do you have all those paper towels?

Tom Alfred got sick in the study. Remember?

Gemma And no one cleaned –?

Tom (*over this*) I don't mind!

Beat.

Gemma What you must think of us.

Tom (*what has been on his mind:*) About the cremation, Gemma. Alice said to me – before any of you got here, when she had no one else to talk to – she said that Harry probably would not have wanted to be cremated. But it was something she believed in, so – she went ahead and did it. (*Beat.*) She asked me if I thought that was OK. (*Beat.*) I don't mean to criticize Alice. But someone should

323

know, I thought. Not that there's anything you can do about it now. I'm only saying, that sometimes Alice can say one thing to you and another thing to me. I wanted you to know that. (*Beat.*) For Christ sake go to bed. (*He turns to leave.*)

Gemma (*desperate*) So where in London do you come from, Tom?

Beat. He stops. From upstairs Alice screams a few times, still like a wounded animal.

Where did you live?

Tom Chiswick.

Gemma That's not too far from –. Do you know Eel Brook Common? In Fulham, off the King's –.

Tom A friend of mine and I used to play tennis there.

Gemma My God, he knows our common!

Tom There's a court –.

Gemma Two! And a playground. It's not a very big common. Not that many people know it, in London.

Tom Why should they!

Beat.

Gemma (*half to herself*) That common is so close to where we lived!

He turns to go.

Tom! Ever since we got here, I've been wanting to tell someone.

He stops to listen.

I've got good news! I've been looking for the chance to . . . (*Beat.*) I'm engaged.

324

He turns back to her. Short pause.

Tom Congratulations –.

Gemma He's American!

Tom Why are you telling me –?

Gemma Like your girlfriend!

  Beat.

Tom I'm sure your family would be very interested in –.

Gemma He's from New Mexico. He's even part Mexican, but his family has been here –. Years and years.

Tom (*over this*) Why do I care about your –?

Alice screams in the distance. This stops them both.

Gemma (*referring to the scream*) What a night. She's realized what she's lost. She's scared. God, let her sleep. (*She turns back to Tom.*) My fiancé. He's big, you think of them as small – the Mexicans, but not him. He's tall. (*Beat.*) Can't read worth a damn though. (*She laughs to herself.*) Can't read at all, I think. He's my gardener. Or works for the man who does my garden. He doesn't know shit about art, music . . . As thick as a brick shithouse, his expression. A big dumb American like you see at the beach. (*Beat.*) I love the way he feels. His body. And he's a nice man. Warm. Open. (*Short pause.*) When I told father – he went crazy. (*She laughs to herself.*) He said – what the hell is wrong with me? (*Beat.*) He said – he'd given me culture. He'd educated me. He'd taught me right from wrong. I don't know what that had to do with –. But it's what he said. Good from evil. Beauty from ugliness. And now – I do this – terrible thing. I told him he wasn't being fair. At least he should meet –. But he just kept screaming at me: 'Where have we gone wrong?' 'Where have we gone wrong?'

(*Beat.*) 'How did we all get to here?' (*Beat.*) I didn't
understand. But I'd never heard him shout like that – not at
me. (*Beat.*) 'The barbarians are sweeping over us and all we
do is kiss their ass.' His words. I don't know what they
mean. (*Beat.*) I tried to get him to calm down. Usually I
could find a way, but this time it was impossible. It just
kept coming out. The anger. At everything. At me . . . I
warned him, Tom – if he did anything to himself, I'd hate
him for ever! (*Short pause.*) This was yesterday – this
conversation. When I called – he was in his study. He'd
been reading he said and – I could hear – listening to music.

Tom Yesterday afternoon?

Short pause.

Gemma At first, when Alice phoned with the news – I
blamed myself. I even thought *I'd* killed him. (*Beat.*) I
know that's unfair to me. I did nothing wrong. I was one
thing maybe – a final straw to someone's . . . problem. It's
taken me until now – to accept that it really had nothing
to do with me.

A single scream from Alice in the distance.

(*to Tom*) Did it?

Tom No. I'm sure it didn't.

Gemma (*suddenly relieved*) I've put myself through so
much today. (*She stands.*) He should have been happy,
dammit! With my news! I tried to tell him, Tom – we
change. You have to. (*She starts to leave.*) Thank you. I'll
try and go to sleep now. Goodnight. (*She goes.*)

Tom Goodnight.

*Short pause. Tom hesitates, then picks up the roll of
paper towels he'd set on the table, and he too heads
into the hall, as Alice screams again.*

SCENE EIGHT

The kitchen. Morning.
  *Alice, Alfred, Gemma, Elizabeth and Sophie are sitting
at the table. The men are in black suits, the women in
black dresses. Two or three are drinking coffee. The table
has been cleared of the papers, etc. and is very neat. In
the centre of the table is an urn – Harry's ashes.*

Sophie (*telling a story*) There's a man – he's American of
course. And he's standing in line to get into Buckingham
Palace.

Alfred For the tour?

Sophie (*nodding*) And he asks the guard. (*American:*)
'When will we see the Queen?' The guard says she's in
Scotland. The man is beside himself, he says, 'The Queen
should be here! When I go to Disneyland Mickey's
there!'

  She laughs loudly, the others smile politely.

My daughter told me that.

Alfred (*to no one*) Speaking of Disneyland, at least we
don't have one stuck in the middle of our country. (*He
laughs.*)

Alice Anyone want more coffee?

  Paul enters, also in a black suit.

Paul (*entering*) He's going to stay.

Alice Thank Heaven!

Alfred (*same time*) I would think –.

Gemma (*same time*) To leave now.

Elizabeth (*same time*) Who did he think was going to take him to the station?

Beat.

Alice And Harry's suit?

Elizabeth (*to Alice*) What about father's –?

Alice (*over this*) He hadn't brought a suit, of course. He was coming for a weekend!

Paul I rolled up the cuffs. He'll be OK. (*He sits.*)

Sophie (*to Paul*) I told them about the Queen and Mickey Mouse. They found it very funny.

Alice Thank God, it's a beautiful day. Did anyone else see the sunrise this morning, or was I the only one up?

Tom enters, wearing one of Harry's black suits which is a few sizes too large. The others look at him.

Tom (*after a moment*) I don't want to look foolish.

No response.

Gemma Sit down and have some coffee. Make room –. Let Tom sit . . .

Tom (*sitting*) I didn't even bring a tie.

Alfred (*to Tom*) I never got to hear all your accents. I hear you do a very funny Midwest. Our Dean's from the Midwest. (*He laughs to himself.*)

Tom I don't think I feel like –.

Alfred I had a student stand up in class once, and say, (*American:*) 'You're nothing. Shut up!' (*He laughs.*)

Tom Paul told me the story –.

Alfred He had a Midwest accent.

Alice We were just saying – it's a beautiful day.

Gemma It's not going to rain.

Tom It rained last night.

Alfred Did it? When we went for our walk –.

Tom Later. I stepped out for a moment. And it was raining. Then I came back in. The guests are due in . . .? (*He looks at his watch.*)

Alice If you see a young woman, blonde, very attractive – Harry's star pupil, the violinist – snub her. (*Short pause.*) I'm terrible with names. Everyone – if I don't introduce you . . .

Pause. Tom notices the urn.

Tom Is that the . . .?

Alice I picked it up this morning. It was waiting for me. Do you want to look inside?

Tom I don't think I need –.

Alice (*to everyone*) The man at the funeral home, not the funeral director, but the little man who sits by the guest book – I think he works there. Anyway, he said to be sure, that when we throw the ashes – to keep our mouths closed.

The others turn away.

It's good advice! (*Beat.*) Obviously there'd been a bad experience . . .

Sophie (*standing and collecting the cups*) If we're not going to have anymore cof–.

Gemma Tom never got –.

Tom (*over this*) I'm fine.

Short pause as Sophie carries the cups to the sink (off).

Elizabeth (*to Gemma*) Did you know that father called her – Fifi?

Alice (*nodding to the urn*) They had a catalogue. I had no idea what Harry'd want. I picked that one out. It's nice, isn't it?

Everyone quickly agrees that the urn is nice.

A couple were quite gaudy. (*She shrugs.*)

Gemma notices Elizabeth looking at something on her lap.

Gemma (*to Elizabeth*) What are you looking at?

Elizabeth (*holding up the photo album*) Has everyone seen these photos –?

Gemma grabs the album and hands it to Alice.

Gemma Maybe you could make a few copies for us.

Alice Just say which ones you want.

Gemma Thank you.

Alice starts to look through the album. Sophie returns from the sink, and goes and stands behind Paul, putting her hands on his shoulders.

Paul (*to everyone*) Excuse me, if we have a minute . . . Sophie and I'd like to clear something up. (*Beat.*) Yesterday – and God it was only yesterday when we arrived, wasn't it? (*He shakes his head in amazement.*) When Sophie and I arrived –. Elizabeth. Well, Sophie felt that you –. When she came up to you to hug you? To console you? She says you turned away from her and ran to hug me.

Elizabeth Oh God! I don't remember –.

330

Paul I didn't exactly see this either, but she says –.

Sophie (*to Elizabeth*) You sort of pushed me away – to get to Paul.

Paul And this hurt Sophie. Correct? But Elizabeth, you didn't mean to hurt her. That too is correct?

Elizabeth No. Of course –. Why would I –?

Paul (*to Sophie*) There. That has been addressed and dealt with.

   Beat.

Elizabeth (*needing to explain*) I saw my brother. I wanted to hug him.

Sophie (*wanting help*) Paul.

Paul My Sophie is your sister-in-law. She wanted to console you. She wanted to be consoled herself. You should have let her do that. She has feelings too. Our father's death – upset her as well. Is that right, Sophie?

Sophie Maybe this isn't the time to bring this up . . .

Paul You asked me –!

Sophie (*interrupting*) But I'm sure your sisters want to know these things.

   Beat.

Alice (*quietly, showing Alfred a photo in the album*) Harry bought me this bathing suit. (*She looks at Alfred, then at everyone else.*) I hope I didn't keep anyone awake last night. Alfred thinks it must have been either the eggrolls or the moo-shoo pork. What do you think?

Paul (*putting his arm around Sophie*) She had just a bite of the moo-shoo and –.

Gemma (*over this*) Elizabeth –.

Elizabeth (*over this*) The eggrolls definitely!

Paul If we were Americans we'd sue!

He laughs, others laugh. Beat.

Alfred None of you probably know this, but last night – Alice and I had the chance to spend some time together.

The others look down.

To talk.

Alice We'd hardly know each other before. We'd only met the –.

Alfred One time. At Paul's wedding.

Alice Paul and Sophie's wedding.

Alfred Alice couldn't make your mother's funeral.

Alice I sent flowers.

Alfred The one time. (*He looks at her.*) I have asked Alice to come to Albuquerque.

Alice To visit!

Gemma (*over this*) That's wonderful! And maybe even stay –.

Alice I don't think –.

Alfred Wait until she sees the colours!

Gemma Uncle Alfred's right – it's the colours, they'll shock you – they're lunar, that's how I describe them. (*Beat.*) Alfred says they're vaginal.

All except Paul and Elizabeth laugh.

Paul (*to himself*) I suppose we see what we want to see.

Beat.

Elizabeth And what will you do about the house?

Gemma Elizabeth, we said we'd talk –.

Alice Close it? Sell it? (*Beat.*) And go West! That's what Americans are always doing, isn't it? At least for a visit. (*Beat.*) I assume you want me to sell it. No one wants to live here . . .?

Beat.

Gemma We'll talk this afternoon – about the things.

Elizabeth Or tomorrow. (*to Paul*) Are you still flying back tomorrow?

Paul We can't stay –.

Sophie (*over this*) Claire –.

Gemma I'm going back tonight.

Elizabeth Tonight! You didn't say –.

Gemma Into New York. I'm seeing friends. I'm hardly ever east anymore.

Paul (*to Gemma*) Tom's on the bus this afternoon –.

Tom Alfred was going to drive me into town –.

Gemma (*to Tom*) I can drive you all the way in if you don't mind waiting until –.

Tom The bus is fine. I have the ticket.

Beat.

Elizabeth (*to Paul*) You're still here tonight.

Paul nods. Beat.

Paul Thanksgiving's in a month. Do we celebrate Thanks–?

Alice Sh-sh!

Everyone is silent. Alice gets up and looks outside.

I thought I heard . . .

Sophie (*to Paul*) Are they late?

Alice, who has been holding a book, opens it. She looks up.

Alice If anyone asks, don't say anything about the college. Or if you do say Harry loved teaching there. Don't say the truth. (*Beat. Looking at the book.*) I thought, this was . . . right. Do you mind? You'll hear it twice.

Everyone: 'No!' 'Of course not!' 'Please.' Alice looks at the urn.

Once, only for the family, Harry.

She reaches and turns the urn so it 'faces' her. She reads (from Keats's 'Ode on Melancholy'):

'But when the melancholy fit shall fall
    Suddenly from heaven like a weeping cloud,
That fosters the droop-headed flowers all,
    And hides the green hills in an April shroud;
Then glut thy sorrow on a morning rose,
    Or on the rainbow of the salt sand-wave,
        Or on the wealth of globed peonies;
Or if thy mistress some rich anger shows,
    Emprison her soft hand and let her rave,
        And feed deep, deep upon her peerless eyes.
She dwells with Beauty – Beauty that must die.'

Pause. She closes the book.

Gemma Father.

Short pause.

Elizabeth Paul? For the family? What did you plan to sing?

Paul hesitates.

Alfred Come on, Paul.

He slowly stands.

Paul I didn't know what to choose.

Gemma (*to Tom*) Have you ever heard him sing?

Tom No, I –?

Gemma Come on, break our hearts. I haven't started to cry yet. You might as well get me going.

Paul I haven't sung in front of people for –.

Elizabeth Why is it we have to apologize for everything?!!

Beat.

Paul OK. 'Those of us who knew my father well' – this is my introduction – 'knew my father well, will always associate this piece – with him. For you – Father. May you now have the peace you sought.' (*Beat. He begins to sing 'The British Grenadiers':*)
   'Some talk of Alexander,
   And some of Hercules,
   Of Hector and Lysander,
   And such great names as these . . .'

With the first line the family bursts out laughing.

Gemma (*over the singing*) Great choice!!

Elizabeth (*over this*) He'd love it!!

Gemma (*to Tom*) Father used to sing this while he shaved! It drove us crazy!

Alice He still does! Did!!

Paul (*continuing*)
'But of all the world's brave heroes,
There's none that can compare,
With a tow, row, row, row, row,
Row, to the British Grenadiers!'

*All except Tom try to sing along, banging the table to
the march beat.*

Everyone
'Whene'er we are commanded
To storm the Palisades,
Our leaders march with fuses,
And we with hand grenades.'

Alice (*to Tom*) Don't you know it?

Tom A little.

Gemma Then sing!

Everyone
'We throw them from the glacis,
About the enemies ears,
With a tow, row, row, row, row,
Row, the –'

Sophie (*shouting out*) French!!!

Everyone 'British Grenadiers!!!'

*The family suddenly sings in a whisper, obviously as
Harry used to do it.*

Everyone (*whispering*)
'And when the siege is over,
We to the town repair,
The townsmen cry –.

The family shout:

336

'Hurrah boys, here comes a Grenadier;
Here comes the –.'

Alice Sh-sh!!!

They stop singing. Beat. Alice goes and looks out.

It's a car. The guests are arriving.

Pause. Alice takes out a cigarette, lights it; takes one puff and puts it out. Everyone is straightening their clothes. Tom tries to straighten his.

Sophie (*to Tom*) You look good.

Elizabeth Paul, you better direct traffic. Tell everyone where to park.

He nods.

Gemma I can take their coats.

Elizabeth Put them upstairs.

Paul I thought it was outside –.

Elizabeth Until everyone comes.

They are on their way out.

Alice Just one thing I meant to tell you.

They stop.

You should know this. (*Beat.*) When people called – I told them, it had just been an accident. That Harry was cleaning his gun.

She heads down the hall. The others look at each other and follow; Gemma tries to straighten out Tom's suit as they go.
The urn is left alone on the table.
Debussy's The Girl with the Flaxen Hair *begins to play.*

337

Off, the sound of greetings, condolences, cars arriving, offers to take coats, car doors closing, directions where to park, etc.

PRINCIPIA SCRIPTORIAE

for Tom Creamer and Gerry Freund

Characters

Bill Howell
Ernesto Pico
Man in prison
Julio Montero
Alberto Fava
Norton Quinn
Hans Einhorn
Soldier

Note:
Each scene has a title that should be projected moments
before the appropriate scene begins, remain in view
throughout the scene, and go out when the scene ends
(e.g., Principium 1: Choose your setting carefully).

The Setting:
Latin America

The Time:
1970 and 1985

Principia Scriptoriae was first performed on 25 March 1986 at The Manhattan Theatre Club (Lynne Meadow, Artistic Director), with the following cast:

Bill Howell Anthony Heald
Ernesto Pico Joe Urla
Man in prison Ernesto Gonzalez
Julio Montero Shawn Elliot
Alberto Fava George Morfogen
Norton Quinn Steven Gilborn
Hans Einhorn Mike Nussbaum
Soldier Ernesto Gonzalez

Directed by Lynne Meadow
Set designed by John Lee Beatty
Costumes designed by William Ivey Long
Lighting designed by Jennifer Tipton
Sound designed by Scott Lehrer
Production stage manager Don Walters

Principia Scriptoriae was subsequently presented by The Royal Shakespeare Company in the Barbican Pit, London, on 1 October 1986 with the following cast:

Bill Howell Anton Lesser
Ernesto Pico Sean Baker
Man in prison Arturo Venegas
Julio Montero Clive Merrison
Alberto Fava Clive Russell
Norton Quinn Oliver Ford Davies
Hans Einhorn David de Keyser
Soldier Steven Elliott

Directed by David Jones
Set designed by Bob Crowley
Costumes designed by Fotini Dimou
Lighting designed by Paul Armstrong
Sound designed by Andrew Ludlam
Stage management by Tana Russell, Eric Lumsden, Susan Dale

SCENE ONE

Projection: PRINCIPIUM I: CHOOSE YOUR SETTING CAREFULLY.

1970. Latin America. A poorly lit room without windows. Door barely visible upstage. A bench to one side. Bill Howell and Ernesto Pico, both in their early 20s, sit on rusted and bent lawn chairs, and talk.
  Pause.

Bill Maybe a million. Depends on who is doing the counting. You understand that, don't you? That it does very much depend upon who is doing the counting.

Ernesto I understand.

Bill So a million people. At least. All coming down Pennsylvania Avenue. What that must look like to Johnson. Think about that. You have to think about that. What Johnson must have thought. Or whoever it was they had holding down the fort, so to speak. (*He chuckles to himself.*) I'd have gotten my tail out of there fast if I was one of them. (*Short pause.*) Over a million people, Ernesto, think of that.

Ernesto Yeh. (*Short pause.*) That's something. That is really something.

Bill The whole god damn government is crumbling. That's what it felt like while we were marching. Like the buildings themselves were toppling. I'm not joking. All the statues. The columns. The private Cabinet dining rooms. (*He laughs.*) The Senate handball courts. (*He laughs. Stops. Short pause.*)

345

Ernesto laughs.

Ernesto Yeh. (*Short pause.*) So where were you? In the middle, I'll bet.

Bill Yeh. (*Short pause.*) In the middle.

Ernesto Right! Hell. (*He slaps Bill on the leg. Pause.*)

Bill Ernesto, things are changing so fast and I do not mean little bitty changes either. I swear to you, in what, something like ten, give it fifteen years – it might only be five, who the hell really knows for sure – but the way things are done in the States is hardly going to be recognizable to us today. To people today. It is all going to be so – completely different. You'll have all these – different people running the place for one. That's one big thing. God can some of them talk, Ernesto. You should have heard them speak at the Mall. (*Short pause.*) You couldn't really hear them at the Mall. But God could they talk.

Ernesto I'll bet. (*Short pause.*) Of course they've got a lot to talk about.

Bill The United States of America is going to be one very strange place in a few years. Given just a few more years, it is going to be one great place all right. All this is only the beginning. It is when you get people cooperating, sharing is really the word. We are sharing now. We are finally doing that. Some of us are. So once this has been firmly established, which it really is now, then we can finally quit all that 'competition' stuff. I mean, what the hell are we competing for? We're all on the same planet, right? (*Short pause; he shakes his head.*) Not only do you have to think it, Ernesto, you must also live it. (*Pause.*) You understand that, right?

Ernesto I think so.

Bill Good. (*Short pause.*) And this is precisely why I

said – I mean, here I am a writer, right – but here I said, sure, I'll be the one to sell the T-shirts. Just tell me what the hell to do and I'll do it. (*Short pause.*) So I did.

Ernesto Huh.

Short pause.

Bill Yeh. I sold the T-shirts. Someone had to. Ernesto, you have to keep remembering that there is nothing you are too good for. That is what sharing means. That is what it means today. (*Short pause.*) You talk revolution then you have to mean revolution and that goes for even revolting inside yourself. This is really the clue for the whole thing. You can't ever stop asking yourself questions. That is how you find out who you are and also who you are not. It is not all just the outside world, it is the inside world of your brain too. But you know what I mean.

Ernesto Huh.

Bill Ernesto, you get all of that into your head and the rest just falls into place.

Pause.

Ernesto When did you sell T-shirts?

Bill When? In the march, Ernesto. The march on Washington. The Mall. What do you think I've been talking about?

Ernesto You sold T-shirts on the Mall?

Bill Yeh.

Ernesto I thought you were in the middle of the march.

Bill Yeh. In the middle selling T-shirts. (*Short pause.*) Ernesto, someone had to sell them. That's how we paid for the bus. I paid for the bus. (*Short pause.*) For part of

347

it. That's how I was in the middle of things. I didn't just march, I also sold T-shirts. The actual march was a lot more than just marching. You can understand that, can't you? That a march is more than marching? That is everything I have been talking about.

Ernesto I understand, Bill.

Bill I would think you would.

Ernesto I was confused for a second, but I understand now.

Bill I was being very clear, I thought.

Ernesto Huh.

Pause.

Bill If you've got a problem understanding, believe me, I can appreciate that. The one thing I do not want to do is come on too strong. Trust me about that, Ernesto. There is nothing wrong with not completely understanding. It has taken me years and years to figure that out. So just don't worry about it. (*Short pause.*) After all, I know you people have not exactly worked things out for yourselves yet. And that I can appreciate. That's not a problem for me. If anything, I am only amazed at how slow you all are at getting things going for yourselves. But that, I do not mean critically.

Ernesto Give us time, Bill.

Bill I'd give you all the time in the world, if I could.

Ernesto Well time is all we need. We do after all have a different rhythm down here. From the States, I mean.

Bill I appreciate that. (*Short pause.*) It wouldn't hurt though for you people to see the sort of thing I have been describing. I am only saying maybe you could find something in it to learn.

Ernesto Bill . . .

Bill And that is not a criticism. Who still can't learn something? I can still learn something. That's all I'm saying. I'm talking about sharing, Ernesto; I am not being critical. (*Pause.*) Maybe it's just learning how to sell T-shirts.

He looks at Ernesto. They both laugh. Pause.

Bill How long do you think they'll make us wait in here?

Ernesto shrugs.

Ernesto Can't be too long. My father's a lawyer.

Bill A lawyer? Huh. (*Short pause.*) If I hadn't been a writer, I'd have been a lawyer. For unions.

Ernesto Good for you.

Bill Must be fairly difficult being a lawyer in a country like this. The things you'd have to accept – people being picked up right off the streets and everybody just seems to accept –

Ernesto People are not accepting it, Bill.

Bill That's not how it looks, Ernesto. Believe me.

Ernesto I can't help how it looks.

Pause.

Bill I'll bet if it weren't for me being American, they'd be beating the shit out of us right now. That is what is standing in the way. Not your father being a lawyer.

Ernesto Bill, I don't think you know what you're . . .

Bill Because I am an American, they can't. They wouldn't dare. I'm right, aren't I? It makes you sick. What a place to have to call home. (*Beat.*) Sorry. I know I've only been down here a week, but still, it must be very hard to call a place like this home.

349

Ernesto I don't.

Bill Don't what?

Ernesto Call this place home.

Bill Why not?

Ernesto Because, dammit Bill, I don't! That's why. (*Short pause.*) It may be my home, but I don't have to call it that. Why do you think I went to school in England? If anything made me not call this home, it's my going to school in England. You wouldn't believe how ignorant people are here.

Pause.

Bill People can be ignorant in England too, Ernesto. (*Short pause.*) At least they could when I was over there with a group from my college.

Ernesto I know that, but that's not what I'm saying. I am saying I don't call this home and people are unbelievably, relentlessly ignorant here. I am saying two different things. (*Short pause.*) And I came back – because of both things. I had to find out about me first. Then I came back. I know who I am now. I didn't before, now I do.

Bill You know who you are now?

Ernesto I think so. Yes.

Bill Terrific. It's great to know who you are. You're lucky.

Ernesto Yes. I think I am actually.

Bill I'm still looking for myself. That's why I went away for a while, you know. Why I'm here in fact.

Ernesto I thought you came down to help us. You had read about us.

Bill I did. Yes, I did. But I also came to look for myself.
You can do them both, Ernesto. At least you can now.
(*Short pause.*) First I thought I'd just go to Cuba. And
that is where I'd be if I hadn't come down here. It turned
out being a lot cheaper coming down here. (*Short pause.*)
I came standby.

Ernesto You got standby from Kennedy?

Bill It was not problem. You should remember that.

Ernesto Yeh. I should.

Bill Still. I almost went to Cuba. I would have had to
have gotten a flight from Paris. And it just didn't seem to
be the time for Paris, you know what I mean? A couple of
years ago, well sure; but I don't think there is much there
now – for me at least; not after what I've been doing at
home. Even Sartre's pretty much out of the picture these
days. (*Short pause.*) He's going blind, you know.

Ernesto Yeh. Like Joyce. Like Borges. It's almost a trend.

Bill I guess. Yeh. (*Short pause.*) Still it can't be at all like
it must have been with Camus around. (*Short pause.*)
Or – in the thirties. If I had been a self-exile in the thirties,
they would have had to have tied me down to keep me
away from Paris. (*Short pause.*) Or was it the twenties?
(*Short pause.*) Anyway, you could not have kept me away
from Paris. But today? Paris is going in the wrong
direction today, Ernesto, if you want to know my
opinion. Even Stockholm's got to be more interesting than
Paris today, what with all the draft dodgers. I'm told the
Swedes just roll out the red carpet for the draft dodgers –
because it's not what they think of when they think of
Americans, which basically means they don't have bombs
and napalm coming out of their ears, which is how they
should see some of us; how I would see some of us, that is
except for the rest of us; anyway that's why I think the

Swedes like them so much. Especially the black draft dodgers. Also there's all that free health care. (*Short pause.*) They know what they're doing in Sweden. Damn. (*Short pause.*) Well, I could have gone there, but it isn't cheap at all. Not like this. Anyway Paris is not where it's happening. And as for Cuba, I couldn't afford it in the end. It was that simple. Cuba is not cheap.

Ernesto You're not the first person to tell me that.

Bill For some reason you would think it would be, right? But it's not. Sort of like San Francisco. Wouldn't you think San Francisco would be pretty damn cheap? Guess again. Of course, you can always live anywhere cheaply – if you're into that – but if not then it is a very expensive city as interesting American cities go. Denver, for one, is a lot cheaper. For some reason I'd have thought it would be the other way around – because of the mountains, I guess. But still, if you can afford San Francisco, it is worth every penny.

Ernesto It is?

Bill Every centimo, believe me. And for writers like us, Christ, I mean you've got Berkeley, you've got City Lights Books . . .

Ernesto City Lights Books?

Bill Don't tell me you don't know City Lights? Ernesto, you call yourself a writer and you don't know City Lights? Now they are really into poetry. And even more important they are into poets. They're into writing per se. They are incredible. They were thinking of publishing my novel; it turns out they can't of course, but they were really thinking about it. Said they'd put it in the window of the bookshop – they've got a bookshop that's mostly what they are, a bookshop, and it has a very big window, so they'd put it in when I did get it published. I was really pleased with that.

Ernesto You should be. I would be.

Bill I was floating, Ernesto.

Ernesto I'm not surprised.

Bill You wouldn't believe the writers that go into that bookshop. There are writers all the time in that bookshop. It's intimidating, really.

Ernesto It would be. For me too. So it's San Francisco then, that's the place to go.

Bill In my book it is, Ernesto.

Ernesto In your novel you mean? It's set in San Francisco?

Bill No, that's just an expression. 'In my book' means, well, it means – yes.

Ernesto Ah.

   Pause.

Bill My novel's set in St Louis. That's not a place you want to go. (*Pause.*) I've been looking for a place to set my next book. Maybe down here. I'd say almost definitely down here, except it might be hard not knowing the language.

Ernesto You must know some Spanish though.

Bill No. None. I know French. (*Beat.*) I know some French.

Ernesto But the leaflets we were handing out when . . . Bill, they were in Spanish.

Bill Yeh. So?

Ernesto You were handing out leaflets and you didn't know what they said?

Bill I knew what they said. You don't have to know the language to know what they said – generally. (*Short pause.*) Oh come on. Did you read them?

Ernesto I wrote them.

Bill Well there you have it. So what's the problem?

Short pause.

Ernesto But Bill . . .

Bill (*standing up*) What's the big fucking deal? (*He moves away.*) I thought you wrote poetry. (*Pause.*) Look, we'll be out of here soon. I'm American, right?

Pause. After a moment Bill goes upstage, unzips his pants, and pees against the wall.

(*while peeing*) I did this once on the White House gate.

SCENE TWO

Projection: PRINCIPIUM 2: ALWAYS LIKE YOUR CHARACTERS.

The same. Bill and Ernesto have metal plates full of food on their laps. Throughout the scene they eat. As the scene begins, they are chuckling.

Ernesto Isn't that a character?

Bill Still, every Englishman is a bit of a character.

Ernesto (*giggling*) Even for an Englishman, Bill. (*He laughs. Pause.*) I love it when you come across people like that. This man would have forgotten to eat. He was that bad. Really. I swear to you, if it hadn't been for his wife, he'd have been – there would be nothing there. You could not make up such a character. (*Beat.*) If it hadn't been for

his wife. (*Beat.*) If it hadn't been for her. (*He laughs.*)
Sweet man, really. Brilliant. His book on Milton.
Standard now, I think. (*Short pause.*) I wrote a poem
about him. (*Beat.*) Part of it was about him. (*Short
pause.*) And you've never been to Cambridge?

Bill I told you, I've been to Oxford. (*Short pause; he
takes a bite of food.*) I went punting there. Just outside
Oxford.

Ernesto Just outside?

Bill I went through Oxford to get just outside.

  Short pause.

Ernesto Two different places, Cambridge and Oxford.

  They eat.

Bill So he never found out about you and his wife?

Ernesto (*shaking his head*) I told you his head was – (*He
gestures 'out there'.*) He was quite a good tutor though.
(*Pause.*) So was his wife. (*Laughs. Long pause.*) You
know – it's not at all like everyone says it is.

  Beat.

Bill (*eating*) Prison?

Ernesto Cambridge, Bill. English universities in general,
actually. (*Short pause.*) Oxbridge, I mean. (*Short pause.*)
They're not all homosexual.

Bill Who said they were?

Ernesto Everyone did – before I left. Everyone who
talked to my mother did. You wouldn't believe the bizarre
conversations my mother and I had before I left. It is not
often that a son gets such a clear picture of just how his
mother's mind works. There is a good reason for that.

There is a humane reason for that. (*Short pause.*) Here is this nice upper-middle-class lady – and what does she start to do: take her only son around to brothels.

Bill You're kidding.

Ernesto Mind you, the better brothels, but still.

Bill That is pretty amazing.

Ernesto I'm not saying she went in. God forbid. She just took me around.

Bill I'm glad she didn't go in.

Ernesto No. She stayed outside. She just hung around outside. And paid. (*He laughs.*) This is true. There can be some really strange shit down here. People can be really fucked up down here.

Bill People can be fucked up anywhere. Take St Louis.

Ernesto Uh-huh. (*Beat.*) She'd pay and stay outside. But first they'd have to haggle though. I'm standing there and they are haggling over the price. My mother and the prostitute. (*Short pause.*) That sort of does something to one's sense of pride. (*Short pause.*) And none of it would have happened if the priest hadn't told her about English universities. The ideas people get into their heads.

Bill Right. Once they latch on to something, it doesn't matter what the truth is. How obvious the truth is.

Ernesto Especially when you're talking about a place they've never been. Like Cambridge. Or Oxford.

Bill I know a lot of people like that. (*Beat.*) Almost everybody where I grew up is like that.

   Beat.

Ernesto That's not to say that some shit doesn't happen

at English universities. Of course it does, but hell no one is pushing anyone around, they've still got English manners after all. Now there's something you don't find here.

Bill No. You only find English manners in England, I'm afraid.

Ernesto Yeh. I think you're right. I am sure you are right. It's a shame too. Still, it turned out that there were prostitutes even in Cambridge. So I wrote my mother that and she raised my allowance. (*He laughs. Pause.*)

Bill I gave up taking an allowance when I went off to school. I thought that was part of the point of going off to school. (*Short pause.*) Of course I didn't go halfway around the world.

Ernesto Right.

Bill And it doesn't take all that much to live in Ann Arbor. I had my dorm room. My meals. But I certainly didn't have money for prostitutes – even if I'd have wanted one. Which of course I didn't.

Ernesto Of course.

Bill No offence.

Ernesto Please. From what I understand about American universities there is no need for prostitutes.

Bill True. (*He smiles.*) This is very true.

He laughs. Ernesto laughs.

Ernesto I sometimes wish I had gone to an American university instead.

They eat. Pause.

Bill And what about your father, Ernesto?

Ernesto About the brothels? He went by himself. He didn't go with my mother. I don't think he went with my mother.

Bill I mean, what did he think of what your mother was doing?

Ernesto Why should he think anything? (*Beat.*) Maybe he didn't even know. I don't know. And what the hell, it was none of his business anyway, this was one of those special mother–son things, you know.

Bill Huh. (*Short pause.*) Odd, isn't it?

Ernesto Not really. Not for here.

Bill No, and that is what's odd – that we have such different backgrounds, Ernesto.

Ernesto That shouldn't surprise you.

Bill Mine is so – I don't know – forgettable, I guess. At least that's what I figure I have to do – forget it – if I really want to be, become, what I know I want to become. But yours is so –.

Ernesto Mine is so what?

Bill Literary almost. You know what I mean.

Ernesto No, I don't think I do. How is my mother taking me to brothels literary? Seems to me that is the exact opposite of literary. That is what I would call not literary.

Bill But Ernesto, Come on, it sounds like it came right out of a book – out of a Spanish novel say. Your mother taking you to brothels is so, it's picaresque really. Surely you see that.

Ernesto Picaresque?

Bill Yeh.

Ernesto It's not picaresque, it's true. It happened.

Bill Of course it happened. And that is just my point. Ernesto, no offence intended, but as a writer you seem to have it so god damn easy that's all.

Ernesto I have what easy?

Bill You seem to have stories – like this one with your mother and the brothels – that must just write themselves. That just need to be written down. And that's why I envy you.

Ernesto You envy me?

Bill If you had come from St. Louis you'd know exactly what I was saying and why, believe me.

Ernesto But what about all that's happening now in the States? That seems to be a pretty good story to me.

Bill It is. Of course it is. But for a journalist more than for someone like me. You understand the difference? What is happening in the States may be a little bit literary but basically it is journalistic. I think that is clear to everybody, Ernesto. So look, I'm not expecting you to agree, I just want you to understand what I am saying – that it seems to me that it has got to be a lot easier for you to write, that's all. That is all I want to say.

Ernesto That it is a lot easier for me to write?

Bill Yes. (*Beat.*) Look, you've got a character like your mother and you're telling me it's not easier?

Ernesto She's my mother, she's not a character.

Bill Don't tell me you haven't thought about writing about her.

Ernesto I don't want to write about my mother.

Bill No?

Ernesto No.

Pause.

Bill Then I'll write about her. Tell me some more about her.

Ernesto I don't want you writing about my mother. You never even met my mother.

Bill I know she took you to brothels. That's a pretty good start, I can build off of that.

Ernesto Damn it, I told you she is not a character!!

Bill I'll treat her sympathetically. I always try to like my characters.

Ernesto She is not your character! (*He moves away.*)

Bill Sorry. (*Beat.*) Sorry.

Ernesto What are you doing down here anyway?

Long pause.

Bill What were we talking about? Cambridge. Right. Cambridge.

Short pause. Ernesto comes back, sits and continues to eat.

Ernesto It's not the homosexuals who are everywhere in Cambridge.

Bill No?

Ernesto It's the politicians. The sons of the politicians. They send their sons from all over the world to be politicians. Shahs' sons. African tribal leaders' sons. (*Short pause.*) They do nothing. They know nothing. It's all just to say they went to Cambridge. No wonder they think of us the way they do. The Europeans, I mean. (*Beat.*) Can't blame them, really. (*Short pause.*) You know

I couldn't even talk to the African Negro kids. No one could. Couldn't speak English. What the hell were they doing taking up space some smart English kid could have used? Couple of Indian kids I could talk to. That was it. The ones from down here – one of Somoza's kids was there – acted like they were retarded. The worst accents I have ever heard. Makes you embarrassed to say where you come from, really. (*Beat.*) Those accents like fingernails over a blackboard. (*Pause.*)

Bill And what about you?

Ernesto What about me?

Bill How did you end up there?

Ernesto I earned the right to be there. (*Short pause.*) I earned the right. (*Pause.*) You would have thought I was English the way I fit in there. (*Short pause.*) I wasn't like the others who came there. I had a lot of English friends. You don't know what that means to people down here. You don't understand shit about us here – so just shut up.

Bill Sorry.

Ernesto Don't apologize. (*Beat.*) Just shut up.

  Pause. They eat.

Fucking Americans. Don't even bother to learn the language. Don't know shit.

Bill I heard that.

Ernesto Right.

  Pause.

Bill This food sucks. If I weren't so hungry, I wouldn't go near it.

Ernesto What did you expect – fried jumping beans?

Short pause.

Bill No. I thought maybe Yorkshire pudding.

They look at each other. Pause. They eat.

Before I walk out of here, I'd love to have a good look around. Wonder who else they've got locked up. Could do a nice piece about this place. I'm not above writing journalism. There's a whole tradition of novelists writing journalism. (*Beat.*) People should know what is going on here. I mean, at home they should.

Ernesto Why?

He eats. Pause.

SCENE THREE

Projection: PRINCIPIUM 3: REMEMBER IT IS 99% PERSPIRATION.

The same. An older man now sits on a bench to one side. He holds his head in his hands; he is barefoot.

As lights come up, Bill is walking away from the man and toward Ernesto, who sits in one of the chairs. Their clothes are now stained with sweat, their shirts unbuttoned.

Bill He doesn't speak English. You talk to him. (*He takes his handkerchief out and wipes his face and neck.*) You talk to him. (*Beat.*) Ask him who he is.

Ernesto doesn't move.

Maybe he knows something. Maybe he knows why the fuck we're still in here. (*Beat.*) Shit, it's close in here. But I guess this kind of heat doesn't bother you people.

362

Ernesto It bothers us people.

Pause.

Bill It is one thing to detain you for a while. They do this in the States, too. They're not supposed to but they got ways to do this too. But when they start throwing you in with other . . .

Ernesto (*getting up*) Bill, give me your handkerchief.

Bill What do you want with my . . .?

Ernesto nods toward the man.

It's filthy.

Ernesto You're using it.

Bill It's my filth.

Bill reluctantly hands him the handkerchief; Ernesto goes to the man.

Ask him what he is in for. That's what I want to know. I've just heard that sometimes they put murderers in with people like us – just to scare us.

Ernesto Where did you hear that?

Bill I heard it. I heard it.

Ernesto (*to man, handing him the handkerchief*) Tome esto. Haber si le ayuda. [Here. This will help.]

Man Si. Gracias. [Yes. Thank you.]

Ernesto ¿Sabé usted, le dijeron porque . . .? [Did they tell you why . . .]

Man No, no se nada. No me dijeron nada. Estaba caminando mi perro cuando me . . . [No. I don't know anything. They told me nothing. I was walking my dog when they . . .]

He turns away, holding his head. Pause. Ernesto returns to Bill.

Bill Well?

Ernesto He was just out walking his dog.

Bill He was arrested for walking his dog? Right. Right.

Ernesto I didn't say that. I don't think he meant that.

Bill You think just because we give him a handkerchief he's not going to try and pull something. Don't be so naive, Ernesto.

Ernesto looks at him.

How fucking naive. I don't know how you survived this long in the world, Ernesto. (*He laughs.*)

Ernesto I gave him the handkerchief, Bill, because he was bleeding.

Bill I know that. (*Short pause.*) But I'm talking about in the bigger sense – you also gave him the handkerchief so he wouldn't do anything to us. I know he was bleeding. (*He laughs to himself again.*) People aren't the way you like them to be, Ernesto. If he's going to do something, he is going to do something. Handkerchief or no handkerchief. Period. You can't change that.

Ernesto Why are you so sure he's dangerous?

Bill He's in jail, isn't he?

Ernesto We're in jail, are we dangerous?

Pause.

Bill Ernesto, when we were handing out the leaflets and that man came up to you. He said what again?

Ernesto I told you.

Ernesto gets up, Bill follows him.

Bill Tell me again. Maybe we missed something.

Ernesto What's there to miss, he said to be sure to pick up any leaflets that might be dropped.

Bill Which we did. Dammit, we did that!

Ernesto Bill . . .

Bill We fucking did that!

Ernesto Bill, they didn't put us in here for littering.

Bill I know that. (*Beat.*) Of course I know that. What do you think I am? I was just thinking out loud. Can't I think out loud?

Ernesto Think out loud.

Pause.

Bill You think I'm panicking, don't you? I'm not, Ernesto. I am nowhere near to panicking.

Ernesto Good.

Bill You don't believe me, do you? Come on. How can I convince you? Tell me how I can convince you.

Ernesto Look, you already have.

Bill I have?

Ernesto Yes, Bill.

Bill Good. (*Short pause.*) How did I convince you?

Ernesto Bill!!!

Bill All I'm asking is . . .

Man ¿Qué tiempo hace que están aquí? [How long have you been here?]

Bill and Ernesto stop. Short pause.

¿Hace cuanto tiempo que están aqui?

Ernesto Horas. Como cinco. Bueno, ahora no estamos seguros. [Hours. Maybe five. We're not really sure any more.]

Bill (*in a half-whisper*) What did he say? (*Beat.*) What did he say, Ernesto?

Ernesto (*ignoring Bill, going to the man*) ¿Y usted? [And you?]

Man ¿Semanas? ¿Qué mes es éste? [Weeks? What month is it?]

Ernesto Marzo. [March.]

Man Meses entonces. [Months then.]

Bill Ernesto!

Man ¿Les entendí bien que ustedes estaban distribuyendo panfletos? [Did I understand right that you were passing out leaflets?]

Ernesto (*nodding; then*) ¿Entiende ingles, entonces? [Then you understand English?]

Man Algo. Un poco. ¿Panfletos izquierdistas? [Some. A little. Leftist leaflets?]

Ernesto El Frente Unido. Estaba yo en Inglaterra, sabe usted. Aun asi, realment no esperaba . . .
[The United Front. I've been in England. Still I didn't really expect . . .]

Man ¿Usted esperaba Speakers' Corner? [You expected Speakers' Corner?]

Ernesto laughs.

Bill What's funny? What is so god damn funny?

Ernesto I told him I'd been in England, so I wasn't prepared for this and he said what had I expected, Speakers' Corner.

Ernesto laughs again. Bill doesn't.

Bill Oh.

Ernesto No habiamos estado en la calle tanto tiempo, no, como menos de una hora. A lo maximo una hora. Ademas, no fueron panfletos radicales exactamente. Seguro que conoce usted la clase de material. [We hadn't been on the street that long. Less than hour. At most an hour. They weren't exactly radical leaflets. I'm sure you know the kind of stuff.]

Man Yo vengo escribiendo esa clase de material por años [I've been writing that kind of stuff for years.]

Ernesto ¿No me diga? ¿Es escritor? [Really? You're a writer?]

Bill What? What? What did he say that's so interesting?

Man Yo escribo para *El Mundo*. ¿Ya les ha hablado alguien? [I write for *El Mundo*. Has anyone talked to you yet?]

Ernesto No. No.

Bill Did he say *El Mundo*? Isn't that a newspaper?

Man Ya veo [I see.]

Bill Ernesto, that's a newspaper, right?

Ernesto A lo mejor conoce usted a mi padre. El ha escrito un poco para los periódicos también. Ferdinand Pico. [Maybe you know my father, he's done some journalism as well. Ferdinand Pico.]

Man nods.

¿Le conoce? [You know him?]

Man nods.

Bill What does he have to do with *El Mundo*?

Ernesto He's a journalist. He knows my father.

Man Prefiero hablar de otra cosa. [I'd rather talk about something else.]

Ernesto ¿Por qué no quiere hablar de mi padre? [Why don't you want to talk about my father?] (*to Bill*) He doesn't want to talk about my father.

Bill So he's a journalist. Big fucking deal. (*He goes to pull Ernesto's arm.*) Come on. You've talked to him enough.

Ernesto Why won't he talk about my father?

Man stands and moves away.

Bill (*pulling on Ernesto*) Look, the cop, you sure you understood the cop, Ernesto.

Ernesto What cop?

Bill The cop who picked us up for Christ sake.

Ernesto I don't know if he was a cop, Bill.

Man ¿El cree que el hombre que les arrestó era uno de los puercos de la policía? [He thinks the man who picked you up had to be a cop?] (*He laughs.*)

Bill What did he say? (*to the man*) Shut up. (*to Ernesto*) You told me he was a cop.

Ernesto I never did, Bill. I said he acted like a cop. Maybe he was one, maybe he wasn't.

Bill Oh. (*Beat.*) Oh. They can't do any shit to us. (*Short* *pause.*) I won't take any shit. You said he knows your father. Ask him where the hell your father is.

Ernesto ¿Qué sabe usted de mi padre? [What do you know about my father?]

The man spits. Ernesto is taken aback.

Bill What can they do, Ernesto? It's not like they found drugs on us or something. This is one country I wouldn't like to be in when they found drugs on me.

Man Ellos pueden decir que les encontraron drogas encima. [They can say they found drugs on you.]

Bill turns to the man.

Ernesto He says – they can say they found drugs on us.

Bill But I didn't have any drugs. I don't travel with drugs.

Man ¿Y qué? [So?]

Bill So they can't prove I did. He knows English?

Ernesto A little he said.

Bill Oh. (*Beat.*) You were with me.

Man ¿El? ¿Quién le prestaría atención a éste? [Him? Who would listen to him?]

Ernesto (*translating*) Me? Who would listen to me?

Man Quizás sea un asesino. Quizás un abusador de niños. [Maybe he's a murderer. Maybe a child molester.]

Ernesto Maybe I'm a murderer. Maybe I'm a child molester.

Man ¿Quién sabe lo que ha hecho? [Who knows what he's done?]

Ernesto Who knows what I've done?

369

Man ¿Después de todo, está en la prisión, no? [After all, he's in prison, isn't he?]

Ernesto After all, I'm in prison, aren't I?

Short pause.

Bill Right. (*Beat.*) Right.

SCENE FOUR

Projection: PRINCIPIUM 4: WRITE OUT OF EXPERIENCE.

The same. Ernesto and Bill on the floor, trying to sleep.
Pause.
From off we hear a round of automatic gunfire. Pause.

Bill He'll be back. They'll bring him back. He's a journalist, right? (*Beat.*) He said he was a journalist, right? They're not about to . . . (*Beat.*) . . . to a journalist, Ernesto.

Pause.

Ernesto They fake shooting you. To frighten you. I read that somewhere.

Bill Right. So that's what they're doing. I get it. (*Pause.*) I cannot believe this is happening to me. I can't believe I am experiencing this.

Bill gets up and goes to a small faucet in the wall, with a bucket under it. He turns the faucet on and sticks his head under the water. Ernesto watches, then stands up.

Ernesto Good idea.

Bill Sticky in here. I think it's night out, don't you?

Ernesto Yes. I do. (*He puts his head under the faucet.*) It feels like night. (*Beat.*) I can't sleep. Can't you?

Bill (*lying down again*) It takes me a while. Even – in college, it would usually take me a while.

Ernesto sits in one of the lawn chairs. Pause.

Ernesto (*pointing to the other chair*) Bill, mind if I . . .?

Bill What? (*He looks up at Ernesto pointing.*) Mind if you what?

Ernesto The chair.

Bill (*turning over*) What are you asking me for?

Ernesto It's your chair.

Bill Do whatever you want.

Ernesto takes the other chair, sets it in front of him and uses it as a footrest.

(*quietly*) It's not my chair.

Pause.

Ernesto My father does some journalism too. I don't mean 'too' like – (*He points to the door.*) I wasn't talking about him. I mean – as well as being a lawyer. He does both. Though he tries to keep those two careers separate. When he can. (*Short pause.*) When he can. You'll meet him.

Bill Yeh. I guess I will.

Ernesto rubs his face. Pause. Bill rolls over and watches Ernesto.

What that guy said about your father, it hasn't – you're not upset, are you?

Ernesto No, of course not.

Bill Good. (*He rolls over.*)

Ernesto If it weren't for my father – I'd have never been a writer. You didn't know that, did you? You couldn't know that. (*Pause.*) Bill . . .?

Bill (*still turned away*) I'm listening.

Ernesto You know it really takes that kind of immediate encouragement – like I got from my father – to do anything here, something different here. It is almost impossible to fight your own family's wishes here. Oh you can try. My father tried. But it is hard here, Bill.

Bill (*turning and sitting up*) Ernesto . . .

Ernesto He didn't upset me! (*He stands and walks to one side.*) My father would never have anything to do with the government. I know this. He has told me this. He wants nothing to do with it. He says – because he doesn't want to end up retiring to Miami. (*He laughs.*)

Bill smiles.

My grandmother wanted him to go into the government. She said, that's where the money is made. I don't think she's ever forgiven him, really. She still pressures him I think. (*He lifts his shirt and dries his face. Pause. He uses his shirt to fan his face.*) He wanted to go to Europe to university. His family had the money. We know they had the money. It wasn't the money. It cost a lot and they weren't rich but they could have gotten up the money. That's what Father always said. So he didn't go to Europe. Not for twenty years. (*Beat.*) Twenty years later I meet him at Heathrow. I think that's why he sent me to school in England, so I could meet him at Heathrow. (*Beat.*) In fact, from the time I was . . . there was never even a question. I was going. Not from anyone. Not from my sisters. (*Beat.*) My father screamed with joy when he saw me at Heathrow. (*Beat. He is fighting back tears.*) We fed the ducks. I knew he'd want to do something like that.

Something English like that. (*trying to laugh*) When he
first got off the plane, he looked to me like a bus
conductor. But he was my father. (*Beat.*) A good man.
Who'd have shit to do with the government. Shit! (*Beat.*)
That's how he raised me.

Pause.

Bill Obviously the guy just didn't know what he was
talking about.

Ernesto Obviously.

Long pause.

Bill Look, even if he did meet . . .

Ernesto He didn't!!!!! (*He stands and moves to one side.*)
He couldn't.

Bill Right. I know that. (*Beat. Quietly.*) But even if he
did, what is so wrong about being seen meeting Manuel
Rosa? Rosa's a pretty well-known poet after all.

Ernesto He's the government's ambassador to Franco.
(*Beat.*) My father would know what anyone would think
if they saw him meeting with Rosa. Poet or not, he's this
government's ambassador to Spain. It's clear to anyone
what meeting with him means.

Pause.

Bill Then, the guy's wrong. It's that simple.

Slowly Ernesto goes back and sits in the chair. Pause.

Ernesto Read much of Rosa?

Bill Maybe a couple of things in an anthology.

Ernesto He doesn't translate well. If you knew his love
poems especially, there's little else like them in Spanish.
(*Short pause.*) Incredible how you'd never guess Rosa's

thinking from his poetry. He doesn't put any of that right-wing shit into his poetry. (*Short pause.*) You're right, Bill – the guy's simply wrong about my father. (*Long pause.*) Tell me about yours. Your father.

Bill Ernesto. . .

Ernesto Please. I'd like to know.

Bill (*sitting up again*) He – teaches chemistry in a college. I grew up on a college campus. He doesn't read much. At least he doesn't read what I read. He reads a lot of journals. (*Pause.*) They must be very upset. My parents. My father becomes pathetic when there is nothing he can do. There is nothing he can do.

> *Suddenly another round of automatic fire. Pause. Ernesto begins to sob. Bill gets up and pats him on the shoulder. Ernesto hugs him. They hug. Finally Bill pulls away.*

Hey, watch that hugging stuff. Remember. I know what kind of school you went to.

> *Ernesto smiles. Bill smiles.*

SCENE FIVE

Projection: PRINCIPIUM 5: LET YOUR IMAGINATION GO.

The same. Ernesto sits in one of the chairs. Bill stands behind him.

Ernesto A trial?

Bill It's the only thing that makes sense. It's why they're keeping us. What other reason, Ernesto, could they have for keeping us? This happens in the States too.

Ernesto I don't know.

374

Bill I'm sure of it. I'd bet on it. They're going to have to let us talk to your father.

Ernesto Leave my father out of this.

Pause. Ernesto stands and moves away. Bill looks at him, then shrugs.

Bill What the hell, we'll get Kunstler then. (*He laughs.*)

Ernesto Get who?

Bill Never mind. The most important thing to keep in mind is how are we going to turn this into – like one of those happenings. That should be the idea. You know what I'm talking about right? (*Beat.*) Oh come on, you know about those. They had them in Greenwich Village, about ten years ago.

Ernesto Oh. (*Beat.*) Oh, right.

Bill People like Cage and Rauschenberg. A lot of people like that. A lot of people who are somebody today, Ernesto. It's really amazing when you think of it.

Ernesto Amazing how many became somebody?

Bill Yeh.

Ernesto I guess they must have found something together, something they could use later – as individuals.

Bill I'm sure.

Ernesto That's what I've wanted, you know. To find such a group – of individuals. It's what I think I need, really.

Bill Who doesn't? Who wouldn't like that? And who says it can't happen here? This could be the start of that sort of thing, actually. Except with a big difference; with this we have to get political, those happenings, they really weren't. They happened too early to get political. But in style they can be the same.

Ernesto I understand.

Bill There's also the stuff from the Chicago trial to learn from. Actually, historically, I do think that was when the happening moved into the political, moved ahead, so to speak, beyond just 'art', you know with . . . (*He makes the gesture of quotation marks.*) And into the realm of politics, politics without . . . (*He makes the gesture of quotation marks.*) You know what I mean. Historically, Chicago is the turning point. Actually all this only proves what a teacher of mine was saying that in fact they are one and the same thing – art and politics, that is. As one develops into one, the other develops into the other. (*Beat.*) Something like that. I only took one semester from him. Anyway, each one has the other inside itself, that much I do remember.

Ernesto What Chicago trial?

Bill The Chicago trial. With the pictures, you know, of the black guy gagged. The judge gagged the black guy. Which reminds me, one thing we have to hope to get, we have to do anything to get, is pictures.

Ernesto Pictures of what?

Bill I am starting to see all the possibilities, Ernesto. As long as we keep Chicago in mind, we will be doing just fine. Look, if they want to ask us their fascist questions, hell, let them, who says we have to answer? Who says we can't say any damn thing we want to?

Ernesto I'm lost, Bill.

Bill Just keep listening and it will all start coming together for you, I promise. Just listen. We are going to turn the whole god damn courtroom into the zoo it really

is, Ernesto. It's going to be real theatre, that's what it has
to be – and that's where the happening stuff comes in.
Understand now? (*Beat.*) Look. They won't know what to
do, right? They never do. They didn't in Chicago. Hence –
the black guy gets gagged. One of us could get gagged,
Ernesto, that would be a trip. Let's not throw out any real
possibility here. If they are like – and I'm sure they are –
like they are everywhere else in the world, then the judge,
we can make him look like a complete fool, Ernesto. This
will be our job. (*He laughs to himself.*) We just have to
keep interrupting him with: Oink! Oink! Oink!

Ernesto Oink?

Bill Yeh. Oink. You know for . . .

Ernesto I know. I know.

Bill So maybe we will be gagged. Maybe I will be. I don't
know Spanish anyway so what's to lose, right? Now in
Chicago, they also had people like Ginsberg. They were
there from the beginning. Like camp followers. That
really helped matters. They talked to the media and
things. It's got to be a zoo outside of the trial too. Anyone
like him down here?

Ernesto Ginsberg?

Bill Yeh.

Ernesto Any poet here like Ginsberg?

Bill He doesn't have to be a poet. But yeh. Like him.
(*Beat.*) Sort of like him. Anything like him.

Ernesto No. (*Beat.*) No.

Bill Oh, Well, somebody right will come along. There's
always somebody. Maybe even a somebody we don't even
know. Something like this is enough to make somebody's
name. Whatever, all we have to do is keep – (*He begins to*

pound the chair on the floor.) Oink! Oink! Fascists! Pigs!
Oink! Oi . . .

> *From the hall, we hear someone screaming as he is
> being brought by. The screaming gets louder as it passes
> the door, then fades in the distance. Pause.*

Ernesto Come on – oink! Oink! Oink!

Bill and Ernesto Oink! Oink! Oink!

> *As they yell, they begin to laugh.*

SCENE SIX

Projection: PRINCIPIUM 6: KNOW YOUR READER.

*The same. The light in the room is off though light now
floods through the open door. The scene then is basically
in silhouette.*

> *Ernesto sits on the floor, against the wall. He holds his
> arm. Bill sits on the bench, his pants down. He rubs his
> thigh. Their clothes ripped, their faces bruised. In the
> silence we are able to hear, from down the hallway, a
> radio playing Spanish love songs sung by a woman. Bill
> coughs; blood comes up out of his mouth, in almost a
> chunk. He begins to wipe it away.*

Bill (*in obvious pain*) There's so much to write about,
isn't there? (*Beat.*) Think about that. And that in and of
itself is enough to keep you going. (*Pause.*) A minute ago I
was thinking about Spenser. God knows why. I haven't
thought about Spenser in – a very long time. I think I
really would like to reread *The Faerie Queene*. I'd like to
read it once when there wasn't a reason to read it. I mean,
now that I'm not in school. It is an odd thing I'll bet to
read when you are not in school. How's the shoulder?

Ernesto I'm sure they didn't set it right. I told them that. I can feel that they didn't set it right. (*Short pause.*) The bone is pressing through. I don't think the bones are even touching.

Pause.

Bill Fuck them.

Ernesto stands and goes to Bill.

Ernesto Get on your back. Let me see.

Bill does. Ernesto looks him over.

Shit. Stay there. (*He goes to the faucet, turns on the water, wets a part of his shirt which he has taken off. As he is filling the bucket:*) If you are looking for something to read . . .

Bill Who said I was looking for something to read? I've got a million things to read. (*Beat.*) What do you suggest I should read?

Ernesto Lorca. (*He begins to rub the cloth over Bill, cleaning his wounds.*) There's a feeling Lorca has – in his love poems. I'm talking basically about his love poems. They are things unto themselves. About nothing – but themselves.

Bill Huh? Are they sort of like Manuel Rosa's?

Ernesto stops rubbing and looks at him.

Like you said about Manuel Rosa's love poems?

Ernesto No. (*He begins to rub again.*) They are nothing like his. Does this burn?

Bill Yes.

Ernesto And this?

Bill Yes.

Beat.

Ernesto What Lorca has, what I wouldn't give to get that into my poems.

Bill How is he in translation?

Ernesto I don't know. I don't know. (*Beat.*) I'm thinking of taking your advice and writing about my family.

Bill Don't listen to me.

Ernesto It'll end up being about me, of course. When I really write it.

Bill That's happened to me too.

Ernesto There's school. (*Beat.*) There's growing up. (*Beat.*) There's my first sex.

Bill With the prostitute?

Ernesto Who said my first sex was with the prostitute? (*Beat.*) Right. With the pros . . .

Bill suddenly coughs up more blood. Ernesto looks at him, then turns away, fighting back tears. Bill begins to clean himself off.

Bill (*while cleaning the blood*)
'Whan the Aprill with his shoures soote
The droghte of March hath perced to the roote,
And bathed every veyne in swich licour . . .'

Ernesto (*without looking at Bill*)
'Of which vertu engendred is the flour.'
(*Pause.*) So you know Old English too.

Bill Middle English.

Ernesto Right. That's what I meant. Middle English.

He takes the rag from Bill and begins to wipe the back of Bill's neck.

Bill *The Seafarer*'s Old English. (*Beat.*) I also took Old English. Middle English and Old English.

Ernesto Really? I never quite went that far. Greek. (*Pause.*) A little Greek. (*Pause.*)

Bill I even translated from the Old English.

Ernesto Like Pound.

Bill Right. (*Beat.*) I was really into Pound then. (*Beat.*) Hard man to figure out, Pound.

Ernesto (*going to the faucet to rinse out the rag*) How he could let the Fascists use him, you mean?

Bill Yeh. (*Beat.*) Doesn't make any sense to me. From the poetry. (*Beat.*) From the great poetry.

Ernesto I know. (*He comes back and continues to clean Bill.*) Take out the anti-Semitism and it's really great poetry. How hard is it to breathe?

Bill (*He breathes and shrugs.*) Not hard.

Ernesto Does this hurt?

Bill No.

Ernesto nods and sighs.

What does that mean? That it doesn't hurt?

Ernesto I don't know.

Beat. They both laugh, though with pain.

Old English?

Bill nods.

Wow.

Bill reaches and takes out his wallet and takes a piece of paper out.

Ernesto Let me.

Bill I can do it. Sit down.

Ernesto What's that?

Bill (*taking the rag from Ernesto and beginning to wipe the blood off himself, he reads:*)
  'So on myself I may utter fragments
  of song, rehearse bits of my history,
  how in labored days, hard ships hours
  I so often suffered, the bitter heart's sorrow
  had long lived through . . .'

Ernesto Yours?

Bill My translation.

Ernesto That's what I meant. There've been so many translations.

Bill When you take Old English you find there's not much there to translate but *The Seafarer*.

Ernesto I never thought about that. See, with Greek –

Bill Greek's a whole different story.

Ernesto With Greek you could spend your whole life translating from the Greek.

Bill People have.

Ernesto I suppose so.

Bill I could think of worse ways of spending your life.

Ernesto Me too. (*Beat.*) Me too.

  Pause.

Bill I keep a copy in my wallet. They never took my wallet. Throughout all that they never took it.

Ernesto They took mine. First thing.

Bill Soon they'll take mine.

Ernesto Yeh.

Bill Next time they call us in. They'll take it then.

Ernesto has sat on the bench, and looks over Bill's shoulder.

Can you read it in this light?

Ernesto nods. Bill reads:

' . . . how upon ships
I so ventured to homes of sorrow;
the terrible rollings of waves there kept me,
a close night-watch at ship's prow
which neared close against cliffs.

Beat.

I heard nothing but the sea's chord,
cold waves. Once the song of the whooper swan
gamed for me. The gannet's hoarse cry
and curlew's caw replaced a man's laugh,
seagull sang in place of mead.'

Bill and Ernesto
'Storms beat the staid-cliffs; the tern
shrieks back through iced feathers;
very often the eagle screams about;
no kinsman can comfort a desolate man.'

Long pause.

Ernesto Wow. (*Beat.*) 'No kinsman can comfort a desolate man.' Sort of jumps out at you at the end. Sort of

383

shocks you. It's beautiful. (*Short pause.*) What's a gannet?

Bill (*putting the paper back*) Some kind of bird. I forget what kind. (*Beat.*) I've never seen one. (*Beat.*) I had to look it up in the encyclopaedia. (*Short pause.*) I've seen a whooper swan though. (*He taps his wallet.*) Next time, they'll take it. (*He puts it in his pocket. Pause.*) I passed out. (*Short pause.*) Did you pass out?

Ernesto doesn't move.

I wanted to pass out. (*Pause.*) When they did that to my cock, that's when I wanted to pass out. I passed out later. After they did this to my cock. (*Beat.*) Fuck them.

Ernesto starts to cry. Bill immediately stands up and now tries to keep Ernesto from thinking about what has happened.

Ernesto, do you ever have days when all you want to do is sit surrounded by your books?

Ernesto Bill . . .

Bill To have all of my books around me, to be hugging them almost, to be hugging them really, I have days when that's all I want in the world. I've never told anyone this before. (*Beat.*) I have some beautiful old books. I think I've been to every used book store in the Midwest. (*Beat.*) The Upper Midwest. (*Beat.*) It's something I do.

Ernesto (*sobbing now*) Bill . . .

Bill (*loud so as not to hear Ernesto's crying*) Ernesto, that gannet's got me thinking. If one could just describe what a bird say, does – think of that – the way it flies. In words. Who wouldn't be pleased with doing that? Having accomplished something like that. (*He turns to Ernesto.*) Am I right?

Ernesto nods.

What do you think, maybe I'll write something about a gannet. What do you think one looks like?

Ernesto smiles and nods; he stands and goes to Bill.

And what are you going to write about? (*He is trying to keep from crying now.*) What are you going to write about?!! (*Pause.*)

Ernesto Cry if you want. I don't care if you cry.

Bill (*screaming*) What are you going to write about?!!!!!

Ernesto I don't know. My family. Me. I'll write about growing up.

Bill What?

Ernesto (*louder*) I said I'll write about growing up.

Bill Good. (*Beat.*) Good. (*Pause.*) Who doesn't like reading about somebody growing up?

Pause. Intermission.

SCENE SEVEN

Projection: PRINCIPIUM 7: IT SHOULD ALSO BE ENTERTAINING.

A men's bathroom. Stall to one side. Fan overhead. The same Latin American country, 15 years later.
   Julio Montero, mid-40s and well-dressed, stands at the sink, looking into the mirror. Alberto Fava, also well-dressed, sits on a stool to one side. He is a middle-aged Italian. Ernesto leans against the door. They are all smoking.
   Pause.

Julio (*without looking at Alberto*) Did you see those

385

pictures of his baby? (*Beat.*) Looks like a pig. His son looks like a pig. (*Beat.*) The son looks like the father.

Alberto He looks like a baby.

Julio Not like babies we have here. Made me sick looking at that kid. (*Beat.*) Same feeling I get looking across the table at him. (*Beat.*) Hans Einhorn has hurt me, Alberto.

Alberto So you keep saying.

Short pause.

Julio I am deeply hurt. I had not anticipated this fact that I was to be hurt, Alberto.

Alberto Enthusiasm, Julio. Nothing is meant by honest enthusiasm. (*Beat.*) If you had let us sleep first. We haven't slept. We should not have met formally until tomorrow. I did suggest that. (*Beat.*) I am suggesting it again.

Julio No.

Alberto (*putting out his cigarette*) Hans did say you'd want us tired out.

Julio See what I'm saying? He doesn't stop. God damn Nazi. And you repeat it.

Short pause.

Alberto Hans may be many things, Julio, but a Nazi he is not. You've read him.

Julio I haven't read him. (*Beat.*) I know what Einhorn writes without having to read him.

Alberto You two were just talking about his last novel.

Julio I can talk about things I have not read. (*Beat.*) I'm human. (*Short pause.*) Where does he get this holier-than-thou attitude? In the end, it's this which gets under the skin. And don't say it is honest enthusiasm. This is how this man thinks. It has not been easy to sit and take what he has been saying.

Alberto Such as? (*Beat.*) For example?

Julio I have no examples. I have my feelings. Hans Einhorn has greatly upset me. You don't upset me. The American writer doesn't upset me. Even though he is a Republican he doesn't upset me.

Alberto I hardly imagine that Quinn is a Republican.

Julio He is, Alberto. He may not even know it himself, but he is. (*Beat.*) Watch him. I've been watching him. You watch him.

  Beat.

Alberto Watch him do what?

Julio Act like an American Republican. (*Pause.*) You're not going to ask me how an American Republican acts? (*Pause.*) They act in funny ways, especially when they are negotiating, which they are doing right now with our people. Very funny ways, Alberto. You mention say – socialist economic policy; or – revolutionary freedom force, or –

Alberto Julio . . .

Julio . . . and they begin to stare at the end of their pens, they stare and twirl their pens. They are biding their time, you see, thinking all this is just bullshit we have to get flushed out . . .

Alberto Shut up!

  Pause.

Julio Those are the Republicans. (*Beat.*) But I like Quinn.

He's not the one who upsets me.

Alberto How long are you going to stay in the bathroom?

Julio It is my fucking bathroom. (*Beat.*) It is the People's fucking bathroom.

They smile at each other; Julio turns back to the mirror.

Look at the grey, Alberto. Soon I shall look as old as you.

He glances at Alberto and smiles. Alberto just looks at him.

And dye my hair too. You do dye your hair, don't you, Alberto?

Alberto Are we going back into the meeting?

Julio Tell me something, Alberto . . .

Alberto I don't dye my hair!

Julio Not that. Not that. (*Beat.*) Are you sure? (*Beat.*) I wasn't going to ask that. Tell me, why you, Alberto? Why a man like you? I have so much admired you. And not just the writing – yours I have read, Alberto – but what you have done. Where you have placed your influence. As one leftist to – (*He gestures to Alberto, then turns away and looks back into the mirror.*) And I find you now involved with this right-wing American group.

Alberto I would not call The Writers Committee for Human Rights a right-wing organization, Julio.

Julio No? (*He laughs.*)

Alberto And its offices are in London, not America.

Julio London, New York, you are splitting hairs now, Alberto. (*He laughs and looks back into the mirror.*) Five hours' sleep. That is all one needs. Too much sleep and you get wrinkles. Did you know that?

Alberto Julio, if we are so god damn right wing, why are we here? Why are we wasting our time?

Julio I don't know. I don't know.

Alberto You asked us, Julio! You invited us!!

Julio Not to argue. (*Beat.*) Not to be hurt. I invited what I thought was a few friends – fellow writers – to see my country. To show it off; there are many interesting aspects of my country to write about. The literacy rate, for instance, in the last three years . . .

Alberto We received the literature – at our hotel. Thank you.

Julio This Writers Committee for Human Rights has been slandering us. We needed to do something.

Alberto So do it! That's all we're asking for. (*Beat.*) Then sit down and explain why you can't. If there's a rational explanation for keeping Manuel Rosa in prison, then . . . (*Beat.*) There's not a man on the committee who hasn't supported what's been happening here.

Julio laughs to himself.

What has been said today cannot come as any surprise to you. We assume that by asking us . . .

Julio Yes. (*Pause.*) Yes. It is only the harsh tone with which one has been confronted. This was not expected. Nor is this appreciated. From such sympathetic friends. (*Beat.*) Keep the fucking self-righteousness out of this. You aren't in Western Europe.

Pause.

Alberto I understand. I'll talk to Hans. He just wants to get this over with, is all. You can't blame him for that. It seems so simple. Just let the guy out of prison. I mean what is the big deal? (*Beat.*) I'll talk to Hans, get him to tone down his arguments a little. (*Beat.*) But in his defence, he is the vice-chairman of the committee, he has the responsibility, and the real understanding; Quinn and I, we're really just here for the . . .

Julio (*suddenly turning*) Hans Einhorn doesn't understand shit about my country. And he doesn't give a damn about human rights.

Alberto That's not terribly fair, Julio.

Julio He's a careerist. Don't fool yourself. You only kid yourself thinking this man cares about shit. The biggest careerist writer I know. Everyone knows about him.

Alberto That's not true. It's not, and you know it.

Julio (*to Ernesto*) Aren't I right?

Ernesto I tried to say a simple pleasantry to Mr Einhorn in the hall, but he looked at me like I didn't exist. I assume because I'm no one important.

Julio Because he's no one important. You see what the people are saying?

Alberto Maybe Hans didn't hear him. Maybe he was preoccupied. We all get preoccupied.

Julio A revolution like ours can mean nothing to him. This is obvious.

Alberto This man has a reputation; he is admired; he personally has supported countless Czech exiles in Vienna; he acts from his heart and he has a big heart; Hans Einhorn is a passionate man.

Julio Hans is passionate, yes, about Hans. Look at the characters he writes. Egomaniacs.

Alberto I thought you hadn't read . . .

Julio Don't you think we know that in Europe now it's not just the work that the critics are looking at, you've got to have the correct posturing to go along with it. Einhorn is posturing, he's been posturing, and he's been getting the reviews. But I am not blaming him for this, I am just saying don't get holier-than-thou with me. I do not see why I have to sit in that room and take the shit as this fat-ass Nazi lectures me on human rights. (*Beat.*) If he wants to talk genocide, I'll listen; that I'm sure he knows something about.

Alberto Julio . . .!

Julio And that's why I'm not going back in there until he's gone, Alberto.

 Beat.

Alberto Are you crazy? (*Beat.*) Julio, you know that's not possible. You have to know that.

Julio I don't see why that's such a big concession to make.

 Pause.

Alberto Concession? (*Beat.*) I thought we were supposed to be airing our views. When did it become a negotiation? (*Beat.*) What's to negotiate? (*Pause.*) What's your secretary's name again?

Ernesto Ernesto Pico.

Alberto Ernesto, go and tell Mr Einhorn we will be a little while longer. (*Beat.*) And ask Mr Quinn to please join us in here.

 Ernesto moves to go.

Julio I have nothing to say to Quinn.

Ernesto stops. Pause.

Get Quinn.

Ernesto goes.

Why not? But I think I have made my terms very clear.
(*He begins to wash his face in the sink.*)

Alberto Now they are 'terms'.

Julio Why can't the German just go back to the Hilton?
What's the big deal?

Alberto I thought you didn't call it the Hilton any more.

Julio Oh right. That's true. We don't. (*He dries his face.*)
How old's his wife anyway – to have a baby?

Alberto She's his second wife.

Julio So he dumped the first. Figures.

Alberto I don't know. Maybe she died. (*Beat.*) She could
have died, Julio.

*Norton Quinn, a middle-aged American, and Ernesto
enter.*

Quinn Hans isn't too happy about being left alone.
(*Beat.*) What is it?

Alberto Julio refuses to meet any more as long as Hans is
present.

Quinn Right.

Beat.

Alberto He's upset.

Quinn Right. (*Beat.*) Sorry, but we came as a group. (*He
turns to go.*)

Julio What's more important to you – your group or

what you came here to discuss?

Quinn I don't like that question.

Alberto Even if we asked him, I don't think he'd just go back to the hotel.

Quinn No. And I don't see us asking him.

Julio Ernesto, call for the car to take the gentlemen away. (*Beat.*) They will be needing assistance in arranging flights back home as well.

   Long pause. No one moves. Suddenly Quinn laughs.

Quinn (*to Alberto*) We have the same publisher in New York. Do you know how many translators he's gone through? He's famous for this bullying shit.

Alberto Listen to him, Norton. Just listen to him. (*Beat.*) Maybe he has a point. If all we're worried about is Hans's pride . . .

Quinn First it'll be Hans. Then one of us. What's the point Alberto?

Alberto The point, I seem to recall – is the life of Manuel Rosa. We haven't, I hope, forgotten this.

Julio (*laughing to himself*) If this were only about Manuel Rosa.

Quinn Wait a minute, what do you mean by that? I did not understand that.

   Pause.

Julio Ask Alberto.

Quinn He probably couldn't help Rosa even if he wanted to.

   Julio laughs. Ernesto laughs.

He hasn't shown us shit that he can do.

They laugh.

I think I've had all the talk I can take for one day.

Julio There won't be any tomorrow.

Pause.

Quinn He's bluffing. He needs us here.

Julio laughs really hard.

If he wants to come back to the table, I'll be at the table; with Hans. (*He goes to the door.*)

Julio Ernesto.

Ernesto goes to the door.

Alberto Norton.

They stop.

We owe Rosa's family at least the rest of the afternoon. (*Beat.*) I feel somehow we can work through this problem. (*Beat.*) I think it is at least worth a discussion.

Long pause.

Quinn (*moving to the stall*) Excuse me, I've got to pee. (*He goes into the stall. After a moment we hear him peeing.*) So discuss. Discuss. I'm listening.

SCENE EIGHT

Projection: PRINCIPIUM 8: STUDY THE CLASSICS.

The meeting room. Table. Chairs. Overhead fan. Hans Einhorn, an older heavyset man, sits at the table, his hands under his chin. Bill Howell sits to one side, looking at some photographs.
Pause.

Hans I know how he works. He wants me out. (*Beat.*)
The games we end up playing, Bill. It's so tiring. To a man
like Julio – everything is politics. The game of politics.
Even a man's life – as in this case, with Manuel Rosa.
How do you argue with that? They suck you in. That's
what they're after. To suck you in. (*Beat.*) I've been
sucked in. (*Beat.*) Think of the energy we waste. I've dealt
with him before. (*Pause.*) The world could be simpler, Bill.
Hand me the water pitcher.

> *Bill pushes the pitcher toward Hans, who has taken out
> a small flask and is making himself a drink.*

Bill (*with the photos*) Beautiful child. You said – sixteen
months?

Hans In the pictures. Eighteen months now.

> *Bill continues to look at the photos. How's your room
> at the Hilton?*

Bill I'm not at the Hilton. I'm staying with Ernesto and
his family.

> *Hans looks at him.*

Mr Montero's secretary. (*Beat.*) We're old friends. Though
it's been years since we saw each . . .

Hans Right. (*Beat.*) My room sucks. (*Beat.*) There comes
a stage in one's life – especially if one is successful,
whatever that means . . . (*He laughs to himself and sips.*)
When certain seemingly trivial things can all but unsettle
one. One's whole day can be affected.

> *Short pause.*

Bill I can talk to Ernesto; maybe he can do something
about your room. I think he made the arrangements.

Hans I wouldn't bother. (*Beat.*) I'm already in my third.

(*Beat.*) They're all the same. (*Beat.*) When you reach my age, Bill – and you will, believe me you will – you too may wish to pamper yourself a little. Even in a country like this. Especially in a country like this. (*He laughs to himself.*) And if you can't, you end up asking yourself what the hell has one worked all these years for? (*Pause.*) I'm shocking you.

Bill No. No, you're not.

Hans I know what you're thinking – how can Hans Einhorn talk about his life's work as if it were all written just so he could live a little more comfortably? (*Beat.*) Don't be shocked, Bill. (*He laughs to himself.*) There's a lot to say for shocking people. I shock people all the time. I feel it's part of a writer's job. (*Beat.*) To shock.

> *Hans takes out the flask and pours another drink.*
> *Pause. Bill finishes looking at the photos and puts them*
> *in front of Hans.*

Bill Thank you. Very handsome child.

Hans (*drinking*) I write for him now. (*He taps the photos.*) Everybody should have one. Even when you're old you should have one. A child keeps you young. Keeps you thinking, Bill. We need youth. We couldn't live without it. (*Pause.*) But you, Bill – or is it William?

Bill Bill's fine.

Hans You, Bill, are still young. (*He laughs to himself.*) And successful. Congratulations.

Bill Not really, Mr Einhorn. Nothing like –.

Hans To be asked by the Writers Committee, Bill. Very nice. Very good.

Bill Actually it was Mr Quinn who asked me along.

Unofficially. I thought everyone knew that. Everyone was supposed to be told that.

Pause. Hans nods and looks away.

Mr Quinn had read some of my pieces.

Pause. Hans nods while looking away. He puts the photos back in his pocket.

You must be very proud.

Hans turns to him.

About your son, I mean.

Hans My wife is. (*He laughs to himself at this private joke. He looks to Bill.*) I enjoyed your book, Bill.

Bill Which book, Mr Einhorn?

Hans Which book? (*Beat.*) You are supposed to say 'Thank you.' Or 'How nice.' I don't know which book. I don't know any book, Bill, I thought you were old enough to understand that. I thought you were old enough to have this conversation with me. (*Pause.*) Grow up, son.

Ernesto enters with a coffee tray.

Ernesto Comrade Julio thought we might enjoy a little coffee. (*He sets down the tray.*)

Hans He thinks I'm getting drunk.

Pause. Ernesto pours coffee.

Bill Ernesto . . .

Ernesto Cream, Bill?

They look at each other.

Bill Thank you. Thank you very much, Ernesto.

397

Hans The first time I came up against him was in Vienna. There was a conference. When isn't there a conference? (*He laughs to himself.*) Yes. Yes. (*Beat.*) Julio had nothing then. He wasn't Minister of Culture. He hadn't even a country to be Minister of Culture of. Nothing. (*He nods towards Ernesto.*) Like him, Bill. No older than him. And Julio stands up – and he starts making demands. This is true. He wants this person made president of the conference, that person treasurer. We all just look at each other. Heinrich Böll is sitting almost next to me – and there is a man with a social conscience; if anyone's got one it is this man. It was this man. And Böll is saying – who is this boy with his demands? What are we: writers or terrorists? What are we: writers or revolutionaries? We are going to have to decide! So Julio says he wouldn't talk until Böll has left the room. (*Pause.*) You see he does this all the time. He has his tactics. (*Beat.*) You learn to expect it. I know what they're talking about in there. (*Beat.*) Böll didn't leave. (*Beat.*) He asked our fellow writers if they wanted him to leave. Writers have to put their foot down sometime. If we don't, who will? (*He pours himself another drink.*) Who will?

Hans drinks. Alberto, Quinn, and Julio enter.

Bathroom break over so soon?

Pause. They all sit down.

Well?

Alberto Let's get back to our discussion, can we? I think I will have some of that coffee, if you don't mind, Bill.

Bill passes the coffee.

Hans Back to our discussions? (*He laughs.*) Very good. Very good. How nice to see our host come to his senses. Don't think I don't know what's been going on.

Alberto Hans . . .

Hans (*to Julio*) You have come to your senses, haven't you? (*He laughs; to Alberto and Quinn:*) I want to thank you both. Thank you. I appreciate the support. Now if we can, getting back to the case of Mr Manuel Rosa . . .

Alberto Hans . . .

Hans I'll call on you in a moment, Alberto. I have a few thoughts of my own which I wish to convey to Mr . . .

Alberto Hans.

Hans looks at him.

Norton is going to chair the meeting for the rest of the day.

Pause. Hans, realizing the compromise made in the bathroom, looks first at Alberto, then to Quinn. He stands and moves away.

Hans Fuck you.

Alberto I'm sorry. Norton.

Hans Fuck you!!!

Julio (*pointing to Hans*) May I just say to Mr Einhorn that I had nothing to . . .

Quinn No! I'm running this meeting now.

Alberto Wait. You had nothing to do with what?

Julio With Norton being made chair of the meeting.

Quinn Alberto . . .

Alberto That's outrageous. How can you say that?

Julio It was your idea. Not mine.

Alberto You wanted him out!

Hans (*to Bill*) What did I tell you?

Julio I only want the record to show that it was Alberto Fava who connived to have Quinn take over the chair. That is only the truth, is it not?

Ernesto (*writing*) I'm writing that down.

Julio I had nothing to do with your humiliation, Hans.

Alberto It was not meant as a humiliation.

Julio But that's how he's taken it. Haven't you?

Hans Perhaps you'd really like me to leave.

Quinn No!!!

Beat.

Julio (*under his breath*) Ask me.

Quinn Shut up. (*Pause.*) Sit down, Hans. Sit down, Hans!

Hans sits down.

Julio Yes. And show us the pictures of your baby again.

Quinn Alberto . . .

Alberto Norton, please. Please!

Beat.

Quinn OK. I believe I was still speaking just before we took our break.

Hans You were still speaking as Julio walked out of the room, yes.

Beat.

Quinn (*looking at his notes*) Uh-huh. (*He looks up.*) Julio, what I personally cannot quite understand is why are you doing this to yourself. I'm talking about Rosa now. It doesn't make any sense to me – political sense – to imprison a man like Manuel Rosa. He can't do any real harm on the outside. For one he's too old and second who's going to listen to him? (*Beat.*) His credibility is questionable after all. In fact, it is only this imprisonment that gives him any credibility at all. So you see, it seems to me that the only real damage he can cause you is by staying in prison. You understand what I am saying?

Julio Rosa is a criminal.

Quinn Maybe. That is not the point of my question.

Julio It is the point of his imprisonment though.

Quinn What I mean is – his books, Julio, they happen to be very well thought of.

Julio I don't understand what that means to this.

Quinn The books are considered good. He's good. (*Beat.*) A good poet, I mean.

Julio And if he were a bad poet, then he would deserve prison? (*He turns to Ernesto.*) What is this, some sort of justice by literary criticism?

Ernesto smiles.

Hans (*to Alberto*) He shouldn't be trying to reason with him.

Alberto Hans . . .

Hans Why don't you just come out and ask him what he wants in exchange for releasing Rosa. Why waste our . . .

Quinn Hans, shut up! (*Beat.*) I didn't call on you.

Hans You didn't call on . . .

Alberto (*yelling*) He said he didn't call on you!!! (*He raises a finger to be called on.*)

Quinn Alberto.

Hans You two a club now?

Alberto Julio, stand back for a moment if you can and try to see how it looks. It may not be how it really is – but appearances can as well have the power of truth; as any of us well knows. I mean – take the fact that we are here. Why would Norton, Hans and myself come here?

Julio I'm sure you have your reasons. I told you in the bathroom what I thought Hans's reasons were.

Hans Which are?

Julio You need the posturing to keep getting the reviews.

Alberto Hans, ignore him. (*Beat.*) We are here because Rosa is a writer. People, many, many people, Julio, have come to be quite sensitive about countries which arrest their writers. It is seen as a sign. A symbol meaning more than it may in fact be meant to mean. (*Beat.*) And people take that symbol and they use it to define for themselves their feelings, their impressions about the whole country. Call this unfair – and no doubt it is in some cases, just as it is very fair in many others – but fair or unfair aside this is just what happens. (*Beat.*) Let's say right now for the sake of argument that Manuel Rosa is a real criminal.

Julio Of course he is. And not just for the sake of . . .

Alberto Julio, sometimes necessity demands us to release one criminal so that a whole country will not be accused of the wrong crimes. There are people prone to use Rosa not because they wish to help him, but because through him they can disparage your country and all your country has been able to achieve in its short life; all your country represents. (*Beat.*) It is not our wish to see this happen. (*Beat.*) Norton was telling us that a magazine in the States

– it's a new magazine, literary and aesthetic, but very conservative in outlook, and naturally quite political in a very subtle way – this magazine is planning on starting a new award. A literary award. The whole point of this award is so they can give it to Rosa. (*Beat.*) You see specifically how he will be used. You see just how your revolution will be victimized. Julio, what is the point? Say he served his full sentence. Say he's ill. Everyone will believe that such an old man is ill.

Pause.

Quinn (*quietly*) Let him out – if you can – Julio. And if you can't . . . (*He shrugs.*)

Long pause. Julio stands, moves away.

Julio (*nodding*) Ernesto . . .

Ernesto I don't know what you are all talking about. Manuel Rosa is not in prison. We have no prisons in our country.

Alberto (*banging the table*) Julio!!!!!

Ernesto (*after a beat*) But if – and I repeat if – the Minster of Justice can be convinced to let Manuel Rosa leave our country, he is going to want to know what will we receive in return?

Bill Ernesto?

Quinn (*to Bill*) Sh-sh.

Hans Didn't I say we just should have asked?

Quinn We'd hoped we could convince you on humanitarian grounds.

Julio What humanitarian grounds? I haven't heard any humanitarian grounds.

Pause.

Quinn (*finally*) There is nothing we have to give – that I can think of.

Ernesto (*opening a folder*) There is a young man – one of ours – presently in prison in Honduras. An excellent poet. Comrade Julio as president of our Writers Union and as Minster of Culture has repeatedly asked for this man's release. Perhaps if you could . . .

Quinn Of course. Of course. That is what we are about. Look, we are interested in hearing about any cases. If you don't tell us, then we can't help. What's the name.

Ernesto (*after a beat*) José Dorio.

Quinn (*writing it down*) José Dorio. We'll wire London in the morning. I'm sure they'll come up with something they can do.

Hans José Dorio?

Ernesto nods.

Hasn't the Committee been informed about him already?

Julio Yes.

Quinn There must have been some . . .

Hans I seem to recall that no proof could be found that this Dorio had ever written a line of poetry in his life. The Hondurans, I believe, even went so far as to claim he was illiterate.

Ernesto He is illiterate. (*Beat.*) That is true. (*Beat.*) But since we want him released, we call him a poet. (*Pause.*) If your organization would support us in this claim . . .

Quinn I don't think . . . Julio I'm sorry, we . . . I don't believe this. What's your name?

Bill It's Ernesto. Ernesto Pico.

Quinn Ernesto, I don't know where you got the idea that we could just proclaim someone a writer. That is, it's . . . I don't know. That is not what we do.

Bill I think Ernesto was being ironic, Mr Quinn.

Quinn (*to Ernesto*) Is that true?

Ernesto If Bill says so.

  Pause.

Quinn Oh. (*Beat.*) Oh.

Julio Actually I thought Ernesto was speaking theoretically. Is it that much harder for a committee such as yours to proclaim an illiterate a writer than a criminal innocent?

Quinn Julio, Rosa's a political prisoner.

Julio What does that mean?

Quinn His crimes are only political.

Julio So is José Dorio's illiteracy. And if one can blind oneself to political crimes why not also to political illiteracy? (*Beat.*) And now that José Dorio is no longer illiterate in our eyes, it is not much more trouble to see him also as a poet. And in regard to Mr Quinn's earlier distinction regarding imprisoned good writers and not so good ones, I believe Ernesto would also ask us to think of José Dorio not only as a mere poet, but as one of distinction and great critical acclaim. (*Beat.*) Perhaps this is the point Ernesto was trying to make.

  Long pause.

Hans May I . . .?

Quinn No. (*Pause.*) Don't misunderstand me – we don't wish to soft-pedal the difficulties you people have had to go through. You have to just believe me when I say I have all the respect in the world for what this country has been attempting.

Hans He's so sincere.

Quinn Also – I can only imagine how a man like Rosa – who chose to be a part of that government and, as you have suggested, may have written the occasional speech for that government – what he must mean to you. (*Beat.*) But my point is this – what Rosa did, well it wasn't exactly like he was here torturing people himself. He wasn't even in the country.

Julio He was the government's Ambassador to Spain.

Quinn That is my point. We are not talking about a war criminal here, are we? What this is, is political. I want that made very clear. I wouldn't be here if he were a war criminal.

Hans Who said he was a war criminal?

Quinn (*to Julio*) You're not questioning that?

Julio No.

Quinn Good, because I wanted that perfectly clear.

Pause.

Hans What's all that about?

Alberto shrugs.

Quinn Now . . . (*He opens another file.*)

Julio But this does not mean that Manuel Rosa bears no responsibility for his government's actions. He did choose to join such a government.

Quinn To be Ambassador to Spain. I'm told he always wanted to live in Spain.

Alberto True. You know his work on *Don Quixote*.

Julio You make him into a very stupid man when you say something like that. (*Beat.*) What you may not be understanding, gentlemen, is what such a government that we had could be like. This I am not sure you understand. Though maybe it is something you can never understand.

Alberto Don't start, Julio. You are not the only persecuted man in this room.

Julio Persecuted, yes. I am sure you have been persecuted, Alberto. (*He pats him on the shoulder.*)

Alberto Don't patronize.

Julio I only think that having the police follow you around and give you parking tickets or – in Quinn's case – what is the worst, Norton – having your taxes audited?

Bill Mr Montero.

Julio (*ignoring him*) There is a difference, that is all I am saying. There is this understanding gap, shall we call it. You talk about how a few fickle people out there may get the wrong impression about my country, when what is most important, is it not, is that the people here, my own people, get the right impression of what we are all about. This is what matters to me. There is much you will never comprehend – you can begin by what we all have had to live through.

Beat.

Bill Mr Montero. Excuse me.

Quinn Bill, sit down.

Bill No. I was here during that time. I do know what you are talking about. Ernesto can tell you.

Ernesto says nothing.

Quinn That's right, Bill, you wrote about that experience didn't you? Sit down, please.

Hans I didn't read that book.

Bill Wait. I want to show you. You want to see – I'll show you. (*He takes down his pants.*) Ernesto, take off your shirt. Take it off.

Ernesto looks at Julio, who shrugs; Ernesto begins to take off his shirt.

(*to the others*) Look here. There. They used this metal wire, like a cattle prod. I found out later that's what it was like. Like a cattle prod. And look at his back. (*He points out wounds on Ernesto's back.*) There. You have pins in there now, don't you?

Ernesto nods.

Look at that!

There is a long embarrassed silence. The others have only glanced at the wounds.

What's wrong? (*Beat.*) I wanted Mr Montero to know that he wasn't the only one. Isn't that what you were trying to say, Mr Fava? (*Beat.*) I do know what it's like.

Julio I guess you do.

Beat.

Quinn For Christ sake, please pull up your pants, Bill.

Bill does. Ernesto puts his shirt back on.

Bill I don't understand.

Quinn Bill, we're talking. Where were we?

Julio I don't know.

Alberto raises a finger.

Quinn What Alberto?

Alberto (*without looking up*) My wife was tortured. Just last year. The fascists wanted me. They cut with a knife across here. (*He points across the breast.*) They also used cigarettes. (*Beat.*) They . . . (*He points to Bill and Ernesto.*) reminded me of it.

Pause.

Hans I read the piece you wrote about that. Very moving.

Alberto Thank you.

Pause.

Quinn OK – where were we?

SCENE NINE

Projection: PRINCIPIUM 9: WORK WITHIN YOUR LIMITS.

The porch of Ernesto's house. Bill and Ernesto sit on two rusted lawn chairs. A child's tricycle in a corner. Crickets. Evening. Pause.

Ernesto Tell me more.

Bill Why?

Ernesto Bill, do I have to have a reason? What is the matter with you?

Bill looks at him.

What's wrong? (*Short pause.*) I'm your friend, remember?

Bill (*turning away, continues*) The book, it sort of set me off as an article writer. Can't keep up with the demand really; people want to send me all over the world.

Ernesto That's wonderful, Bill. I envy you.

Bill You know, I can't tell if you're being sincere or not.

Ernesto Why wouldn't I be sincere? I don't understand. (*Beat.*) Bill, really it is not me who's been acting strange.

Bill Right. Right. (*Beat.*) Sorry. (*He continues.*) Funny how you plan things and then . . .

Ernesto Then what?

Bill Then something, like what happened to us, happens and it changes everything. It changed everything – eventually.

Beat.

Ernesto I don't quite understand, Bill.

Bill looks at him.

Come on, why do you keep looking at me like that?

Bill Like what? (*Beat.*) Forget it. (*He continues.*) I am saying that I wouldn't be writing articles if I hadn't written that book and I wouldn't have written that book if . . . if it hadn't happened. That's what I mean, so that's what my advice to someone would be now – don't plan. Because why bother, everything is going to change anyway so what's the point, you'll only get yourself frustrated. I was getting myself frustrated until I realized that.

Ernesto I see what you are saying now. Yes. That is very, very interesting.

Pause.

Bill You son of a bitch, will you stop that! And don't say stop what, you know what I mean. What's happened to you?

Ernesto What's happened to you?

Bill Why do I feel that everything you say to me is a lie? It is driving me crazy – all this lying, Ernesto. The reason I came down here was to see you. The whole committee thing gave me the chance, but I came to see you.

Ernesto Ah. (*Beat.*) Julio mentioned to me something about how you'd been commissioned to do an article on Norton Quinn. I thought that's what you were doing down here. Working on your article about Norton Quinn.

Bill I'm doing that too. (*Beat.*) I would have come . . .

Ernesto Who's lying now, Bill? (*Pause.*) I asked you, who's . . .

Bill gets up and moves away.

I thought it went OK today. People got their points across. (*Beat.*) We'll have to see what happens tomorrow.

Bill I thought we agreed we wouldn't talk about . . . I thought we wanted to hear about each other.

Pause.

Ernesto I'm sure you figured out that we planned all that about the illiterate poet. We even rehearsed it. We didn't know Quinn. Sort of took a flyer on him by making him chairman, you see we didn't know how he'd . . .

Bill Ernesto . . .

Ernesto 'Bendable', that's the word. You understand. (*Beat.*) But tomorrow's another day. Julio's thinking of

411

demanding that Einhorn become chairman again. (*He laughs.*) If you can have him removed why not also have him put back? That makes the point, I guess, doesn't it? I guess maybe I shouldn't be telling you all this.

Bill You know what you're doing.

Ernesto Excuse me? (*Beat.*) Sometimes friends bring out of one more than they wish to say.

Bill Right. (*He laughs.*) Excuse me, Ernesto, but I think I would like to go to bed now. It has been a tiring – draining – day.

Ernesto I hope you haven't been disappointed? (*Beat.*) In me? (*Beat.*) Is it in me? Or in you? (*He puts something in Bill's hand.*)

Bill What's this?

Ernesto Your hotel room key.

Bill But I thought I was staying . . .

Ernesto My wife and I thought you'd be more comfortable . . .

Bill Oh. (*Beat.*) I see. It doesn't look so good having an American in your . . .

Ernesto My wife and I thought you'd be more comfortable . . .

Bill (*suddenly yelling*) Bullshit!!!!!! (*Pause.*) Please. Ernesto, I do understand. Just don't bullshit me. Not me. OK? Not me. (*He turns and starts to go.*)

Ernesto I'm not bullshitting.

Bill (*suddenly turning back*) Fuck you!!!!!

   Pause as they look at each other.

Ernesto Bill, they can't complain if you happen to fall asleep on the couch.

Bill Are you sure?

  Beat.

Ernesto No. No, I'm not.

Bill Then I don't want to . . .

Ernesto Do you want to stay?

Bill Ernesto?

Ernesto Do you want to stay? You can stay here if you want. We would like you to stay.

  Pause. Bill sits back down.

Bill What are you writing?

Ernesto Nothing. (*Beat.*) A poem. A long poem. (*He gestures out.*) A natural history of that countryside. Flowers. Trees. Birds.

Bill Any gannets?

Ernesto What's a gannet? (*Beat.*) No. No gannets. Sorry.

Bill We were so stupid then.

Ernesto Not stupid.

Bill Young then. Young!

Ernesto Yes. We were young.

Bill And silly. The things we thought. (*Beat.*) We were stupid.

Ernesto Right. (*Beat.*) Right. We were.

SCENE TEN

Projection: PRINCIPIUM 10: MAKE IT NEW.

1970. A courtyard of the prison. Bright sun. Ernesto and Bill sit, tied to posts, at a distance from each other. They are blindfolded.

   A few shots of gunfire from another section of the courtyard – at some distance.

Ernesto (*twisting his body toward Bill*) Bill?

Bill I'm here.

   Pause.

Ernesto And then what happens?

   Pause.

Bill Robert decides it is just time he put his foot down, so he tells his father. He tells him that if he is ever going to do anything, it is not going to be in St Louis.

Ernesto Yeh.

Bill But, Ernesto, what his father hears is that Robert, whom he calls Bobby just to put him down – that I make very clear in my novel. That 'Bobby' is his father's way of putting him down. (*Beat.*) In the manuscript I underline 'Bobby'. To make this clear. (*Beat.*) When it's printed it'll be in italics.

   Another set of gunshots, which sound closer.

Ernesto Bill?

Bill I'm still here. (*Beat.*) I think they're getting closer. I think they are like coming down a line. (*Beat.*) They fake it to frighten you. I heard that somewhere. (*Beat.*) Shit, I will bet you anything he's already getting telegrams.

Ernesto Who is getting telegrams?

Bill The general. His people are getting telegrams. About us, Ernesto. (*Beat.*) Someone's sending telegrams. (*Beat.*) My parents are sending telegrams.

Long pause. A dog barks in the distance.

They just laugh at him, Ernesto.

Ernesto Who?

Bill Robert's parents. In my book. When Robert tells his parents that he has to get out of St Louis before his brain blows up they just laugh at him. And when his father – he teaches economics at a local university – when he asks Robert just how he plans to live, Robert finally confesses that he hopes to be a musician. He plays the bass. He had a group. They broke up the previous winter, but he did at least have the experience of having a group. It wasn't so foolish as they thought, Ernesto.

Ernesto No. It doesn't sound foolish to me, Bill.

Bill Thank you. So he runs away without telling them exactly where he is going. Fuck them, he thinks.

Another round of gunfire.

Ernesto Bill?!!

Bill (*loudly*) But they come after him! There's a whole chapter just about this chase. This escape. (*Beat.*) It's written all in one sentence. The entire chapter is one very long sentence. With a lot of parentheses. (*Beat. He almost yells.*) So he escapes!!

Ernesto Good for him.

Bill begins to break down. Ernesto twists toward him again.

415

Bill I'm all right. I'm all right.

Ernesto I'm hugging you. Do you feel me hugging you?

Bill Yes. (*Beat.*) Ernesto?

Ernesto tries to turn.

And you said they wouldn't use the machine on my cock.

Pause.

Ernesto Hey Bill, we're writers right? And people are always sending telegrams to get writers out. Other writers are always sending telegrams to get other writers out. Hug me back. Thank you.

Beat.

Bill His father, Ernesto, just could not understand him. He would not even try to understand him. Shit!

Ernesto I'm sorry.

Bill Robert was suffocating. His soul cries out for new places. New people. Things are changing and he wants to be a part of that. He's dying to be a part of that. He wants to matter, Ernesto. And his father will not understand that!

Ernesto No. No.

Bill He isn't a kid any more. He isn't some kid. He has things to do. He fucking has things to do!

A soldier enters with a revolver.

Soldier ¡Callense ahorales troca a listedes! [Shut up. You're next.]

Ernesto ¿Qué vas a hacer con nosotros? [What are you going to do to us?]

Soldier Cállate y di tus oraciones, chiquito. Voy a contar

416

hasta diez. [Shut up and say your prayers, sonny boy. I will count to ten.]

Ernesto He said – he will count to . . .

Bill OK. OK.

Soldier ¡Tu también, Americano! [You too, American.] (*He pushes Bill with his gun.*) Uno. Dos. Tres. Cuatro. Cinco. Seis. Siete. Ocho. Nueve. (*Beat.*) Diez.

> *He raises his gun in the air and shoots a single shot in the air. He looks at them, laughs to himself and walks off. Pause.*

Ernesto Bill?!!!

Bill I'm still here.

> *Pause.*

LEFT

(a reworking of *Sensibility and Sense*)

for Rob Marx and Jim Ragland

Characters

Older Marianne Rinaldi, *early seventies*
Younger Marianne Rinaldi, *early twenties*
Older Elinor Blair, *early seventies*
Younger Elinor Blair, *early twenties*
Older Edward Chandler, *early seventies*
Younger Edward Chandler, *early twenties*
Peter, *Edward's nephew, forties*
Therese, *late twenties*

Left was first presented under the title *Sensibility and Sense* on American Playhouse Television (Lindsay Law, Executive Producer) on 24 January 1990. The cast was as follows:

Marianne Rinaldi Elaine Stritch, Lili Taylor
Elinor Blair Jean Simmons, Trini Alvarado
Edward Chandler Tom Aldridge, Eric Stoltz
Peter Jeffrey DeMunn
Therese Lori Singer

Directed by David Jones
Produced by Timothy Marx
Associate producer Shirley Abraham
Production designed by Edward Pisoni
Lighting by Alan Adelman
Costumes Jane Greenwood
Edited Girish Bhargava
Casting Judy Courtney and D. L. Newton

Act One

SCENE ONE

Projection: AN EARLY DAY IN JUNE 1986. 4.05 P.M.

A summer vacation home on a lake in the Adirondacks, New York State. Accessible only by boat, the house and its various cabins overlook the large lake.

The living-room of the main house. Doorways to hallway and kitchen; door to porch. Kerosene lamps on the walls – there is no electricity. There is a small dining area with table and chairs. The area around the fireplace has sofas, chair, table. There is also a card table and chairs, a bar and a desk.

Marianne Rinaldi, a woman in her seventies, sits on a couch. Edward Chandler, her husband, also in his seventies, sits in a chair, a drink on the arm of his chair.

Pause.

Marianne Did I tell you that –?

Edward Yes. (*Beat.*) I'm sure you have. You tell me everything. You have told me everything. (*Beat.*) At least once. (*Beat.*) What were you going to tell me? (*Beat.*) I am sorry I interrupted you, Marianne. Forgive me. (*Beat.*) Then don't forgive me. Fuck it.

Marianne begins to take off her grey stockings.

Edward Now what are you doing?

Marianne Taking off my stockings. What are you blind now too? I thought it was perfectly obvious that I was taking off my stockings. Don't go blind on me, Eddie. Not now. Now when I need you.

425

Edward (*taking a sip of his drink*) I'm as young as I ever was. (*Beat.*) I said –.

Marianne (*ignoring him*) I hate these stockings. I hate this whole kind of stockings. My legs are sweating. It's summer, so what am I doing wearing stockings that make me sweat? Why did you put stockings on me this morning?

Edward You asked me to.

Marianne Not these particular stockings. I would never want her to see me wearing stockings like these. Surely, this, at least, would be obvious to you. It would be obvious to anyone else, Eddie.

Edward I can get other stockings. (*He makes the gesture of beginning to get out of his chair.*) Should I? You want me to get up and get you other stockings? (*He sits back down. Beat.*)

Marianne This kind of stockings makes me feel like a matron. My assistant at Bryn Mawr wore stockings like these. (*Beat.*) Don't bother to get up and get the stockings. I wouldn't want you to trouble yourself. (*Beat.*) Not Bryn Mawr. Holyoke. My assistant something when I was Provost at Holyoke. When I was there. When I was at Bryn Mawr I had a positively gorgeous assistant dean. She wore mini-skirts and could she ever talk with the girls. She could *rap* with them, Eddie. Went into business eventually. I wrote her recommendation for Wharton. (*Laughing to herself.*) I didn't mention the mini-skirts. (*Laughing harder.*) When she went for her interview she wore a grey suit. (*Beat.*) People. (*Turns to Edward.*) You slept with her I think. (*Beat.*) Or did you? I stumbled in on you two – in my office?? The President of the College's office?? I have this memory of pulling apart some couple in my office. It's not a bad memory, Eddie.

Edward It wasn't me.

Marianne Perhaps. But as I say, it's not a bad memory at all.

Short pause.

Edward You won't get my goat today, Marianne. So you might as well stop trying.

Marianne If you say so – then I better stop. (*She hears something.*) Is that a plane? She could be coming by seaplane. That would be like Elinor to arrive by plane. It would be typical.

Edward Peter is meeting her with the boat. You know that.

Marianne Then I guess that's not Elinor. (*Beat.*) If she'd sold the excerpt to *The New Yorker* then I'll bet she would be the one in that seaplane. That's what I started to tell you before you interrupted me, Eddie. That she tried to sell an excerpt of her memoirs to *The New Yorker*. And she thinks of herself as almost a communist! To *The New Yorker*! What –. (*She laughs.*) The hypocrisy. But it's so typical, isn't it. That is Elinor. (*Beat.*) One of my lawyers told me. They called up Shawn. We would have sued *The New Yorker* too. My lawyer made this perfectly clear.

Edward Peter never mentioned –.

Marianne Who said anything about Peter? I have other lawyers than your nephew, Peter. I have many many lawyers from which to draw. This particular one you have never heard of, Eddie. I have never before spoken of him in your presence. A very handsome lawyer too. Well dressed. Very contemporary. And he hears things before they actually happen, like this and *The New Yorker*. You should meet him sometime. He could teach you a thing or two. He's a very good listener.

Short pause.

Edward Would you like me to get your other stockings? I would, you know.

Marianne (*smiling*) Eddie, I know you would do anything in the world for me.

He smiles to himself.

You're smiling. You haven't stopped smiling since I told you Elinor was coming up.

He stops smiling.

Edward You didn't tell me. She called me.

Marianne You didn't tell me that –.

Edward Yes, I did.

Marianne What did she do – call you up for more alimony? That's what I'd do in her shoes – bleed you dry with alimony. Perhaps we should get divorced, Eddie.

He smiles to himself, she smiles, then suddenly:

Is my wig straight? I'd hate to have her see me with a crooked wig. You'd tell me if it wasn't straight, wouldn't you? You wouldn't let me humiliate myself. (*She stares at him, then:*) The last time I saw her she'd gained weight. (*still staring*) Say something about the wig. Pay me a compliment. Don't you think I need to hear compliments? The fact that I will no longer believe them doesn't mean I don't want to hear them, Eddie. (*Beat.*) If she pities me, I'll spit in her face.

Edward twitches in his chair.

That got a reaction out of you. (*She smiles, then:*) A tuft of hair is growing back. That's something. I noticed this morning. (*She listens.*) I don't hear the boat. What I heard wasn't our boat. (*Beat.*) I nearly bought another wig. What a perfectly gorgeous wig it was. The colour I

428

have always wanted to have. I had my purse out and I was paying for that wig. The clerk should have told me first it was made in South Africa. It wasn't my fault he'd gone and fitted it. I'd said I wanted it, but I hadn't paid for it. Clerks should know better. One still has one's beliefs, even when one is bald-headed. (*She looks at Edward's thinning hair.*) At least I do mine. You'd have been proud of me. That clerk was sorry I ever walked through his door. Ever – come through his –. Been brought through –. I had fun at least. He was so angry he didn't pity me. And he didn't seem to want to talk about South Africa at all. Like so many young people today. Don't you agree? Young people today –. How many drinks have you had since lunch? How are you going to defend me? Once in my life I need your help and look at you.

He looks at her. She studies him, then:

Nah. You don't look so bad.

He smiles.

No, you don't, dear.

Noise, off.

There's the boat. I hear the boat. Elinor's here.

SCENE TWO

Projection: AN EARLY DAY IN JUNE 1937. 4.40 P.M.

Marianne Rinaldi, early twenties – the Marianne of the previous scene nearly fifty years earlier, the younger Edward Chandler, early twenties, and Elinor Blair, early twenties are suddenly in the middle of a conversation.
   1986: Older Marianne and Older Edward remain on

429

the couch and chair, not frozen, but rather waiting, thinking, throughout.

Edward Marianne, he's our host. He invited us. We just got here.

Marianne He invited you, Eddie. You invited us.

Edward Elinor, you talk to her.

Elinor turns away.

(*back to Marianne*) When I said I wanted to bring two colleagues from *The Review*, he –.

Marianne (*to Elinor, over this*) Did he say 'colleagues' or did he say 'girls'?

Elinor smiles.

Edward I said colleagues. Of course I said colleagues. Maybe I said female colleagues.

Marianne Jesus Christ, what did I tell you?

Edward (*to Elinor*) And he said that was fine! Bringing you two was just fine with him! (*to both*) So damnit you were invited!

Marianne (*over this*) Why does none of this surprise me?

Edward If you're going to make up your mind before we even talk with Gene –. Then I'll shut up. You want me to shut up, I'll shut up.

Marianne Shut up. You interrupted me. (*She turns to Elinor.*)

Edward You won't even give him a chance? Just because he's rich?! Who's the real snob here?!

Marianne (*to Elinor*) So we're getting out of the boat –.

Edward Damnit, there is just one thing I want to say!!

Marianne stops her story and waits. He says nothing, then suddenly charges to the porch door, opens it, goes out, door slams, and immediately comes back in, goes to the bar, and begins to pour himself a drink as:

Marianne (*to Elinor*) So we're getting out of the boat. And Mr Hopkins –. (*A half glance to Edward.*) Eddie's good friend. Gene-the-millionaire-Hopkins. I mean look at this place. The money it must take to just keep the grounds –. You know Eddie's spent the last two summers up here with his pal, Gene. Eddie better be careful or he's going to start to think like a rich person. Even think he is a rich person. He better be real – [careful].

Elinor Marianne, please. So Gene is there and we're getting out of the boat.

Marianne He's helping me out and it was so obvious, Elinor, that this man is staring at my legs. In fact, he doesn't even try and hide the fact that he's staring at these legs. (*She turns to Edward.*) Maybe he's thinking, Eddie, that he can afford to buy these legs.

Edward Oh, for Christ's sake!

Elinor (*looking at her legs*) You have nice legs, Marianne.

Marianne Thank you. You have nice legs too. Don't disparage your legs.

Elinor I wasn't –.

Marianne (*continuing*) And then we're walking up from the dock, and he turns and says: 'Does Imperialist Japan mean anything to you?'

Edward (*to himself, as no one is listening*) I doubt if Gene just turned to her and said –.

Elinor (*to Marianne*) Unbelievable!

Marianne Not really. Not for a rich boy. You expect this kind of thinking from a rich boy.

Edward (*to himself*) What kind of thinking?! So he just asked –.

Marianne Elinor understands.

Elinor I understand.

Marianne So I say – 'Imperialist Japan? Why sure, Mr Hopkins. I hate old Imperialist Japan. What kind of girl do you take me for?' I'm exaggerating, but almost that. But it's just so – yech! Him trying to be so 'political' with me by throwing around this 'Imperialist Japan'.

Elinor (*to Edward*) Just like with the Williams' boys. You could always tell a Williams' boy at Smith. It was like they'd just read a newspaper in the car on their way to Smith.

Marianne Or a Dartmouth boy.

Elinor Or a Dartmouth boy.

Marianne But I still don't get exactly what Gene's trying to say, then – this is amazing – gets better – or worse – and he says to me 'silk'. And there he is staring down at my legs again. I'm beginning to wonder if it's just some affliction with his neck – it is that obvious – when I realize he's referring to my stockings. I was wearing these silk stockings.

Elinor I remember.

Marianne I took them off a little while ago. They were hot. And he says to me 'Marianne, you don't mind if I call you Marianne, do you?' 'Of course not – Gene.' (*She laughs.*)

Edward (*into his drink*) He's a good man. He's as far to the left as –.

Marianne He says 'I hope I won't offend you by saying this but most *progressive* women, these days, wouldn't be caught dead wearing anything silk. Because of –.' And I chime in – 'Imperialist Japan. Of course, I know that.' (*Beat.*) Actually I didn't. Did you?

Elinor No.

Marianne I don't remember anyone at Smith saying a word against wearing silk.

Elinor And the women at Smith are progressive if they're anything. (*to Edward*) It's not exactly Vassar after all.

Marianne Well I made it very clear that I am progressive. More than progressive. And if he knew me better he'd see just how ridiculous it was to even suggest I wasn't.

Edward (*into his drink*) He's helped a lot of people. Knows a lot of people. A lot of smart, political, good people.

Marianne (*over the end of this*) So this is what I said to him – I take him by the arm, put my arm in his –.

Elinor I saw you do this –.

Marianne (*over this*) And said: 'Gene, when I saw you staring at my legs down on the dock, I thought to myself – what a dull, juvenile, selfish, spoiled rich-boy creep. How relieved I am to find now that that leg-stare – was meant politically.'

She and Elinor burst out laughing.

(*laughing*) 'Yes, yes,' he says, 'I'm glad you understand that now. A political stare. Not uncommon for me really.'

More laughter. As they begin to calm down, Elinor suddenly starts laughing harder again.

What?! What?!

433

Elinor (*laughing*) I just remember – that on the dock, Gene took a good long look down my dress. He must have thought my chemise was silk!

She laughs hard. Marianne stops laughing, then:

Marianne You just remembered that?

Elinor (*laughing*) Yeh.

Marianne It happens to you that often, it just slipped your –?

Elinor Yeh.

Marianne Oh.

Marianne makes herself laugh with Elinor. Finally they finish.

We're done now, Eddie. Now you can say whatever you want. Even defend your good buddy, Gene – if you want.

Edward Gene doesn't need me to defend him.

Elinor (*laughing*) I think he should take who he can get!

This makes Marianne laugh.

Edward And certainly not from you two. His commitment to the left . . .

Marianne Oh please. (*to Elinor*) He means the *left breast*!

They are almost hysterical with laughter now.

Edward But if you need to attack him before you can ask him for money – if that's what this is about – that's your problem.

Marianne (*calming down*) I'm not asking him for money. *The Review* is. And even that wasn't my idea.

Pause. They calm down. And for a moment no one knows what to do or say, then:

Elinor (*to Marianne*) What do you say we go for a swim?

Marianne (*getting up*) Why not? You remembered to bring a suit. Or do you think Gene would rather we didn't wear bathing suits, perhaps that'd clinch his support.

Elinor Marianne. (*Beat.*) I brought my suit. Though I haven't worn it since Smith. I hope it still fits.

Marianne I thought you loved to swim.

Elinor I do. Why?

Marianne You just said you hadn't been swimming since –.

Elinor Marianne, I said I hadn't worn it since Smith.

Elinor smiles. Marianne suddenly laughs. They head out the door.

Edward (*pointing to his watch*) Gene said he'd see us at six.

They are gone.

(*calling*) We make our proposal to him at six!!

SCENE THREE

Projection: 4.55 P.M.

1986: Older Edward still in the chair, drink still at his side. Older Marianne still on the couch. The porch door has just opened and Elinor Blair, early seventies, stands in the doorway.

1937: Young Edward sits upstage, looking out the

435

window, waiting. He is directly behind the Older Edward.

Elinor Don't get up. Please.

Edward (*turning to the door*) Elinor! We were beginning to wonder. We heard the boat ages ago.

Elinor I was washing up in my cabin. (*She looks to Marianne, who avoids her.*) Don't get up, Eddie.

He starts to get up.

Sit down. Eddie –.

He is up and goes to hug her.

Edward You look wonderful.

Elinor And you.

They hug.

And you.

Edward (*moving to the bar*) What is it, Scotch or Bourbon this year?

Elinor Later. My stomach. The ride – I'd forgotten what it was like when the water was choppy. As you both know, I always have had a delicate stomach.

Marianne laughs to herself.

Edward (*pouring*) One for me then.

Marianne Edward.

Edward (*ignoring her*) Well, the place hasn't changed. At least that hasn't changed.

Elinor Still no electricity?

Edward Across the lake they have it now.

Elinor I hope you never get it here. It would be so

different. To think that George and I could have –. And at that price. You were the smart ones, let me tell you. (*Beat.*) But it wasn't like George –. I don't blame you. If it hadn't been – friends, it'd have been strangers. Old man Hanson asked us first. If we wanted to blame anyone, we should have blamed ourselves. There are buyers in this world and there are renters. Good for you. It must be a gold mine now. You must get offers all the time. The summers here with George, I shall always –.

Edward I haven't gotten any offers, Elinor. It's not Manhattan. You want to make an offer? (*Beat.*) Marianne, have we gotten a single offer for this place?

For the first time Marianne lifts her head and looks at Edward.

Elinor Hello, dear. How are you feeling? That's a gorgeous wig.

Marianne turns to Edward.

Edward It's on straight.

Elinor How lucky you are to have such a peaceful relaxing place to – get better in. (*to Edward*) It was such a shock when I heard. You can imagine how it seemed – after going through it all with George just last –.

Edward Marianne is sitting right there, Elinor.

Beat.

Elinor I would like a Scotch please, Eddie.

He moves back to the bar. Finally, Elinor turns to Marianne.

You and I have been best friends since –.

Marianne Eddie, where's my lawyer? I thought I made myself perfectly clear that I wanted him here. What does he think I pay him for? We feed him. He spends the day fishing.

Elinor Peter's in my cabin.

Marianne My lawyer, and already she's calling him –.

Elinor (*to Edward*) He said he wanted to make my bed. I told him –.

Marianne (*to Edward*) I asked you to make her bed! You promised me you'd make it!

Elinor (*over the end of this*) Where in the world did you find a lawyer who makes beds, drives motorboats –? (*She takes the drink from Edward.*) Thank you. All my lawyers seem to know how to do is have lunch. (*She laughs at her joke. No one else does.*)

Edward Peter is my nephew.

Elinor Ah. (*She sips.*) You always knew how to make a drink. I say if you can't taste it . . .

Edward Peter should be here any minute. It can't take that long to make a bed.

Marianne (*under her breath*) How would you know?

Edward We can talk when Peter gets here.

> *Long pause. No one knows what to say – all we hear is the sipping of drinks, then:*

Elinor (*suddenly standing*) Oh let's not talk yet! I'm not here just to talk – but also to visit! I think that's why I'm really here – to visit. I could have 'talked' through my lawyer.

> *Marianne laughs to herself.*

Why are you laughing? (*to Edward*) I know what she thinks. (*to Marianne*) You couldn't be more wrong. My lawyers told me your case is ridiculous. They've never seen such a waste of time. They've begged me not to give it a second's thought. (*Beat.*) Most people find it rather pathetic. I'm sorry to tell you this, but they do. I thought it best if I were the one to tell you this. This is why I came. And did I come with a lawyer? Do you see *me* with a lawyer, Marianne? (*Short pause.*) Don't talk to me. Use your illness against me.

Edward Would you like a snack? Can I get you anything? That is, if your stomach –.

Elinor Not one of our friends blames me! I only wrote what I remembered. I didn't write history. So write what you remember, Marianne. I won't sue you for libel. Why don't you settle it that way. Write what you want. Remember what you want! The one thing I do not appreciate is the begging for sympathy. That has hurt me. I have never seen anyone use an illness like –. You'd never have seen me behave this way, if I were the one who . . . (*She turns to Edward.*) There are friends of ours who won't even talk to me!!

Marianne (*suddenly smiling*) Really? Hear that, Eddie?

Elinor I spent the whole of last year at George's bedside, I resent this, this . . . (*She starts to choke up.*) I'm sorry. (*Sudden burst at Marianne.*) I can't sit here and take this! Marianne, dear, how are you? No matter how you behave towards me I am still happy to see you. (*almost crying*) No matter how much you try to hurt me. I –. (*Fighting back tears. To Edward*) I love her. She can't make me not love her. (*Elinor cries. Beat.*)

Marianne I told you she'd start with the crying, Eddie. Please, I'd like my nap now, Eddie.

Edward stands.

Elinor Can I help? Let me get Peter to help.

Marianne My husband will carry me. Thank you.

Edward, with effort, picks her up. Elinor continues to cry.

(*to Edward*) If you drop me in front of her I'll kill you. Watch the wall. Watch it. (*As they go:*) Hold me tighter.

They are gone down the hallway to the bedrooms.
Elinor stops sobbing and wipes the tears from her eyes. She opens her purse and takes out make-up, which she begins putting on while watching herself in a small mirror.

SCENE FOUR

Projection: 5.55 P.M.

1937: Young Edward stands, as the Young Marianne enters from the kitchen, notebook and papers in hand, eating a celery stick or carrot. She speaks loudly, looking through her notes, to the Young Elinor, who is still in the kitchen.
1986: Older Elinor remains seated, fixing her make-up. When she finishes, she sits back and thinks.

Marianne (*loudly*) Fact: *The Leftist Review* was founded by members of the Communist Party, yes, *but* not by the Party itself! I'm not sure he knows that! Fact: financial support for *The Review* came not directly from the Party but rather through a guaranteed pre-sale to John Reed clubs.

Elinor (*off*) Good point!

Marianne This arrangement then can be seen as nothing more than that say between a publisher and a book club.

Elinor (*off*) That's true!

Marianne So elements within the Party may claim we stole *The Review* out from under them, all we in fact have done is tear up a contract between a publisher and a book club.

Elinor (*entering with a tin of biscuits, eating one*) Clever girl.

Edward (*turning from looking outside*) Gene wasn't around the boat house. I don't know where he is.

Elinor (*looking at her watch*) It's not quite six.

Marianne (*continuing*) But we promise him that our plans for *The Review* will include no attacks upon the Party or Party members. A man such as – yourself, Mr Hopkins, who is well-known to generously support numerous progressive causes, would not want to find himself funding one which attacks another. This won't happen. So, supporting *The Review* cannot be construed in any way as criticism of the Party. After all, don't we too have the Party in our recent past? That's my bit. (*She sticks her fingers in her mouth, pretending to gag herself.*)

Elinor Right. I know what you mean.

Edward You know what what means?

Elinor Grovelling, Eddie. Have a biscuit, they were on the counter in the kitchen. They're imported.

Marianne Of course! Some import revolution, others import –.

Edward I'm not grovelling. And I have no intention of –.

Marianne Anyone else want a Manhattan? (*She goes to the bar.*)

Edward As a matter of fact, I would.

Marianne (*to herself*) Why did I ask? Elinor?

Elinor shakes her head.

Edward I have had one drink. Two drinks, all afternoon.

Marianne So who's counting?

Elinor After Marianne, then it's your turn, Eddie.

Short pause. Marianne pours drinks.

Marianne (*holding up the half-made drink*) Are you waiting for –?

Edward I'll talk about how we need now to go *with* history.

Marianne laughs to herself.

Why is that – [funny]?

Marianne It just sounds like bullshit – in the context. Here. Begging for money.

She hands him his drink. He doesn't take it, she sets it down.

Sorry.

Edward Go where history, where events take one.

Marianne Talk to me. I'll be Gene. (*She sits next to Elinor and suddenly pulls open Elinor's blouse to look at her breasts.*)

Elinor Stop it!

Marianne I'm – Gene. (*She smiles. Sips her drink. Beat.*)

Edward An ideology – any ideology, holds one back, we believe, Gene. Narrows one's mind –.

Marianne (*as Gene*) But without some sort of ideology, how is your *Review* going to choose what to and not to publish?

Edward We'll –.

Marianne Upon what will you base – choice?

Edward We'll publish what *we* believe is worth publishing. We will select on the basis of merit – artistic, intellectual – both with regard to the writing and the writer. Without the Party – or any other strong ideological force breathing down our necks – we look forward to a broad range of writing and opinion –.

Marianne You mean by taste, then? You'll choose – by taste.

Edward No – Gene – not simply by –.

Marianne Call it what you will, Mr Chandler, but that's what it amounts to – your taste. And a taste derived from –? Your bourgeois upbringings?

Elinor I don't think Gene would talk like –.

Marianne Taste formed by your reactionary cultures? Tastes so ingrained will not change by themselves. Without the spine of beliefs –.

Edward We have beliefs!

Marianne Without ideology, such 'beliefs' are based on what? More tastes?! Derived from the same bourgeois –?!

Edward Not tastes! From our minds! Our open minds! Our consciences!

Elinor (*over this*) Hey you two –.

Edward This (*pointing to his head*) and this (*heart*) and this (*gut*) will tell us what to and not to publish! What we know in our brain, hear in our heart, feel in our stomach to be good writing!!

Marianne What you and these two (*very*

443

condescendingly) girls say is good, you mean.

Edward Initially, yes, then we –.

Marianne And what if you – can't agree? (*Beat.*) What? I think we should be prepared for that sort of argument.

Elinor (*looking at her watch*) It's past six.

Marianne I was just being Gene –.

Elinor (*ignoring her, holding out a paper*) The editorial statement.

> *She tries to hand it to Edward, who takes his drink instead, then reads.*

'In a world that is changing blah blah blah. It is the hope of the editors, blah . . . A forum for free thought, debates, blah, etc.' It reads well. Maybe we should read it out loud to him.

Edward You're not a Jew, are you, Gene?

> *The others look at him.*

Neither am I. My father's the Chaplain of Hamilton College. None of us is Jewish. But imagine – that you are. And if you're like the Jews I know, you've been brought up, raised by your parents – progressive. Maybe even to the left of progressive. Maybe even communist. Certainly socialist. In any event you possess a set of beliefs under which you try and live. (*Beat.*) You've sought to make a world that is fair, without class, devoid of poverty and exploitation, greed and waste. And nothing's mattered more to you than achieving such an end. Nothing's mattered more – until you hear Chancellor Hitler say what he'd like to do to you Jews. (*Beat.*) If and when he gets his hands on you. (*Beat.*) What – to do? Who to turn to? To others like you who have worked to make a better world? (*Beat.*) Comrade

Stalin says – let him be the standard bearer for anti-
fascism in the world. Trust Stalin to be the Jew's best
hope. (*Beat.*) But is he a Jew? Are his interests – really
yours? (*Beat.*) The world changes every day in ways we
cannot predict or prepare ourselves for. Can any ideology
have the flexibility to accommodate unforeseen change?
(*Beat.*) It is my hope that *The Leftist Review* will become
a forum for questioning, for discussing the meaning of
events as they occur and wherever they lead – with total
freedom and an open unfettered mind. I can think of no
greater political use – or moral use – or intellectual or
artistic use of a magazine.

Pause.

Elinor (*turning toward the porch*) I thought I heard
something.

Noise off.

Marianne What's that?

They go to the porch door.

Edward It's Gene. (*He calls.*) Gene!!! (*He charges out.*)

Elinor He's taking off in his seaplane.

Edward (*off, shouting*) Gene?!! Where are you going?!!!

*The girls follow him out, shouting 'What's going on?',
'What's happening?' as Edward continues to yell
'Gene!!'.*
*1986. Peter, forties, enters from the kitchen. He holds
up a box of kitchen matches. The shouts outside fade
away. Older Elinor turns to him.*

Elinor You found them? Where I said they'd be?

Peter nods.

Same drawer as three years ago. Old people get into such

445

ruts, Peter. It's so tiresome. Do you know how –? Do you want me –?

Peter I can do it. (*He begins to light a couple of kerosene lamps.*)

Elinor Of course, a man of your talents – motor boat driver, bedmaker, lawyer. Anything else you can't find?

Pause as he lights the lamps, Elinor turns toward the bedrooms.

Perhaps we should disturb them. Remind them that we're here. Maybe they forgot. It's been –. (*She looks at her watch.*) On second thought, better not, what if they're fooling around?

Peter Right.

Elinor You think they're in there fooling around?

Peter No. I heard them talking.

Elinor I heard nothing.

Peter (*finished with the lamps*) Anything else you need? Otherwise, I'll go back and – [the kitchen].

Elinor (*ignoring him*) What were we just talking about? Old people. It seems I'm spending so much of my time now with old people. Perhaps it's my calling. Like Florence Nightingale among the sick. Elinor Blair among the old and decrepit. Take a biscuit with you, eat while you cook. I always did. Here. (*She holds up the tin of biscuits.*)

Peter (*taking one*) Thank you. (*He starts to go back to the kitchen.*)

Elinor I bought them for her. They're English. She'll never eat them though. She'll think they're poisoned.

Peter tries to smile.

But tell me, Peter, why would I poison her when she's already dying?

Peter grimaces.

Why would I?

Peter I don't know. Excuse me. (*He hurries off into the kitchen.*)

Elinor (*calling*) It was a joke! I was making a joke! It's always the young who can't take a joke. The young and the lawyers! (*Beat.*) Peter?! What's the difference between a dead snake on the highway and a dead lawyer on the highway?! In front of the dead snake there are skid marks! (*Beat.*) My godson told me that! He learned it at his school! Harvard Law School! They take such jokes as compliments there! (*Short pause. Takes a biscuit, then to herself*) Eddie would eat a biscuit. He'd love it if I poisoned him. His posthumous literary reputation would be made. (*Beat.*) Abandoned. I could have stayed home and felt abandoned.

SCENE FIVE

Projection: 8.05 P.M.

1937: A few more gaslights have been lit. The Younger Marianne, Elinor and Edward all stand, having just come out of the kitchen, followed by Therese, an attractive and very well dressed woman in her late twenties. Therese has put on an apron.

Older Elinor remains on the couch, lost in thought, throughout.

Therese Lucky I happened by with all this food. Gene's left nothing in the ice box.

Marianne We would have managed.

Edward Thank you for sharing with us. I hope we aren't –.

Therese Hey, it's nice to be with people. There's no one at my place now. So I'm lucky too. I'll start getting the plates.

Elinor Let me – [help].

Therese No. No. Gene wouldn't hear of it. You're his guests.

Marianne And you?

Therese A friend. I drop by all the time. (*She goes back into the kitchen.*)

Edward (*half whisper*) Who is she?

Elinor Therese, she said.

Edward I don't mean her name.

Elinor A friend of Gene's? (*shrugging*) I guess she lives around here. She's certainly attractive.

Marianne You think so? I don't. Eddie, you think she's attractive?

Edward No. Not really. Not that attractive. It's the clothes that make her seem attractive.

Therese (*entering with plates*) The one thing you could do is get me that drink.

Edward Sorry, forgot! Manhattan, wasn't it? (*He is at the bar.*)

Therese Anything. I forgot to ask if you all like chops. (*Before they can respond:*) I believe he keeps the silverware . . . (*She opens a drawer.*) I was right.

448

Elinor You're sure we can't –.

Therese (*taking out silverware*) Gene's going to be sick when he realizes he's abandoned you. He'd be mortified as well if he also heard you set your own table. (*to herself*) Some more candles would be nice. (*She heads for the kitchen, stops. To Marianne and Elinor*) You two aren't in the theatre by any chance?

Elinor Us?

Therese Actors?

Elinor No. No, we're not –.

Therese It's the faces. They're so – interesting. Beautiful. (*She touches Elinor's face.*) Gene has a lot of friends in the theatre. (*She starts for the kitchen.*)

Edward And me – do I look like I'm in the theatre?

   She stops and looks, then:

Therese No. (*She is off. Calling back*) You can bring that drink in here, if you don't mind.

Edward (*realizing he has two drinks in his hand*) Sorry. (*He hurries after her.*)

Elinor She's wearing a wedding ring.

Marianne A diamond and a band. Two rings.

Elinor So she's married.

   Marianne shrugs.

Her husband's not up here. She said no one was up here. She seems nice.

Marianne When you are rich you can afford to seem nice. And besides, it's cheap.

Elinor Come on, what has she done?

Marianne It's what she is. There were girls like her everywhere at Smith.

Elinor Rich girls.

Marianne Rich girls like her. They think about nothing. They care about nothing. She's so transparent. I'll bet anything she's having an affair with our Gene. In fact, tonight, she came to see –. The reason for all the food.

Elinor Maybe. So what?

Marianne When she saw us –. All this politeness, it's to disguise what we in fact walked in on. Elinor, use your eyes for God's sake.

Elinor It's none of our business.

Marianne My point. I just don't like rich people dragging me into their fickle frivolous lives.

Edward laughs from the kitchen.

Eddie. I can't begin to describe how disappointed I am in him. First Gene, now this DAR bitch.

Elinor I wouldn't think 'Therese' was exactly –.

Marianne (*over this*) Has he no pride?!

Elinor He's talking to her in the kitchen!

Marianne He's attracted to her. Can't you see that? He pretty much said as much.

Elinor She's an attractive –.

Marianne You too? Now I can't talk to you? I had some hope for you!

Elinor (*over this*) You can talk to –.

Marianne Both of you – go to hell! Forget it! Forget I'm even here!! (*She heads for the porch.*)

Elinor Marianne?

Marianne I'm going to my cabin. Have fun. Enjoy 'Therese'! As for me, I think the dinner conversation alone would drive me to murder. (*She goes out, the door slams.*)

   Immediately, Edward and Therese, carrying candles and flowers, enter.

Edward (*laughing*) You won't believe this. Therese has just been in –. (*realizing*) Where's Marianne?

Elinor She went to her cabin.

Therese The dinner's nearly –.

Elinor I don't think we should wait. (*to Edward*) Therese has just been – what? You were saying when –.

Edward In Spain. For how many months?

Therese Five. (*She puts the candles on the table.*)

Elinor You've just been in Spain??

Therese (*about Marianne*) Your friend. I hope it wasn't something I –.

Edward If you knew Marianne you'd understand it has nothing to do with you.

Elinor (*to Edward*) What does that mean?

Therese (*as she continues to set the table*) I seem to have left my glass . . . (in the kitchen)

   Edward hesitates, then goes and gets it.

(*to Elinor*) She's a very striking woman, your friend, Marianne. Eyes like flames. Striking.

   Edward returns with her drink. She takes it and downs it in a gulp.

Could I have another please. American liquor tastes like water to me after Spain.

Edward goes to make her another drink.

Elinor What exactly were you doing in Spain?

Edward She was in an actual militia.

Therese There was a woman's militia.

Edward With guns and cannons. They gave the women guns.

Elinor I think I knew that.

Therese You haven't been to Spain?

Elinor I was thinking of going last year.

Therese Take it from me, when you do go, go with as few expectations as possible. That's what I did and brother did it help. He seems not to believe in soup spoons. (*She is off to the kitchen.*)

Elinor Marianne should hear about this. (*at the door*) Marianne?! Marianne?!

Edward (*to Elinor*) Think of the courage it must have taken –.

Therese (*off*) Not courage. Courage had nothing to do with it. Maybe, curiosity. I simply wanted to experience this great thing happening. (*She returns with breads, and a bottle of wine.*)

Elinor And your husband, Therese? I noticed the rings. Didn't he try to –?

Therese Talk me out of going? Actually, no. But don't be too surprised by that. Harvey and I have been having sort of a hard time of it lately.

Edward I'm sorry.

Therese Don't be.

Elinor He's not up –?

Therese No. Not this week. (*noticing Edward holding her drink*) Thank you. Put it on the table. (*She strikes a match from the box Peter brought in and begins to light the candles.*) It's all my fault really. I never should have introduced him to my friend, Josie. See – she was my friend first. I met her first. Beautiful girl. We'd spent the whole summer camping together in Montana. The sky out there. It's everything they say it is. So – romantic. You and your friend, Marianne, should try camping out there sometime.

  Beat.

Elinor Yeh.

Therese Josie and I had met in a bar in Chicago. I was changing trains. I mean who knew that this girl with those big brown eyes could also type? (*She smiles to herself.*) I don't know how it happened, but somehow Harvey made her his secretary. She travels with him all the time now. Sometimes I go along too – but I find that sort of thing really confusing. Anyway, instead of trying to argue me out of it, Harvey got me a press card from *Time/Life*. He said that was something he could do for me. So off I went to Spain. I guess what it comes down to is he called my bluff. (*Beat.*) On the other hand I've often wondered if Harvey didn't see it as a plus – my being over there fighting the fascists. When you're dealing with defence contracts all the time like he is, having some tie to someone with a belief, well it helps create the illusion that there is more to you than just greed. (*shrugging*) Who knows? (*She downs her second drink.*) One more and then let's open the wine. (*She hands her glass to Edward.*)

453

What are you three, still in college? (*She heads off for the kitchen.*)

Marianne No.

Edward and Elinor turn to Marianne, seeing her for the first time on the porch behind the screen door.

No, we're not in college.

Therese is off. Marianne slowly enters.

Therese (*entering with a soup terrine, from which as she talks she'll dish out soup*) Speaking of wine. Do you know how they open wine bottles in Spain? Not all bottles. I only saw this once, but –. They take a male dog. I saw them do this with a collie. Part collie. And they take the dog's penis and then they start rubbing its balls and the idea, see, is that the erection will push in the cork. (*She laughs to herself.*) Never saw it work. There are things happening in Spain that you or I never even imagined.

Edward hands her her drink.

Thank you. (*seeing Marianne*) Hello. (*As she serves:*) There was a particular cabo – that's corporal. She was the one who convinced me to join the woman's militia. A huge woman. She was Russian. (*Beat.*) Burgundy okay with everyone? And she had us – the women – out chopping wood in the forest one morning. Except for these two English comrades who were going to stand guard between us and the line, we all had set down our rifles so we could chop. We needed wood. It gets pretty damn cold in Spain in January. And now it is bitter cold. (*Beat.*) Suddenly we see this man come through the woods. We all stop and freeze. The two with their guns – the English girls from Manchester – point them. Then, this man, unaware that here are forty or so young women with axes a few yards away from him, he pulls down his

454

pants and squats. (*She pours soup.*) Well, the Russian comrade – the cabo – she gestures for none of us to move, and she silently picks up her gun, and then – she screams 'Stand up!' in Spanish. The man stands up, with his pants now –. And you see his face as he sees himself standing there, and we are a crowd of women not only with rifles but also with these very sharp axes. (*She laughs to herself.*) I think he was an anarchist actually. P.O.U.M most likely. You should have seen his boots – nothing left of them. Also he had a lot of body hair – so he looked like a farmer, not a fascist. So – P.O.U.M. Anyway, the cabo, she goes up to him and without so much as hesitating –. (*She smiles to herself.*) She grabs a hold of his penis and gives it a huge tug. And he's on the ground now and she says – 'I wanted to ring your bell.' (*She laughs to herself.*) In Spanish she says this. 'Ring your bell.' That's an expression we had, there was a song – it's a pun really. (*She laughs.*) It was very funny. That's war for you. That and body lice. (*She finishes serving the soup.*)

The others take their seats at the table.

For some reason international proletarian solidarity and body lice will be for ever linked in my mind. (*She downs her drink.*) Dinner is served. Eddie – (*she winks to the other girls*) would you like to open the wine?

SCENE SIX

Projection: 8.50 P.M.

1986: The Older Elinor and Edward with Peter now sit at the table, eating their dinner (the bread, soup, etc. served by Therese in the previous scene). As they eat, Edward reads a newspaper, which he holds next to his plate.

1937: the Younger Elinor and Marianne sit at the card table, waiting, throughout the scene.
Pause.

Elinor She's had a very long nap. She's been in there all afternoon. Perhaps someone should . . .

Peter begins to stand up.

I didn't mean you, Peter. You can't do everything in this house.

Peter sits back down.

When George was ill I tried to do everything. I felt I owed it to George. He was my husband. We were married. I cared about him. If he'd taken such a long nap . . .

No reaction from Edward.

Delicious soup, Peter.

Peter Thank you, Elinor.

Elinor (*to Edward*) Anything in the paper? I'm glad to see you enjoying the paper. I brought it so you would enjoy it. (*Beat.*) You're welcome, Eddie. Actually, Peter, I bought it for me to read on the train. And then I just kept it. At the last minute I remembered Eddie and kept it. He was a last second's thought. (*She spoons out a lump of potato from the soup, starts to eat, then stops:*) I don't eat potato skins. Did you know that's where the vitamins are? In the skins. You'll put them in the compost.

Peter I –.

Elinor That compost has been there for ever. Think of what has been thrown out. What's been lost.

Edward looks up from his paper, takes a sip from his drink.

456

Peter, do you play golf?

Peter Yes, I do.

Beat.

Elinor That's it. I only had that one question.

That made Edward smile. Elinor begins smiling, realizing she is slowly getting Edward's attention.

My biggest fear, Peter, in coming here – and did I have fears – do I – I never thought of myself as courageous before, but now, sitting here . . . (*Beat.*) What was I saying?

Peter Your biggest fear about coming here.

Elinor Eddie. I hoped he wouldn't blame me. Marianne – really what do I care about what she thinks?

Peter But I thought Marianne was your closest friend.

Elinor Young man, I am not on a witness stand so I would appreciate it if you would not speak to me in that tone of voice.

Peter But –?

Elinor And I'm only going to tell you once.

Peter Sorry. I'm very sorry.

Elinor Look at him, Eddie, he believed me.

She smiles. Edward tries not to laugh.

When you're ready, Peter, you can take my bowl. I've had all I can take.

Peter (*standing*) I'm finished as well. (*He wasn't. He begins to collect plates.*) Eddie?

Edward No.

Peter takes the two dishes into the kitchen.

Elinor The flowers are lovely. Daffodils have always been a favourite of mine, as you know only too well. The ones in my cabin are even lovelier.

Peter returns, picks up more dishes, except for Edward's.

Peter (*leaving*) I'll do the dishes.

Elinor What a strange experience it is to walk into a cabin and know that you were expected by the flowers on the dresser. I almost felt hurt.

Edward stops reading.

Being known like that. Sometimes such gestures are touching – they mean: be comfortable, you are among friends. Other times, they mean – we know who you are, we know everything, you are among friends.

Edward, listening, turns a page of the paper.

You were always a man with a newspaper. That's how I remember you. You were always interested in things. What interests you now, these days? (*Beat.*) This interest in things is what always made you so . . .

Edward I'm getting interested in writing my memoirs, Elinor. (*He eats.*)

Elinor Good for you.

Edward That doesn't frighten you?

Elinor Why should it?

Edward Perhaps you'd give me a decent advance.

Elinor I don't acquire books any more, Eddie. Not since the Brits bought . . .

Edward I'd take half the advance Dorothy Gilbert got.

Elinor I know what people say but I had nothing to do with the cancellation of Dorothy's book. I don't even know what she said about me in her book. I wasn't the editor. I wasn't involved in the decision. I don't care what people say about me. People can say the moon about me. But that's not me. I don't work like that. Dorothy and Fred were great friends. (*Beat.*) There were a great many errors of fact in Dorothy's memoir. The legal department cancelled the contract. People could have sued. With cause.

Edward (*eating*) It was only a thought. I simply wanted you to know that I can be bought off. With the right advance our three-year marriage will be erased from time.

Elinor I would not want to see those years erased.

She goes to touch him, he does not respond, then:

(*coldly*) I had no idea you were looking for another publisher. What's Robert done? You've been with him for years and years. (*Beat.*) I talked to Robert this week. He thinks Marianne's lawsuit is pure garbage. There are so many people on my side. If I were the one dying I wouldn't want to look so foolish. What's so bad about what I said about her. I hardly mention her. I talk about her politics – not so much about her, Eddie. The fact that she takes everything so personally – I do not see this as my problem! If there is any point I wish to make while I'm here, it is this. I do not think this is my – [problem].

A thud off. Beat. Then a bell.
Peter enters from the kitchen, looks to Edward who remains expressionless, then hurries to the bedroom.
After a moment, Peter returns.

Peter She fell. She won't let me pick her up.

Edward sets down his napkin and goes off to the bedroom.

Elinor (*without looking at Peter*) With something like that, it's not the lungs but the brain that's going to kill her. That's what happened to George. If it is the lungs, it'll be slow and long.

Peter goes back into the kitchen. Elinor goes and sits on a couch (passing the younger Marianne and Elinor). Edward returns and sits back at the table.

Edward In my memoirs –. (*He stops himself, gets up and goes to the bar and pours himself a large drink. As he pours:*) Remind me to change the sheets in there before I go to bed. They need changing now. Sometimes I forget. By the time I get to bed I often have forgotten everything. (*He goes back and sits at the table.*) Back in the city I have a closet full of pornography. Floor to ceiling of pornography. (*He begins to eat again.*) *The New York Review of Books*, of all people, wanted me to do an essay on pornography. It was going to become a book. The people there helped me collect the stuff. I had these nice assistant editors take me around to buy the stuff. That was the most fun. I would open a book – like this and show them – show the kids. The boys were even more embarrassed. I thought we had lived through a sexual revolution? (*He eats.*) A closet full – all bought by the staff of *The New York Review of Books*. I would put that into my memoirs. Never got around to writing the piece, Elinor. Kept getting caught up in the research. (*He smiles.*) Whenever I feel old I start doing more research.

She smiles.

When Marianne and I finally bought this place and stopped visiting – (*nodding to Elinor*). It wasn't that long

ago when you think about it. Five years maybe? No more
than five. I remember we closed and Marianne and I – we
went swimming in the lake. Naked. Why not? It's private.
Even last year. Once or twice. Those three or four years.
Before she started getting dizzy. They said it was her ulcer
acting up. Another ulcer. So she stopped drinking. (*He
sips his drink.*) It wasn't an ulcer. I'd stopped drinking
with her. Then it wasn't an ulcer. (*Beat.*) You'd think the
doctors would have known better. Don't they deal with
this all the time? Maybe seven months ago we could have
gone swimming naked. She has some body. (*He turns to
Elinor.*) Let me tell you, Elinor, she's got a lot better body
than you do.

Elinor smiles, trying not to cry.

What a body. If she hadn't drunk – what an amazing
body. But still – even with – [the drinking]. We could have
gone swimming just months ago, except it would have
been too cold. But in principle. And now it is definitely
warm enough.

*Elinor has gotten up and now approaches Edward,
again with tears in her eyes. She puts her arms around
him, hugs him. He nestles his head into her shoulder.
She rubs his head, then he turns, putting his mouth to
her neck, and bites.*

Elinor Ow! What did you bite me for?

Edward (*calmly*) I thought you liked that. I remember
you always liking that.

Peter (*entering*) I could put some coffee on. Or is it too
late?

SCENE SEVEN

Projection: NIGHT.

1986: The Older Marianne now sits alone at the table, eating her dinner.

   1937: A shuffle of cards and the Younger Marianne and Elinor begin to play cards (two-handed bridge) at the card table.

   Eating, the Older Marianne laughs to herself.

Younger Elinor What's trumps again?

Younger Marianne Clubs. (*Beat.*) Spades. Two spades.

   Beat.

Younger Elinor You think she really meant that? Inviting us to her house. Meet her friends?

Younger Marianne She didn't say when, did she? It's not an invitation if you don't say when. Rich people. (*She shakes her head.*)

Younger Elinor What?

Younger Marianne The things they say.

Younger Elinor You're probably right.

   Short pause, they play.

He's taking a long time helping her to her boat.

Younger Marianne Just because a woman has a big mouth and is willing to say anything – even very personal things, pathetic things in my mind – to strangers, this makes her interesting? (*She shakes her head.*) Eddie disappoints me so much sometimes.

   Older Marianne laughs lightly to herself.

462

Younger Elinor How many cards do you have?

Marianne shows her.

Then it's still my play. (*She plays.*) She is very attractive you have to admit.

Younger Marianne She's nearly thirty. It's at thirty that women reach the absolute peak of their beauty.

Younger Elinor (*seriously*) I thought it was much younger.

Older Marianne laughs out loud at this. Older Edward enters from the porch.

Older Edward She was still reading. That's what the light was for. She's fine. She said she was so tired she was afraid she couldn't sleep. What were you laughing about? Just now. When I came in you were laughing.

Older Marianne I was thinking.

Beat.

Older Edward I'm going to get ready for bed.

Older Marianne So soon? We usually have a drink together before you go to bed.

Older Edward I'll change the sheets and come back out. (*He starts to go, stops.*) I told her it was your idea to check on her. That you were the one concerned. She said she didn't believe that.

Older Marianne I was concerned – about the lamp battery. They're expensive.

He smiles, goes to her, kisses her. She kisses him back. He begins to kiss her neck, then bites her.

Ow. That was nice. You're very sexy.

463

*Smiling he goes down the hall to the bedroom. She
continues to eat.*

Younger Marianne Listen.

Younger Elinor What is it? A bird?

Younger Marianne A loon. I'm sure it must be a loon.

They listen.

Younger Elinor That's a lonely sound. Makes you cry.

Younger Marianne Everything makes you cry, Elinor.

Younger Edward (*coming in from the porch*) Well she's
off. Anyone else want a drink? (*He goes to the bar.*) She
really wants to have us to her house. (*No response. He
pours.*) I had a good time tonight and I am not going to
say I didn't. Therese may be eccentric, but eccentric
people have their place in the world.

Younger Marianne (*interrupting*) Eddie, what are our
plans, if I may ask?

Younger Edward Tomorrow, I thought we'd go –
[swimming].

Younger Marianne How long do we stay?!!

Short pause.

Younger Edward We can go whenever you want.

Younger Marianne I am not the one who brought us
here.

Younger Edward Elinor? (*Beat.*) How long can Gene be
gone? He's left us the boat . . .

The young women ignore him and play cards.

(*finally*) We were out by her boat talking, and suddenly
she stops and asks – which of you two did I sleep with.

464

Beat.

Younger Elinor (*playing a card*) She did?

Younger Edward Yeh.

Younger Marianne (*playing a card*) What did you say?

Younger Edward (*shrugging*) That we're colleagues. We work together.

Younger Marianne Right. (*Short pause, she plays.*) You know I'm not surprised she asked him that.

Younger Elinor Why?

Younger Marianne Some people aren't happy unless they can drag everything down to the personal.

The Older Marianne suddenly starts laughing as if she just heard the funniest joke in the world.

Act Two

SCENE ONE

Projection: THE NEXT DAY, 8.15 A.M.

The lawn which overlooks the beach and lake.

Cabins and main house off (unseen). Stairs down to the beach and dock. Two reclining deck chairs facing the lake. Outdoor wooden table and chairs.

1986: The Older Marianne sits in a reclining deck chair. She wears a sun hat and is reading Elinor's memoirs.

1938: Younger Marianne, Edward and Elinor sit around the table, having coffee. They wear robes, having just gone skinny-dipping.

Younger Elinor puts back her head and closes her eyes.

Younger Elinor Mmmm. The sun does feel good.

Younger Edward Doesn't it? Nice after a swim.

Younger Elinor Very nice.

Younger Marianne You know, Elinor was right.

Younger Elinor (*without opening her eyes*) I know.

Younger Marianne You don't even know what I was going to say. I meant – about swimming like this. Without suits.

Younger Elinor (*still with eyes closed*) I knew what you were going to say.

Younger Marianne It's great. It really is.

Younger Elinor opens her eyes, picks up her sun lotion, folds down her robe – exposing her bare breasts – and

466

begins to put the lotion on her shoulders, etc.

Younger Elinor (*as she does this*) I can hardly stand to put a suit on anymore. It changes the whole thing.

Younger Edward (*a bit uncomfortable*) I agree. (*Then smiling*) But I wouldn't want to do it with someone like Therese, she'd probably try to 'ring my bell!'

He laughs at his joke. No one else does.

Younger Elinor (*ignoring Edward, still putting on the lotion*) There is really something pure about it.

Younger Edward (*trying to get back into the conversation*) I agree. Very pure.

Younger Elinor *We* put the clothes on our bodies. We weren't born with clothes.

Beat.

Younger Marianne Who do you usually go – swimming with?

Younger Elinor shrugs [anyone].

Really?

Younger Elinor Sometimes I just go by myself. If someone else is there – you ignore him. In a way it's a private thing. (*She finishes with the lotion, covers herself again with the robe.*) More coffee?

The others shake their heads.

Younger Marianne It is pure. That is the word, isn't it?

Younger Elinor That's not to say there isn't a – sensuality about it.

Younger Marianne Of course. I didn't mean –.

Younger Edward Yes, there is that.

Younger Elinor (*over his*) Drifting. Stretching. I like to just float. It's comforting, I find. And stimulating.

Younger Marianne I wouldn't call it 'sexual'.

Younger Elinor No, no 'sensual'. I chose the word carefully. And, Edward, 'sensual' has a lot more to do with than just one's sex parts.

Younger Edward Why do you say that to me –?

Younger Marianne Though there can be some of that –.

Younger Elinor You really think so? I think what it essentially has to do with – is being free. Without encumbrances. Your bare body alive, to everything, water, ripples, the sun. Maybe it's not the same for a man.

Younger Edward No, it's –.

Younger Elinor Suddenly feeling unshackled I mean.

Younger Edward It's very freeing –.

Younger Elinor You'd do it again?

Younger Edward (*starting to stand*) Now?

Younger Elinor (*smiling to Younger Marianne*) I'm still not sure if the pleasure's the same. (*to Younger Edward*) Would you do it alone? Was there this wonderfully sensual joy of just being nude in the water? Or was the real thrill having a couple of naked girls floating around you? (*She smiles at Younger Marianne.*)

Younger Edward I . . .? Sure I'd do it alone. I said I enjoyed it. What do you want me to say?

The girls laugh, very much excluding Edward from their joke. Both girls lean back, Younger Elinor closes her eyes, then rolls down her robe again to catch the

468

sun. Younger Marianne, catching this, rolls down her robe, though just a little to expose a shoulder.

(*finally*) Have either of you read that Henry Miller book?

Younger Elinor (*eyes closed*) Who? What book is that?

Younger Marianne (*eyes closed*) I know what you mean.

Younger Edward I'll show it to you. You can't buy it. A friend sent it from Paris. If they'd opened it at customs –.

Younger Marianne (*eyes closed*) It wouldn't have been your fault.

Younger Edward They'd have taken it. I could have been fined.

Younger Marianne (*opening her eyes*) What if you didn't even know what it was? What if I sent you something that I wasn't supposed to and you didn't even know what it was? They couldn't fine you.

Younger Edward I knew what it was! I asked my friend to send it. I was taking a big chance. (*Beat.*) Incredibly graphic. But not at all sensual.

Younger Elinor (*eyes closed*) Doesn't sound –.

Younger Edward Not at all erotic.

Younger Elinor (*eyes closed*) You're not equating sensual with erotic??

Younger Marianne (*again eyes closed*) I don't think he meant –.

Younger Edward I wasn't equating anything. All I said was it wasn't sensual *and* it wasn't erotic.

Younger Elinor (*eyes closed*) Define what you mean by 'erotic'.

Younger Edward It means –. Something that is erotic, it stimulates. Causes physical stimulation. Verifiable physical stimulation.

Younger Elinor (*eyes closed*) That's good. That's a good definition.

Younger Marianne (*eyes closed*) It is.

Younger Edward Miller goes way overboard. Actually by the end it's become quite political. I don't think intentionally. But you can't help but see these people as decadent. As if nothing exists but their . . .

Younger Marianne (*eyes closed*) Cocks?

Younger Elinor opens her eyes.

Younger Edward Yeh. Their 'cocks'.

Younger Marianne (*eyes closed*) Why don't you review it? Sounds like you have something to say about this book.

Younger Edward I was thinking of doing that. That's why I took the chance and had my friend send me the copy.

Younger Elinor, eyes open now, pours herself more coffee.

(*to Younger Elinor*) Whitman's 'erotic'.

Younger Elinor You think so?

Younger Edward Definitely.

Younger Elinor What about Joyce?

Younger Edward I've never thought of him as –.

Younger Elinor Have you read Molly Bloom out loud? If you think Whitman's –. (*She suddenly gets up.*) I saw a copy in the house.

Younger Marianne (*opening her eyes*) Elinor –?

Younger Elinor (*over this*) Let me get it. (*to Younger Marianne*) He's not going to believe this. (*She hurries off.*)

  Beat.

Younger Marianne She's read it twice to me. (*She smiles. She reaches over and picks up Younger Elinor's sun lotion. She rolls down her robe, exposing one breast, and begins to put it on her shoulders.*) You really should do that review of the Henry Miller. How graphic does he really get?

Younger Edward I'll loan you the book –.

Younger Marianne If it's junk –.

Younger Edward It's fascinating to see just how far –. By the end you're just angry at these people, who think about nothing but themselves. And their 'cocks'.

Younger Elinor (*returning with a copy of* Ulysses) I'll just read from the very end. I'll start at random.

Younger Marianne With him how do we know it's at random? (*She smiles.*)

Younger Elinor Marianne –.

Younger Marianne Give me Dreiser any day.

Younger Elinor Just the last . . . Here.

  She stays standing and begins to read. Occasionally, she has to retighten her robe which starts to open.

'. . . where I was a Flower of the mountain yes when I put the rose in my hair like the Andalusian girls used or shall I wear a red yes (*She looks up knowingly at this, then:*) and how he kissed me under the Moorish wall and I thought well as well him as another and then I asked him with my eyes to ask again yes and then he asked me would I yes to say yes my mountain flower and first I put my arms around him yes and dress him down to me so he could feel my breasts all perfume yes and his heart was going like mad and yes I said yes I will Yes.' (*She closes the book.*) It's the rhythm with the 'yes's –.

Younger Edward I caught that.

Younger Elinor You get some of it just reading, but then you hear it . . . I diagrammed the whole last three pages for a paper. (*She has handed Younger Edward the book.*)

Younger Edward Look at this.

Younger Elinor What??

The girls lean over and look.

Younger Edward He capitalizes the very last 'Yes.' I wonder if anyone's written about that.

SCENE TWO

Projection: 9.25 A.M.

1986: The Older Marianne still sits, reading Elinor's memoirs.
    1937: The Younger Edward, Elinor and Marianne remain at the table, reading, sunning, etc. throughout.
    Older Edward slowly enters from the direction of the cabins. Older Marianne, before seeing him, suddenly slams the book shut.

Older Edward Getting ourselves pumped up for the fight? You've been out here for a while now. That much sun –.

Older Marianne Is it time yet? I hope she doesn't chicken out and try to settle. Though that would be just like her.

Older Edward No it wouldn't.

Older Marianne (*ignoring him*) No guts that woman. (*She holds up the book.*) You feel that on every page. You know what really bothers me? It's not what she writes about me. I couldn't give a damn about that. What people say about me, who cares? It's what she's written about you, Eddie, that has me very upset. Even at our age one can still be shocked by how low people will stoop. Actually I'm a little surprised you're not more upset with her than you are. But you always did hide your feelings pretty well.

Older Edward I'm not in the index. I'm never named in the whole –.

Older Marianne Anyone who knows you, Eddie, knows who you are in this. Don't kid yourself. To take apart an old friend, an ex-husband! What could be more cowardly. What could be easier. I'll bet you know things about Elinor that –.

Older Edward If I can ignore what's written about me, and you don't care what she wrote about you, then why are we –?

Older Marianne (*ignoring him*) Look here. Not one word of what I achieved as an educator. Instead, I'm –.

Older Edward They're her memoirs, not yours –.

Older Marianne (*over this*) She's hurt me. A sick woman like me. Hold my hand.

He takes her hand.

Why don't you tell me you love me?

Older Edward I love you.

Peter enters from the direction of the cabins.

Peter (*entering*) I can't get her to change her mind.

473

Older Marianne (*confused*) What??

Older Edward She doesn't want to leave her cabin. She wants to have the discussion about her book there.

Older Marianne But I said I wanted to meet in the main house. Wasn't she told that?

Older Edward That's when she said she wanted to meet in *her* cabin.

Older Marianne She's that insensitive? She expects you to carry me –.

Peter She says she's ill too.

Older Edward Ten minutes ago she said nothing about being –.

Peter It came to her, I think, while she was talking to me.

Older Marianne There's no food in that cabin, we'll starve her out. Or better – call over to the motel, see if there are some people to rent the cabin for the night. Pick me up.

Older Edward Just a –.

Older Marianne She's made her move, now we make ours. Pick me up!

Older Edward What is so wrong about meeting in her cabin??

Older Marianne just stares at Older Edward.

Peter I'll talk to her again. Maybe there's some compromise place to meet.

Older Marianne How about here on the lawn? I'm already here.

Peter That would be her problem. (*He starts to hurry.*)

Older Marianne Whose side are you on?!

Peter I'm on no one's side. (*He goes.*)

Older Marianne You hear that? He's on no one's side! So
what do we pay him for?!

Older Edward (*shouting back*) We don't pay him! He's
my nephew! He's here on vacation!

   Pause.

Older Marianne (*hurt*) Pick me up, if it isn't too much
trouble. I'm getting hot.

   He starts to pick her up.

Be careful of your back, Eddie.

   They start to head for the main house.

SCENE THREE

Projection: HIGH NOON.

*1937: Younger Edward, in his robe, sits alone at the table,
reading a newspaper.*
   *1986: Older Elinor and Peter stroll in from the
direction of the cabins.*

Older Elinor You're right, Peter. It does feel good to get
some air. You know I couldn't get my window closed last
night. I think it must have been because of the window
that –. (*She touches her 'sore' throat.*)

Peter I'll close it. She was out here. I'm sure they're just
inside. Why don't you come in, you haven't had anything
to – [eat].

Older Elinor I'm taking a stroll. I'll be down by the lake
if anyone's interested. (*She starts to go.*)

Peter Elinor.

Older Elinor (*with sudden anger*) I'm as old as she is! I deserve at least as much respect! Tell her I came four hundred miles. She can come one hundred feet.

Peter She can't walk.

Older Elinor She gets around. Half my friends won't see me because she's gotten around to them. (*sudden charm*) You want to accompany me? (*She holds out her arm.*)

Peter Sorry.

Older Elinor She must pay you a lot.

Peter Edward's my Uncle.

Older Elinor Nepotism. So you're cheap. Can't get your own clients. Have to rely on the family. That's good to know. She was always cheap.

Peter goes off toward the main house, Older Elinor starts to move, but stays, lost in thought, leaning against one of the chairs.

1937: Younger Elinor, still in robe, comes from the direction of the main house (passing Peter), shuffling a deck of cards.

Younger Elinor (*entering*) I found them. They were under a cushion in the couch. You still want to play?

Younger Edward (*putting the paper down*) It's last week's. Where's Marianne?

Younger Elinor Going through Gene's bookshelves looking for something to read.

Younger Edward You can deal. And no doubt criticizing everything Gene has.

Younger Elinor Not everything. She hasn't gone through everything.

As Younger Elinor begins to deal, Younger Marianne enters with a book. She too is still in her robe.

Younger Marianne Look at this. Jack Wells' book. I didn't know it'd come out.

Younger Elinor Let me see. Neither did I.

She reaches for the book. Younger Marianne doesn't give it to her.

Younger Marianne It's even inscribed to Gene.

Younger Elinor To Gene??

Younger Marianne Maybe he helped him out financially with the research.

Younger Edward (*to Younger Marianne*) You playing?

She shakes her head.

Who's Jack Wells?

Younger Elinor (*trying to grab the book*) Who's it dedicated to?

Younger Marianne No one. There's no dedication. I thought for sure it'd be for Kitty. (*to Edward*) Professor Wells was my adviser. He's the one who suggested that for my thesis on *The Canterbury Tales* I research the wool trade of the fourteenth century.

Younger Elinor Jack was very to the left.

Younger Marianne You called him Jack too?

Younger Elinor I guess I did. (*to Edward*) I thought we were playing cards. Bid.

Younger Edward Two diamonds.

They play.

Younger Marianne (*still looking through the book*) I used to babysit his kids. That's how I started calling him Jack. Elinor, he wasn't your adviser.

Younger Elinor No.

Younger Marianne You didn't take Chaucer.

Younger Elinor shakes her head.

So why did you call him Jack?

Younger Elinor shrugs.

(*to herself*) Handsome binding.

Younger Elinor (*playing a card*) I give him a month before he disowns it. He's disowned everything he's written. He's very hard on himself.

Younger Marianne Is he? I didn't know that. Why should I know that, we weren't that close. (*Beat.*) I was closer to Kitty.

They finish the game.

Younger Elinor Are we keeping score?

Younger Edward I don't care. (*He shuffles.*)

Younger Marianne (*out of the blue*) I think I was the first person – certainly the first student friend – Kitty told. When she suspected . . . (*to Edward*) She thought Jack was seeing someone. A student.

Younger Edward deals.

Never found out who it was. When she confronted him, he put up a good show. Denied everything. But then, the very next day – and this is what convinced her – he went out and bought all new underwear.

Younger Edward Why would he do that? Was there a sale?

Younger Marianne I don't know.

Younger Elinor (*suddenly laughing*) You are so funny.

Younger Marianne Why –??

Younger Elinor As if making some big point you repeat what Kitty told you about him buying underwear, but then you don't even know what the point's supposed to be! (*She laughs.*)

Younger Marianne To Kitty it was serious!

Younger Edward (*to calm her*) Marianne –.

Younger Marianne You stay out of this! (*to Elinor*) Forget the goddamn underwear!! What I'm trying to ask – as tactfully as I can – is if you were the student, Elinor?

   Beat.

Younger Elinor Who slept with Jack? (*to Younger Edward*) Let's play.

Younger Marianne You were. I don't believe this. She was Kitty's friend too!! How could you betray a friend –?!

Younger Elinor He asked me out on a date? Okay?!

   This stops Younger Marianne.

He asked *me*.

Younger Marianne And you went.

Younger Elinor And I went. He took me to a bar. He liked to sit at the bar. He said it made him feel working class. He's a pretty confused man, Marianne. Kitty, he said, would never sit at the bar with him.

Younger Marianne Excuse me. (*She starts to hurry off toward the main house.*)

Younger Edward Marianne!

Younger Marianne (*over this, holding up the book*) I just want to put this back. (*She is gone.*)

Pause.

Younger Elinor (*finally*) I didn't sleep with Professor Wells.

Younger Edward That's not what she –.

Younger Elinor Nothing happened between us. Promise.

Short pause.

Younger Edward Then why did you let her think –?

Younger Elinor I don't like being accused.

Younger Edward She only accused you because –.

Younger Elinor I think you should stay out of this.

Younger Edward But you're arguing about nothing.

Marianne bursts back in.

Younger Marianne If you think it's because I'm jealous!

Younger Elinor Jealous??

Younger Marianne Nothing could be further from the truth. It's only because Kitty was our friend. That's why I'm disgusted at this rich girl game playing – not caring about who the hell you hurt!!

Younger Edward Marianne, Elinor did not –.

Younger Elinor Be quiet. (*She turns to Younger Marianne.*) How dare you talk to me like that. I had no more money at school than you did. Maybe less.

Younger Marianne I didn't grow up with servants. With chauffeurs. I was the daughter of a – [chauffeur]!!

Younger Elinor (*over this*) Since I was fifteen I've had nothing!

Younger Marianne (*over this*) I didn't attend Mary Baldwin's School for Young – [Ladies]!!

Younger Elinor I left when we had no more money!!

Younger Edward Why bring this up??

Younger Marianne People should not be cavalier with other people's feelings! That's what I believe. That's how I was brought up!

Younger Elinor Right. Eddie, ask her about freshman year. A certain Saturday. I was working at Lyman, the plant house.

Younger Marianne I've told you what I remember. I've apologized. I was a freshman.

Younger Elinor I'm on work study. Watering plants. Marianne comes in with these boys.

Younger Marianne From Amherst. Friends of someone my father was driving for! I didn't know any better. I realized later they were only out to have a good time with a chauffeur's daughter. They got me drunk.

Younger Elinor She comes in drunk.

Younger Marianne That's rich people for you!

Younger Elinor And for the hell of it, because she thinks it's funny, she kicks over my water bucket. All I say is, watch it, and she starts screaming at me like I'm some servant!!

Younger Marianne (*over this*) I was drunk!

Younger Elinor (*over this*) Did that happen?! Did that happen?!

Younger Marianne (*over this*) It was the third week of freshman year!!

Younger Elinor So – I'm the rich person?! (*Beat.*) Your father didn't hang himself in the garage because he couldn't pay what he owed to a lot of rich people. I had nothing in college. I had nothing since Dad did that. Get off my back. Whose bid?

Younger Edward I don't want to play.

Younger Marianne Before our freshman, Eddie –.

Younger Edward Talk to her.

Younger Marianne I receive a note from the dean's office – my room-mate – someone named Elinor Blair.

Younger Elinor You've never mentioned –.

Younger Marianne When I get to Smith, I learn Miss Blair has asked for another room-mate –.

Younger Elinor A friend of a cousin's.

Younger Marianne (*over this*) Because – of course this wasn't actually spoken. Because – Little Miss Blair did not want an Italian for a room – [mate]!!

Younger Elinor (*erupting*) That's not true!!

Younger Marianne And who do I get – the only other Italian in the whole freshman class!! What a coincidence.

Younger Elinor There were other Italians –.

Younger Marianne You counted, I'm sure.

Younger Elinor Who told you I –?

Younger Marianne Some student! I don't remember any more.

   Beat.

Younger Elinor Look at me. It wasn't true. I promise.

Why haven't you ever mentioned –.

Younger Marianne I knew it wasn't true any more.

Younger Elinor It never was. (*Beat.*) Do you believe me?
After all you know about me – could I have done that?
(*Short pause.*) Do you believe me?

Younger Edward Marianne?

Younger Marianne I believe you.

Younger Elinor sighs – the storm has passed.

Younger Edward Where did that come from? And
Marianne, Elinor did not sleep with this professor of
yours. She told me when you went in.

Beat.

Younger Elinor We went out that one time. Sat at the bar. I
ended up throwing beer in his face. As I said, he's confused.

Short pause.

Younger Edward Why don't we switch to rummy so
Marianne can play?

Younger Elinor Do you want to?

Younger Marianne (*smiling*) I haven't found anything I
want to read.

He starts to shuffle, when there is a boat horn, off.

Younger Edward (*standing*) What's that? A boat.
Who's –?

Younger Elinor (*standing and looking*) That's Therese,
isn't it?

Younger Edward She's waving to us. (*He goes toward the
steps to the beach and waves.*) Therese! Therese!

Younger Marianne (*still sitting*) Elinor.

Younger Elinor Come on.

She pulls her up and they follow Younger Edward off down the steps, as the horns continues and Younger Edward continues to shout 'Therese!'
  1986: Older Edward hurries out from the main house.

Older Edward (*to Older Elinor*) I just saw you out here. Did you have a pleasant walk? Would you like something to eat? I could bring it out here. I'll see what there is.

He hurries off. Older Elinor finally sits down on one of the reclining chairs.
  Peter hurries out, obviously just sent by Older Edward.

Peter It's a beautiful lake.

Older Elinor I've been here before.

Peter That's right. You lived –.

Older Elinor You wouldn't happen to have an aspirin?

Peter In the house. Do you want me to get it?

Older Elinor I'm thinking that, yes.

He starts to go, stops.

Peter You'll stay here?

She looks at him.

So I can bring you the aspirin. (*He turns and stops again.*) And a glass of water?

Older Elinor Please. Always a step ahead, aren't we?

He hurries off. Short pause.
  Older Edward enters carrying Older Marianne.

Older Marianne (*seeing Older Elinor*) What are you doing? Take me back inside.

Older Edward does not move.

Feeling better, Elinor?

Older Elinor A little.

Older Marianne You look just awful.

Older Edward carries her to a chair next to Older Elinor.

What are you doing?!

Older Edward My arms are falling asleep.

Older Marianne No they're not.

Older Elinor (*standing up*) Excuse me. (*She turns to go.*)

Older Edward (*at the same time, to Marianne*) If you want to run away.

Older Marianne Set me down. Quick! Hurry! Then I'll be the first one sitting.

Older Elinor (*hurrying back and sitting first*) I'm sitting down!

They are next to each other. Pause.

Older Edward (*to Elinor*) I'll see what there is to eat. (*He hurries off.*)

Older Elinor (*turning to Marianne*) Oh dear, did you come to join me?

Pause. Marianne has picked up Elinor's book.
    1937: The Younger Edward, Elinor and Marianne hurry up the steps and run across the lawn toward the cabins. They are still in their robes.

Older Marianne Fascinating book. Have you read it? I understand it's been shortlisted for this year's Pulitzer for fiction.

Older Elinor (*beginning to leave*) I'm not here to listen –.

Older Marianne You're right. This isn't the best time or place. Later maybe – in the main house.

Older Elinor decides to sit back down.

Older Elinor (*calmly*) Marianne –.

Older Marianne That is if you are feeling better. Trust me, dear, I know what a strain being ill puts on one. I wouldn't dream of criticizing a friend when she's ill. Who would do such a thing?

Older Elinor (*without looking at her*) I am deeply deeply sorry that you are ill. (*She covers her face in her hands.*)

Older Marianne That hasn't worked on me for years. I never understood why people – men especially – could fall for so obvious a –. Does Eddie still fall for that? There is nothing wrong with a little manipulation, but hell what happened to subtlety?

Older Elinor (*looking up*) You've become so old and bitter.

Older Marianne Wise. Wise. Perhaps your book is the perfect expression of its author.

Edward has returned, drink in hand. Peter follows with aspirin and water.

Who was saying just the other day that the only honest statement expressed in the whole thing was the price? (*She laughs and turns to Older Edward.*) Who said that?

Older Edward You did. (*He turns to Older Elinor.*) I
forgot your food, but I remembered my drink.

Older Elinor Peter, is that my aspirin?

He gives it to her.

Thank you, dear. I have such a headache. (*She takes the
aspirin.*)

Older Marianne Maybe it's brain cancer and you caught
it from me.

Pause.

Older Elinor Eddie, what I don't understand about
Marianne's suit – we are here to talk about the lawsuit,
are we not?

Older Edward I'd hoped we'd get around to it.

Older Elinor It's the only reason why I'm here. What I
don't understand – Peter maybe you will explain it to me,
as you, like Eddie, are an intelligent man.

Older Marianne Quit the flattery and talk.

Older Elinor Marianne has said that what I wrote hurt
her. And that I hurt her – on purpose. This thinking
misses completely the kind of book this is, what I
intended it to be. Which is not to say it's without faults –
the reviewer for the *Post Book Review* had a few
grumbles that I, for one, agree with. (*Beat.*) My book was
never meant to be merely – simply – a life story. This is
the mistake that Marianne makes. My book is a history.
And as a history it attempts to present a world, a time, a
place in that world from a particular perspective. In other
words – I have points to make.

Older Marianne Axes to grind.

Older Elinor About our time. From a definite point of

view. I admit I have a point of view. Marianne has a point of view. And they are no doubt different. And so within a discussion of history in which one is striving to present the case for one particular point of view – examples, specifics become unavoidable. (*Beat.*) This is what Marianne has misunderstood.

Older Marianne Eddie, I don't know what she's talking about. Here, read from the book.

Older Elinor In my book I use Marianne only as an example of a larger idea. She is not the idea itself. She is not the reason for the discussion. My intention was not to criticize her. To hurt her. If you don't understand, let me try to make my defence a little clear.

Older Edward Defence? What are you talking about? We're sitting outside, old friends, having a nice relaxed –.

Peter (*interrupting*) Edward, I think what she's telling us is that she has a lawyer –.

Older Elinor More than one.

Peter Who has advised Elinor that legally, according to libel law, Marianne, as a public figure is going to have to prove intention to harm. Is that correct?

Older Elinor Yes, it is. That has been my advice.

Older Marianne You coward.

Older Elinor (*over her*) That has been my advice!

Peter Wait a minute, Elinor, the real problem with this defence, in my opinion, is whether Marianne is indeed a public figure. If she isn't then –.

Older Elinor Of course she's a – [public figure]!

Older Marianne (*at the same time*) Who knows me?! Nobody knows me!

Older Elinor President emeritus of Bryn Mawr –
[College]!!

Older Marianne If my work as an educator is so
important, why didn't you put it in the book?!! There's
not one mention –!!

Older Edward (*yelling*) Peter!!! (*He stares at Peter. They
quiet down.*)

Peter Right. Edward's right. Let's leave the law to the
lawyers. We're here to have a totally open, friendly
discussion of the problem. (*to Edward*) Sorry.

Older Edward You're a real estate lawyer!

Peter I was just trying to help. I said I was sorry.

*1937: The Younger Edward, Elinor and Marianne hurry
back across, heading for the steps to the dock. As they
run, they carry shoes, button shirts, etc. – now dressed
for their visit to Therese. They hurry down the stairs.*

(*to Marianne*) What did you want Edward to read?

Older Edward (*refusing the book, to Marianne*) You read
it. You read what you want to Elinor.

Older Marianne I thought you were here to support me.

Older Edward I am supporting you. I'm supporting this
whole thing. Read what you want to Elinor.

Older Marianne Coward.

Older Edward I'm supporting you by trying to get you
two talking to each other. I think that's a lot of support.

Older Marianne (*to Older Elinor*) He always was a
coward. No spine. Was he with you too?

Older Elinor It was terrible. I had a friend who called
him Eddie Jelly.

Older Marianne Wasn't that me?

Older Elinor I finally couldn't take it. I mean, with a drink in his hand he talks a good fight.

Older Marianne He has a drink in his hand.

Older Elinor I talk about people like him in the book. He's symptomatic of a lot of academic liberals I know. He's part of a whole chapter of ex-radical men I have known.

Older Marianne That chapter I liked. (*She opens the book.*) I'll read a passage then. (*reading*) 'And then there's Marianne Rinaldi, a very old friend. To be sure, Marianne is an intelligent woman and as a young woman one of my circle of leftist friends. (*Beat.*) Today her roots in radicalism can hardly be discerned; not a declared conservative, rather that breed of anti-communist liberal whose moral contradictions have long since been well established but who has hung on to the accoutrements of a political philosophy fashionable under John F. Kennedy. (*Beat.*) There is the well-appointed upper West Side apartment – rent-controlled of course – subscriptions to one or two of the more intellectual theatres – such as they are – the house in the Adirondacks – much less showy than one in Connecticut or on the Shore, but also twice as large – which recalls a more pastoral time when socializing the land was the topic instead of today when it is learning how to water ski when you are sixty-eight.' (*She turns to Older Edward.*) That refers to you.

Older Edward I know, I know. I read the book.

Older Marianne (*reading*) 'There are the bookcases filled with *The Times* bestseller lists of the last decade and the endearing maid, Ethel, who has been like a "sister" to Marianne for years.' (*She slams the book shut.*)

Older Edward You'll lose your place.

Older Marianne It's marked. I come off like a hypocrite. You may not have meant that, Elinor, but I do. Did you mean that? Is that what you think? I am not a hypocrite!! What about your possessions?!!

Older Elinor I do not hide my property in the book. I make everything I have very clear, and even confess that for a few things I harbour very strong feelings. But on the whole I make the point that I have not lived for my possessions, I –.

Older Marianne And I have?!

Older Elinor Your type has, yes. *I* think. Maybe not, actually. But I was using you to define a type.

Older Marianne You attack a friend. A fifty-year-old friendship, to make a point about a type?? That doesn't make sense to me. When I read this book it did not make sense to me.

Older Elinor It was an important point to make I thought. Marianne, I criticize myself throughout the book. In fact, one could even read it as an act of self-criticism.

Older Marianne With the subtitle, 'Elinor Blair, Heroine of Our Time.'

Older Elinor It's 'Elinor Blair, A Woman in Our Times.' (*Beat.*) If I really wanted to hurt you –. Did you read the chapter on Vietnam? I talked about a cocktail party? I didn't name names. I chose not to name names, but that was your cocktail party, remember? (*Beat.*) I was late and I came in saying – 'Did you hear about what happened at Kent State?' And no one had. And I said – 'They are now murdering our children!' We then spent –. *You* then spent the whole evening arguing if 'murder' was the right word. That perhaps all we knew for certain was that a 'killing' had taken place. I never had such a headache. If I really wanted to attack you –.

Older Marianne Attack for what?! I remember you sitting there half-crocked sobbing on somebody's knee. 'My children!' What children?? You don't have any children! The closest you had was that eighteen-year-old co-ed George was seeing on the sly! (*to Edward*) One of George's students. I held her (*Marianne's*) hand through the whole thing. George was going to leave her.

Older Elinor I don't want to make this into a personal thing.

Older Marianne Aren't you a little late?

Older Elinor My point was only that you sat there – debating definitions while other people were out in the street making something happen. If it had been left up to you there would still be a Vietnam.

Older Marianne And there still is a Vietnam thanks to us. Who do you think kept Johnson's people from blowing up the whole place?!

Older Elinor And being such pals of Johnson that's why you supported Humphrey. You loved Humphrey. (*She laughs.*)

Older Marianne I supported McCarthy and you know it. I supported Kennedy and then I supported McCarthy.

Older Elinor Not in the election.

Older Marianne McCarthy wasn't in the election. You wanted Nixon?

Older Elinor We got Nixon.

Older Marianne No thanks to me. Maybe to you. But not to me.

Older Elinor I don't want to talk just elections. Elections are meaningless.

Older Marianne Now you do sound like a communist.

Older Elinor There are worse things to sound like.

Older Marianne (*laughing, to Edward*) She never learns! But I want to get back to your book. (*She opens the book.*)

Older Elinor So I used her name. Big deal.

Older Marianne Why did you do it?

Older Elinor I thought I needed to be specific. Have examples.

Older Marianne It's like you were getting even for something. What were you getting even for?

Older Elinor I was making a point! How many times do I have to say that?! I wasn't getting even for anything! This was not personal. Everything isn't personal!!!

Older Marianne suddenly flinches in pain.

Are you all right?

Older Marianne I'm fine.

Beat.

Older Elinor (*to the others*) She's probably faking it.

Older Marianne That's right. I'm faking it.

Older Elinor Just like that quote unquote heart attack she had in the mid-fifties. Right after she let that teacher be fired. Right after they forced you to let him go and you succumbed. I remember that. Do you? We all took great notice of that. That wasn't a heart attack. I'm not sure you're even sick now.

Older Edward Elinor –.

Older Marianne No, Edward. She's right. I am just fine. And I have been faking it all along. Now that you know – I can stop pretending. It also means I don't have to pull my punches with you anymore, Elinor. Because I don't need your sympathy. I am not sick. (*She struggles to sit up in the chair.*)

Peter looks to Older Edward to see if he should help.

Let's talk politics some more. (*She opens the book.*) Before we get back to me, let's talk Stalin, Elinor.

Older Elinor I see we've put to rest the witch-hunted teacher . . .

Older Marianne (*slamming the book shut*) Did you know him? A very gentle good man. Had I left with him, he'd have had nothing. By staying I got him a year's severance.

Older Elinor So you fired him for his own good. Oh, Marianne –.

Older Marianne At the time it was the best option we had!

Older Elinor Best for him or for you?!

Older Marianne (*opening the book, reading*) '. . . equating Marxism with Stalinism, a ploy used by even those one-time friends of socialism, to taint one and all with the *sins* of Stalin.' (*She looks up.*) 'The sins of Stalin.' You don't want to go any farther than just 'sins'? (*Another page. Reads*) '. . . Stalinism was as much a cultural movement in the course of Russian history, as it was the result of one man's quest for authoritarian control . . .'

Older Elinor Read the rest.

Older Marianne looks up, then reads.

Older Marianne '. . . authoritarian control. A nation's propensity for self-disfigurement can, I believe, be called "cultural", but should in no way diminish the destruction wrought by Stalinism itself.' (*Beat.*) Not exactly a disclaimer. (*Another page.*) 'Nixon, like Joseph Stalin, looked for bodies to throw into the path of –.'

Older Elinor (*to Edward*) Listen to her, now she's defending Nixon! I knew this would happen!

Older Marianne (*throwing the book on the table*) Excuses! Smoke and mirrors! Clouded comparisons! Do you never learn?!

Older Elinor I am not a communist. You know that. I never have been. All of a sudden anyone to your left, you call a –.

Older Marianne I call stupid!!! (*Short pause.*) Have some sense woman. Grow up. The world's not like you thought.

Older Elinor So what's it like? (*Beat.*) Stalin, I have never defended.

Older Marianne You've defended his defenders.

Older Elinor Good writers, teachers. Not because they were anyone's defenders. Friends. I couldn't just cut off people. That's not how I am. When someone's a friend –. (*Beat.*) That is not how I see the world. I went to Russia!

Older Marianne (*laughing*) Right! On a USIA trip. (*to Edward*) A last minute substitute. George had two weeks of lectures in Chicago and she didn't want to stay home alone.

Older Elinor That was not the reason.

Older Marianne That's what she told me!

Older Elinor I had many reasons for going.

Older Marianne So committed. So pure. So ridiculous.

Older Elinor Are you going to throw everything I've ever said back in my face, as if you knew the true and real reason for anything I've done?

Older Marianne What are friends for? You've taught me that. Here. (*She picks up book and opens it. Reading*) 'Chapter Twenty One: Living With Dying.'

Older Elinor I don't mention you in that –.

Older Marianne (*to Edward*) I read this first in the *Times Magazine*. Laughed myself silly. She spends a couple of months holding George's hand – how many nurses did he have to actually take care of him? Three, wasn't it? She holds his hand and suddenly she's an expert on the dying.

Older Elinor Obviously not such an expert as you yourself are now.

Peter (*to Edward, wondering whether this should be stopped*) Edward –.

Older Edward says nothing, just watches.

Older Marianne You have to turn everything into a statement. A commitment, Elinor. Everything needs to be something big. George dies. That has to signify something. Can't it just count for what it was?

Older Elinor And what was that?

Beat.

Older Marianne Your husband died. You are old. I may go first. But you'll be following.

Older Elinor And that comforts you?

Older Marianne It doesn't keep me up at night.

Older Elinor After you're gone, perhaps Eddie and I will get back together. Two lonely people. Who've known each other . . . Does that comfort you?

Older Marianne We've shared men all our lives. There was George.

Older Elinor (*stunned*) That I do not believe!

Older Marianne smiles.

He would not have done that.

Older Marianne looks through the book.

This bitterness fascinates me. Maybe I'll write about it once you're dead. Add a chapter for the paperback edition. You hadn't thought of that – who's going to have the last say.

Older Marianne (*reading*) 'What happened to radicalism? If you were to ask a Marianne Rinaldi today, would she simply respond with a listing of her recent contributions to Amnesty International, The Sierra Club, and the ACLU? In a recent conversation she talked proudly to me about having positively refused to use Saran Wrap, the plastic kitchen wrap, a product of Dow Chemical, the maker of Napalm, since 1967, and about her stand against Barclay's Bank and its association with South African businesses. Though she did not say that the closest branch of Barclay's New York was eighty-two blocks from her apartment, thus there was little fear of this "stand" causing much inconvenience.' (*She closes the book.*) Saran Wrap. Something I mentioned in passing. We were making coffee in the kitchen together. You complained about the plastic wrap I had. You said I was cheap. I was not making a political point to you.

Older Elinor Then who were you making it to?

Beat.

497

Older Marianne As for Barclay's – we were going to Britain that summer. You could get their traveller's cheques anywhere. I was making a point of not buying *them*. You make me sound . . . . Those are not important things. (*She looks to Older Elinor.*)

Older Elinor Where did I lie? Why have you sued me? I am not saying I'm any better, Marianne.

Older Marianne Next time you write a book write that in. 'I'm not saying I'm any better, Marianne.'

Older Elinor I thought I did.

Older Marianne flinches in pain. Closes her eyes. Peter looks to Older Edward.

Marianne???

Older Marianne slowly opens her eyes, then nods – she is all right. She takes a deep breath, then:

Older Marianne Where were we?

Beat.

Older Elinor (*staring at her friend*) After the war you thought Eisenhower would make a great Democrat.

Older Marianne Let's talk about Hungary. And Poland. And Czechoslovakia! Let's talk Afghanistan!!!

SCENE FOUR

Projection: 7.40 P.M.

1986: A kerosene lamp is now lit and on the table, though the sun is still up. Peter is alone, holding the back of a chair, looking out over the lake. In the distance the cry of a loon.

Older Edward comes in from the direction of the house. Beat.

Older Edward Hear the loons?

Peter turns to him.

They're a regular feature of this place. Always have been. (*He sits.*)

Peter I'm sorry, Edward.

Older Edward Have you eaten anything?

Peter I don't think I could. Not after that boat ride.

Older Edward (*distracted*) Did I thank you for getting the doctor? I could not have done that any more.

Peter nods a 'You're welcome.'

Peter I've been calling around for a hospital bed. I've got a lead or two. The doctor thought –. We've assumed you don't want to take her to a hospital. What would be the point?

Older Edward I hope you called Barbara and –. What's my godson's name again?

Peter Sean. They send their sympathies. I will stay as long as you need me.

Older Edward What a terrific life you must lead. Real estate lawyer. Wife. Handsome what? He must be ten years old by now.

Peter Seventeen.

Older Edward Time flies. (*He turns to Peter.*) You think I should have stopped all that.

Peter A disagreement wasn't the cause. The stroke could have happened at any time. I asked the doctor.

Older Edward You asked the doctor? You were afraid we'd killed her? (*Beat.*) But it wasn't an easy thing to watch.

Peter No. And half the time I didn't even know what they were fighting about. Seemed like they were splitting hairs. Both seem to have beliefs that are so much farther to the left than the vast majority in this –.

Older Edward Peter.

Peter That's just an impression, for whatever it's worth.

Older Edward It's not worth anything.

Peter, hurt, turns away.

You can't understand and I have no patience for listening to ignorant opinions right now. (*Beat.*) You should see how Elinor's holding up. They are best friends.

Peter hesitates, then goes off toward the cabins. At the same time:
1937: The Younger Edward and Elinor enter up the steps from the dock, holding the Younger Marianne, who is trying not to vomit.

Younger Elinor We're almost there.

Younger Marianne I feel –.

Younger Elinor We know how you feel.

Younger Edward It was a rough boat ride.

Younger Elinor Eddie, she drank too much. I told her she was drinking too much. I'm surprised her stomach's made it this far.

Younger Marianne grabs her mouth.

I have you. I'll take her, Eddie.

She helps Marianne toward the cabins.

We'll get something cold on your face. Hold on to me,
I've got you. I've got you!

> *They are gone.*
>   *Younger Edward, tired, sits at the table, next to his
>   older self. They sit together for a moment, when
>   Younger Edward suddenly notices the lit kerosene lamp.
>   He picks it up.*

Younger Edward *(realizing)* He's back. *(calling)* Gene!
Gene!! *(He runs off with the lamp.)* You're back!!!

SCENE FIVE

Projection: NIGHT.

More lanterns have been lit.
    *1986: Older Edward remains seated at the table, a
drink now in front of him.*
    *1937: Younger Edward and Elinor sit, also at the table,
laughing.*
    *Younger Marianne, looking pale and hung-over, enters
from the cabins.*

Younger Marianne *(seeing them laughing)* What?

Younger Elinor How do you feel? He's not laughing at
you.

Younger Marianne I'm okay. I thought I was counting my
drinks. I guess I was nervous. I'm sorry if I embarrassed –.

Younger Elinor Nervous about what?

Younger Marianne I don't know. I guess rich people
make me both angry and nervous.

Younger Edward Rich people can go to hell for all I care.

Younger Marianne looks to Younger Elinor, confused.

Younger Elinor He talked to Gene.

Younger Marianne He's back? Where's he been?

Younger Edward just laughs.

Younger Elinor (*explaining*) Gene was in the city. He'd remembered some business. He said he –. Well, Eddie has the feeling that he just sort of forgot about us. When Eddie called to him on the porch? When we just got back? For a moment –.

Younger Edward He didn't even recognize me. For a second, I think he thought I was some neighbour.

Younger Marianne Are you serious? But I thought he was your good friend –.

Younger Edward So did I. (*He laughs to himself.*)

Younger Elinor We're leaving tomorrow morning.

Younger Marianne You won't get an argument out of me.

Younger Elinor We have to leave. It seems Gene had invited some other friends to come tomorrow.

Younger Marianne (*laughing*) You're joking?

Younger Edward (*laughing*) He'd forgotten that he'd invited them.

Younger Elinor (*laughing*) After he saw Edward he said he'd forgotten them too.

Younger Marianne So he's kicking us out?

Younger Edward He said he could get us reservations at an inn in the town. He didn't offer to pay.

Younger Marianne Rich people –.

Younger Elinor We're not done. His friends whom he'd forgotten he'd invited at the same time he had invited us –.

Younger Edward . . . whom he'd also forgot about.

Younger Elinor (*continuing*) They are sort of a Leftist theatre group. They're talking to Gene about him helping them out.

Younger Edward But he said not to worry. (*big smile*) He wasn't planning on giving them a dime. So I shouldn't feel like it was some sort of competition –. He said that when people approach him for money – he can't say no. He's learned not to say yes – he just can't say no. (*He laughs.*)

Younger Elinor He wouldn't take a copy of our editorial statement.

Younger Marianne He wouldn't even –?

Younger Edward (*over this*) I tried.

Younger Elinor He tried. But Gene said he was tired. He was going to bed. And Gene doesn't read in bed.

Younger Marianne cannot believe it and starts to laugh. They all laugh, then suddenly Edward stands, throws a chair to the ground and screams toward the house.

Younger Edward You son of a bitch!!!! (*Silence. He sits back down.*)

Younger Marianne Eddie?

He turns to her.

I told you so.

He flinches.

Younger Elinor She did, Eddie. We both did, but you wouldn't listen. You knew better.

Younger Marianne You wouldn't listen to anyone –.

Younger Edward I feel stupid enough already!

Pause.

Younger Elinor (*getting up*) I'm going to take a walk. See how the lake looks. Maybe a swim. (*to Younger Marianne*) Want to come?

Younger Marianne It's dark.

Younger Elinor Take a lantern.

Younger Marianne Okay. Maybe it'll help me feel better.

Younger Edward Don't blame me for that. That was your own stupid fault.

Beat.

Younger Marianne Thank you for reminding me of that.

Younger Edward What are friends for?

Younger Elinor and Marianne stand, pick up a lantern, and head for the steps.
   Younger Edward looks off toward the house.

Elinor?

They stop.

May I join the two of you? Gene's at the window. (*nodding*) I guess he heard me. I don't want to go in there now.

Younger Elinor Marianne?

Younger Marianne Sure. What are friends for?

They head off down the steps toward the lake.
   1986: Older Edward laughs to himself and mumbles:

504

*'What are friends for?' The Older Elinor has entered
from the house.*

Older Elinor Who are you talking to?

Older Edward Daydreaming.

Older Elinor (*noticing his empty glass*) You want another
drink? I'll go back in –.

Older Edward Peter can do that.

She sits.

He was going to talk to her brother. I thought he should
hear. I suppose we should call Bryn Mawr. They'd want to
know. She was such a force there.

Short pause.

Older Elinor (*sighs, then*) You can't sit in there for ever.

Older Edward No.

Older Elinor Why can't the dead just die? She seems
comfortable.

*From the distance the sounds of people, kids,
swimming, laughing, playing in the lake.*

What's that?

Older Edward Kids down the lake. There's a new cabin.
They have kids. Must be out swimming.

Older Elinor You never used to hear anything.

Peter enters with a couple of drinks.

Peter (*entering*) I reached her . . .

Older Edward (*startled*) What?! Don't scare me like that.
Don't hurry around like that. (*to Elinor*) I thought she . . .

Peter I'm sorry I –. Her brother's flying into Albany.

(*Beat.*) I thought you'd both like a drink.

They take the drinks.

I was going to call Bryn Mawr. Leave a message at the switchboard at least. Someone there should be told.

Older Edward Good idea, Peter. You're a smart fellow. We never would have thought of that ourselves.

Peter goes back inside. They sip. Pause.

I've been thinking about your book, Elinor.

Older Elinor I –.

Older Edward I'm talking. Let me finish. I think she would have died five, six months ago if you hadn't written about her like you did. You got her so angry –.

Elinor smiles.

That book kept her alive. (*He stares out at the lake.*) I've wondered if maybe that's why you wrote about her like that. To get her angry. You know her better than anyone else. And I'll bet you thought – if I could only get her fighting –. That would keep her alive. So. You –.

Older Elinor No, Eddie.

Older Edward Even if it were unconscious on your part, still –.

Older Elinor No. (*Pause. Then she turns to him.*) Yes. Maybe that's why.

He nods, sips his drink.
She tries to fight back tears.

Older Edward The funeral will be at Riverside.

Elinor nods.

She always said she didn't want a memorial service.

Beat.

Older Elinor When I get back to the city, I'll begin to arrange for one.

Older Edward Good.

Beat.

Older Elinor (*staring off at the lake*) I look forward to that. It'll be interesting to see who's left.

Laughter and the sound of kids playing is heard from the lake.